RENEWING CHRISTIAN ETHICS:

THE CATHOLIC TRADITION

RENEWING CHRISTIAN ETHICS:

THE CATHOLIC TRADITION

Michael E. Allsopp

Scranton: University of Scranton Press

Library of Congress Cataloging-in-Publication Data

Allsopp, Michael E.
  Renewing Christian ethics : the Catholic tradition / by Michael E. Allsopp.
      p. cm.
  Includes bibliographical references and index.
  ISBN: 1-58966-109-5 (pbk.)
  1.   Christian ethics--Catholic authors. I. Title.
BJ1249.A455 2005
241'.042--dc22

                                                        2005042244

Distribution:

The University of Scranton Press
Chicago Distribution Center
11030 S. Langley
Chicago, IL 60628

PRINTED IN THE UNITED STATES OF AMERICA

CONTENTS

Part III

Chapter VII – Christian Ethic of Responsibilities: Ethics, Unifying Metaphor

Chapter VIII – A Christian Ethic of Responsibilities: Informing Beliefs, Key Images, Central Narratives

Chapter IX – A Catholic Ethic of Responsibilities: The Ground of Morality, Right Actions, Ethical Principles

Chapter X – A Christian Ethic of Responsibilities: Moral Development, Moral Decision-making

Chapter XI – A Christian Ethic of Responsibilities: Cases, Illustrations

Introduction

What has revealed the love of God among us is that the
only-begotten Son of God has been sent by the Father into
the world, so that, being made man, the Son might by His
redemption of the entire human race give new life to it and
unify it.

Vatican II
Decree on Ecumenism

T he call for the renewal in Roman Catholic ethics during the last
fifty years has come from many voices. Back in 1947, Paul
Tournier said that the time looked ripe then for Catholic
leaders to shoulder the task of making Christ alive and present to the
modern world.[1] Tournier based his opinion on the fact that, after years
of hubris, those who held commanding places in the physical sciences
had become more moderate and circumspect about science's ability to
create utopias (ibid., 146). While boldly reminding his readers that
"Our religion is the religion of the incarnation and we have all too often
forgotten this," Tournier thought that the Catholic Church had a definite
opportunity to "make Him heard" (ibid., 148)—an historically "rare
opportunity" to inspire physicians like himself and business, military,
religious, and political leaders to embrace a more authentic
Christianity— "a life inspired by the Holy Spirit" (ibid., 156).

Twenty years after this call, following similar exhortations from
other well-placed Christians, Pope John XXIII's pastoral letters and
public statements began to echo Tournier's words, no doubt due to the
pope's years as a papal diplomat in France, as well as his understanding
of "the signs of the times." Learning from these experiences, and convinced that the Church was in need of a thorough "renewal," John
made the bold decision to call the Church into ecumenical council
expressly to engage with the modern world, to heal the bleeding
wounds of economic, religious, and cultural division—to make
Christ's voice heard by actively responding to "the signs of the times."

Forty years after Pope John opened the Second Council of the
Vatican on October 11, 1962—a dark Saturday morning during which

his words of welcome were drowned out by the roar of thunder—few can deny that many of the renewal decisions that were set down in the Council's final decrees have been realized: The Church now has a revised body of canon law, its liturgy has been radically changed, and great strides have been taken to heal the wounds of religious division. Furthermore, the Council's specific recommendation that the Church's moral theology should be brought up-to-date has been the focus of major effort. Specialists in literature and biblical languages have wrestled with how to use the Bible in theology and religious ethics; those with expertise in economics, medicine, nursing, psychology, sociology, and military affairs have scrutinized Catholic social teaching in the light of Augustine, Aquinas, and Jesus' moral teaching. Theologians and philosophers, psychologists and experts in the humanities have devoted their lives to this enterprise.

As a result, Catholic moral theology as preached and taught today is quite different in many ways from the 1960s: It is more positive and more optimistic; it is scriptural and respectful of the past—without being simplistically beholden to dated and worn-out notions about the human person, conscience, the goals of sexuality and marriage, or the dignity of the Christian life.

However, writing in 1978, Gerard J. Hughes found it necessary to open his book *Authority in Morals* with the words, "This is a book about method in moral theology, written in the conviction that the present state of the subject in the Christian community at large as well as in the Roman Catholic Church to which I belong is bedeviled by a lack of any clear understanding of how Christians ought to approach moral problems."[2] Hughes was troubled by the debates still raging within the Church about the authority of Scripture, the weight that should be given to papal teaching, and the authority that Catholics should show to the dictates of individual conscience. Hughes might have included the debates about the place of autonomy and self-determination in Catholic morality and the divisions over the roles of inspiration, guidance, and shared leadership in place of the authoritarian, triumphalist, and patriarchal approach that still characterizes papal and episcopal theological leadership.

Renewing Christian Ethics: The Catholic Tradition is a book about autonomy and authority in ethics; it has been written because, although twenty-five years have passed since Hughes's work was published, Catholic and Protestant theologians who work in religious ethics are still deeply divided about the place of the Bible's authority, papal teaching, and the weight that individual Catholics should give to the dictates of their consciences, as they formulate specific moral principles and articulate ethical arguments in the business, military, social, or health care fields.

Renewing Christian Ethics: The Catholic Tradition has been inspired by the calls made by Paul Tournier and Pope John XXIII; it is a conscious response, as well, to Vatican II's call for the renewal of Catholic moral theology. It builds upon the efforts of theologians such as Bernard Haring, Richard McCormick, Josef Fuchs, Lisa Sowle Cahill, Margaret Farley, Germain Grisez, and Enda McDonagh, who have responded wholeheartedly to the Council's mandate. Like Hughes's, this is a book that examines morality and moral decision-making; it assesses the place of self-determination and creativity, of respect for papal authority and regard for one's own God-given ethical intuitions; it strives to incorporate the insights of developmental psychologists into women's moral development and decision-making, as well as the widely accepted positions of Scripture scholars, sociologists, and cultural anthropologists.

In large part the book has been written because of the "conviction that the present state of the subject in the Christian community at large as well as in the Roman Catholic Church to which I belong is [still] bedeviled by a lack of any clear understanding of how Christians ought to approach moral problems." *Renewing Christian Ethics: The Catholic Tradition* is a book that deals with the place of the social sciences in Christian ethics, the power of outdated beliefs that linger too long, and the hardships faced by new insights, as they struggle to gain footholds and acceptance. Indirectly, this is a book about current Catholic thinking in the areas of sexual, medical, environmental, military, and business ethics.

This book has been arranged for those who conduct courses in Christian ethics, as well as those who have a casual interest in the subject. Throughout each chapter, a conscious effort has been made to explain and illustrate, to let authors' voices be heard and to allow them to speak for themselves—in keeping with postmodernism's respect for the singular and distinctive, for the important discontinuities that quickly get lost in summary and paraphrase. The first chapters look at the developments in Catholic moral theology during last 100 years, in particular, since WWII; they examine the forces that have produced dramatic changes within the academic disciple, and, to a lesser degree, within the lived expressions of Christianity—Protestant, Catholic, and

Orthodox—especially in the United States. The second part of this book surveys the most important efforts to renew Christian ethics: those by Roman Catholic theologians, as well as Protestant ethicists whose publications have had major impact on Catholic moral theology. These chapters focus on the efforts of those who have remained within the "natural law" tradition, and those that have developed ethical approaches grounded on other foundations (feminist, liberation, virtue, and theocentric).

Each of these chapters provides critique as well as illustration, and they have been written to allow readers of different backgrounds to assess the strengths and weaknesses of these attempts to present Protestant and Catholic moral theories that preserve the Church's ethical heritages, while at the same time creatively and thoughtfully incorporating what their authors see as valuable advances in literary, theological, and philosophical scholarship, as well as useful insights from their experiences as teachers, chaplains, research psychologists, and pastoral counselors.

Renewing Christian Ethics: The Catholic Tradition (in its third part) offers an original ethical approach that builds upon the Catholic Church's past and present insights into ethics, as it responds to the need to renew Catholic moral theology: its shape and structure, as well as its practical application in the areas of health care, business, personal relationships, and the environment. These chapters develop the work of Richard McCormick, James Gustafson, Sidney Callahan, Jean Piaget, Malcolm Knowles, Lawrence Kohlberg, Hans Urs von Balthasar, Karl Rahner, Paul Ricoeur, N.H.G. Robinson, Enda McDonagh—and, in particular, the twentieth century British philosopher, translator and civil servant Sir W. David Ross, author of *The Right and The Good*, and *Foundations of Ethics*, best-known for his ethic of *prima facie* duties.

The chapters in this third part of the book focus on morality, moral development, and moral decisionmaking; they address the questions, "What makes a right action right" and "What is the ground of morality?" They provide a theological framework and a set of ethical principles for a twenty-first century Christian moral theory that, while standing squarely within the Catholic tradition, embodies the insights of thinkers whose work can update and strengthen that tradition.

The final chapter in this book provides "cases" from the lives of Christian moral "giants" (Robert E. Lee, and the Irish educator Nano Nagel, who did not seek Vatican approval for the Presentation Sisters because such an act of obedience would have severely limited the congregation's mission among Cork's poor). This chapter provides other kinds of "illustrations" from characters in Sean O'Casey's *The Plow and the Stars*—in which Jack Clitheroe, the commandant of the Dublin battalion of James Connolly's Irish Citizen Army during the Easter Uprising in 1916, and his desperate wife Nora (who desires nothing more than to be Jack's "dearest comrade"), are both destroyed because of their twisted moral development and flawed decisions about what they owe to themselves, their partners, and Ireland's freedom.

A deliberate effort has been made throughout this book to explain how readers might use the proposed moral theory in their lives as parents, educators, business managers, or healthcare professionals—to highlight the important differences that this ethic makes not only in approaching and formulating moral opinions, but also in making specific, personal, or communal decisions. Because there is a great truth in Oscar Wilde's observation that "the English have a miraculous power of turning wine into water," in presenting this Christian ethic of responsibilities and in justifying it, conscious efforts have been made to avoid such an embarrassing act.

Readers educated in classic philosophy will see that the ethic presented here has its roots in pre-Christian Stoicism, in Ambrose's *De officiis ministrorum* that has been called "the sole Christian example of a comprehensive ethical treatise before the time of the *Summae*."[3] Others trained in the Catholic Church's moral tradition will appreciate that the moral theory stands clearly in the Thomistic tradition that has consistently described human life not in terms of "rational self-interest" or "greatest happiness," but in terms of "responsibilities"—toward God, oneself, neighbor, church, and society.[4]

At the same time, this ethic links Thomism with post-WWII developments in psychology, linguistics, philosophy, and theology, in keeping with Pope John XXIII's call for the renewal of the Church, and Vatican II's mandate that Catholic moral theology be more closely associated with contemporary thought and Scripture that emphasizes the dignity of the Christian life and the rights and duties of the "people of God."

Michael Polanyi said that research into human knowledge shows conclusively that because the process of knowing always binds the knower to the subjects of his or her knowing, "choosing our beliefs from zero is absurd"—a statement that James Gustafson echoes in defending the "original" (some would say eccentric and quirky) features that one finds within his Reformed theocentric ethic. In the same way, while they stand firmly within the Thomistic and Catholic traditions, the historical surveys, critiques, and ethical theory found within *Renewing Christian Ethics: The Catholic Tradition* embody my own conscious—and largely unconscious—religious preferences and biases; they reflect my years as a Roman Catholic who has lived and studied in Australia, Italy, and the United States; they contain "features" resulting from my work as a university educator, hospital chaplain, and college administrator.

Like those features that critics (literary, historical, philosophical) focus upon when examining Augustine's *Confessions*, Aquinas' *Summa Theologiae,* or T. S. Eliot's poem "The Waste Land," this book's language and style, its scope and goals—what it says and what it omits—contain the fragments and residuals of a unique journey that has been colored and shaped by the elements, friends and colleagues, and great blessings, as well as by the vivid sense (at times) of being "fortune's football"—("This Jack, joke, poor potsherd, patch, match-wood, immortal diamond"),—who will one day experience—I still hope—that extraordinary moment (coming each day closer) when he—through the Almighty's kindness and mercy—is "immortal diamond."

Toward the end of his Nobel lecture *Toward the Splendid City* (1971), Pablo Neruda makes the wise observations, "There is no such thing as a lone struggle, no such thing as a lone hope. In every human being are combined the most distant epochs, passivity, mistakes, suf-ferings, the pressing urgencies of our own time, the pace of history."[5] Because of the truth contained in Neruda's words, I know that my ini-tial hopes of completing this book have been constantly nourished and kept alive not only by a sense of "the pressing urgencies of our own time," but by other life-giving forces associated with family (my brothers and sisters by birth and marriage who had have been there for me over the years), students, undergraduate and graduate (their ques-tions in class, their written responses), and friends and colleagues with their generosity and encouragement.

In special ways, I must once again acknowledge Harry Davis, past-president, St. Patrick's College, Manly, who gave me my start in theology, and who has supported my research throughout the years; Charles Howard, former General of the Marist Brothers, who trusted my judgment while teaching at St. Patrick's College, Manly, and who has been a constant inspiration; Charles Curran, who was a gracious host during my first visit to Washington, D.C. in 1974, and who has been an understanding colleague since that first meeting; Edouard Hamel, Dean of the Faculty of Theology at Rome's Gregorian University during the 1970s, who guided my doctoral studies and encouraged my interest in religious ethics, as well as in Gerard Manley Hopkins and John Henry Newman; Bruce Malina, who has been both an inspiration and a support since we first met twenty years ago when I began teaching at Creighton University. Edward van Merrienboer, Shaun Sommerer, John O'Grady, and Edward Sunshine added to these efforts during my years at Barry University, Miami Shores, Florida.

I owe a special word of thanks as well to Geoffrey Hicks, headmaster, Christ Catholic College, Sydney, who has been the best of friends since the 1950s when we both attended St. Joseph's College, Hunter's Hill. Also to Desmond Egan, one of Ireland's great contemporary poets, as well as artistic director of the Gerard Manley Hopkins Summer School held in Monasterevin, Ireland, for the last 17 years, for his interest and support, and his unsolicited willingness to promote my books and essays. William P. Frost, founder of the College Press in Dayton, and editor of the journal *Explorations,* has been a loyal friend: a source of trust and encouragement for more than twenty years. Vincent Twomey, St. Patrick's College, Maynooth, editor of the *Irish Theological Quarterly*, has been a true friend since our first contacts during the 1980s. I am ever in his debt because of his kindness, interest, and generosity.

I am deeply indebted as well to Richard Rousseau, who directs the University of Scranton Press, for agreeing to publish this, as well as two earlier books. Also to Patty Mecadons, the Press's Production Manager, for her valuable editorial decisions.

Finally, I dedicate this book to my wife, Rosemarie O'Connor, who has encouraged and supported me at every point throughout the years it has taken to complete this work, and who has provided me with many of the book's significant insights and emphases.

While this book's chances of success are no greater than that of a tiny salmon starting life in one of Alaska's mountain streams, the surveys and moral theory that it contains are offered in the hope that they will "do good," as Gerard Manley Hopkins said about his sonnets. The book is presented in the hope, as well, that it will advance the work of renewal in Catholic moral theology mandated by Vatican II—both by its inherent strengths, as well as by its unnoticed weaknesses that will spur (I trust) others to go beyond it, and to develop their own theories that will differ—as they must—from what they find here, largely because of their own intellectual and spiritual journeys—and their own insights into the fact that Christianity (as Paul Tournier said) involves existential choices that are not made on the basis of simplistic or logical deductions from rational or moral standards, but of a person, of the living God, of Christ.[6]

Michael E. Allsopp
All Saints' Day, 2004

Notes:

[1] Paul Tournier, "The Task of the Church," in his *The Whole Person in a Broken World,* translated by John and Helen Doberstein (New York: Harper & Row, 1964). This work was originally published in French in 1947.

[2] Gerard J. Hughes, *Authority in Morals: An Essay in Christian Ethics* (Washington: Georgetown University Press, 1978), xi.

[3] James Gaffney, "The First Christian Ethics Text," in his *Matters of Faith and Morals* (Kansas City: Sheed & Ward, 1987), 214–230, at 215.

[4] On this subject, Paul J. Glenn, *An Introduction to Philosophy* (St. Louis: Herder Book Company, 1944, 10th printing 1955), 383–395.

[5] Pablo Neruda, *Toward the Splendid City* (New York: Farrar, Straus & Giroux, 1972), 31.

[6] Paul Tournier, *The Meaning of Persons* (New York: Harper & Row, 1973), 221.

Part I

Chapter I

Catholic Moral Theology During the Twentieth Century: Changes, Forces of Change

Academic theology seems to have lost its voice, its ability to command attention as a distinctive contribution to public discourse in our culture.

Jeffrey Stout
Ethics After Babel

Einstein once remarked that with the arrival of the atomic age everything had changed except our thinking. Unfortunately the remark is true.

David Tracy
Plurality and Ambiguity

The last 100 years have been an extraordinary time in the history of Christian ethics. Whether we are speaking about the academic discipline taught in universities, or we are using "Christian ethics" to refer descriptively to a distinctive construing of the behavior of Protestants, Roman Catholics, and Orthodox Christians (as well as all other lived expressions of Christianity), nothing equals the last century in terms of the debates, controversies, and changes (fruitful and unfruitful) that both have experienced.

Looking briefly at the high points and low points of these changes, as well as what caused them, will enable us to better appreciate the focus of this book, its call for further renewal in the disciple of Christian ethics, and in what is called Roman Catholic moral theology, in particular.

Roman Catholic Ethics in the Twentieth Century: Features Old and New

After WWII, Lutheran and Anglican theologians responsible for conducting courses in Christian ethics at universities in England, America, Canada, Australia, France, and Germany began to feel that the sky was falling. Likewise, Jesuits and Dominicans who taught courses in Catholic moral theology (as it was called) progressively saw that they too were no longer able to keep order within the rigid sub-discipline of theology, whose multi-volume textbooks (those used in Roman Catholic seminaries were still written in Latin well into the 1960s) were crammed with gnomic quotations from arcane scholars and tidbits of wisdom from armchair "pastoral" psychologists who usually knew much more about Aristotle's psychology than Freud's.[1]

A 2003 survey of the population of the state of Iowa ("America's heartland") found that 10% of those polled thought that putting a bet on a racehorse was a sin, 36% thought that drinking hard liquor (whiskey) was a "minor" sin, and 52% of those questioned were convinced that homosexual acts were "major" sins. However, similar surveys of the academic discipline or the American moral landscape reveal large areas where ethical opinions are radically different today from what they were when Bishop Fulton Sheen was an icon on religious broadcasting, or G. K. Chesterton, Hilaire Belloc, and C. S. Lewis were the darlings of conservative English Christians.[2]

Some notable examples:

- As the twenty-first century begins, U.S. universities with Roman Catholic affiliations are proud to have Protestant, Jewish, and Muslim teachers on their campuses, as well as scholars with Ph.D.s from Paris, Munich, Oxford, Yale, Columbia, and Harvard; they are less interested in attracting graduates from Boston College or Notre Dame, from Rome's Gregorian University or Washington's Catholic University. As one Jesuit chairman expressed it to a department that included senior faculty with Ph.D.s from Oxford, Rome, and Jerusalem's *Ecole Biblique,* when he announced the hiring of a brand new Ph.D. from Yale, "We've made a quantum leap!"
- Descriptions of courses in Christian ethics conducted at Protestant and Catholic institutions feature textbooks and defend positions

that would not have been permitted by deans, presidents, faculty committees, or boards of trustees during the 1950s–1960s.

- Lectures given today, whether undergraduate or graduate, at Loyola University in Chicago or Southern Methodist University in Dallas, reflect the culture and spirit of college-educated American United Methodists, Episcopalians, Presbyterians, and Catholics. Generally speaking, they are ecumenical, liberal, enquiring, and multicultural. Toleration, ambiguity, diversity, fair-mindedness, and pluralism are visible everywhere.[3]

Of course, some Christian communities (Missouri Synod Lutherans, Quakers, Southern Baptists, Mormons) have experienced less change than the United Methodist, Episcopal, and Catholic communities during these years. However, large numbers belonging to the latter denominations, and who live in Chicago, Los Angeles, Seattle, and New York, now openly express views about the morality of divorce, abortion, homosexuality, capital punishment, premarital sex, IVF (in vitro fertilization), and euthanasia that differ markedly from mother to daughter, father to son—while the publications of Protestants and Catholics who conduct courses in business ethics or consult in biomedical ethics at Catholic or Methodist medical centers, indicate the disagreements (friendly, not-so-collegial) among authors,[4] as well as those that Catholic writers have with the Vatican's Joseph Cardinal Ratzinger.[5]

Gales, Storms, and Gentle Breezes: Forces That Have Changed American Catholic Moral Theology

Religious change does not follow the life-path of the rose; it comes about only through struggle and conflict—as Paul, Aquinas, Luther, John Wesley, John Henry Newman, Karl Rahner, Yves Congar, Bernard Haring, and Archbishop Romero found. Consequently, change in religious ethics is a source of anxiety and stress. Unlike their more secular or more liberal neighbors, Jews, Muslims, and Christians who dread modernity and find truth only in sacred Scriptures and ancient traditions, lapse more easily into fundamentalist sects that, unless checked, produce polarizations within communities, witch hunts, and purges, together with the rise of aggressive and defensive responses that have characterized Israel, Iran, and a number of

Protestant denominations (as well as the U.S. Catholic Church) since the 1970s.[6]

Although firmly rooted in the theology and ethics of the universal church, U.S. Catholic moral theology bears signs of local debates, cultural distinctions, and other shaping influences that allow one to speak about "American Catholic moral theology." And some of the major forces responsible for reshaping aspects of U.S. Catholic moral theology since WWII are not hard to identify. Like the great glaciers that gradually changed the American landscape, they have left their distinctive marks.

During the years immediately following the end of hostilities in Europe and the Pacific, Protestants and Catholics in their thousands from Irish, Polish, Italian, Greek, Danish, Norwegian, and German families, in which parents still had strong immigrant attitudes toward religion, work, family, language, and college education, left coal-mining communities in Pennsylvania, ghettoes in New York, and farming communities across Iowa and Nebraska to attend college (thanks to the provisions of the GI Bill).

After graduation, the majority of these men and women did not return home, but relocated to America's new and "exciting" cities where there were futures: Chicago, Miami, Phoenix, Spokane, Denver, Dallas, San Diego, Los Angeles, and Honolulu. They took positions as realtors, high school teachers, accountants, pharmacists, nurses, insurance brokers, and bank managers (while a smaller number became lawyers, physicians, architects, dentists, and college educators). Progressively, these sons and daughters of immigrants were invited to join private golf clubs, accept partnerships in prestigious legal firms—or to make their own fortunes in banking, real estate, medicine, and insurance.

Then, during the 1960s–1980s, the daughters and sons of these first generation college-educated Americans went to university with higher ambitions than their parents: to gain M.D.s, J.D.s, and Ph.D.s, and secure top faculty positions at Yale, Princeton, Harvard, Columbia, Michigan, Notre Dame, and Stanford. With the arrival on campus of this new generation of Ph.D.s—some of whom were quite alienated from the "official" church, because of the its teaching on women, sexuality, marriage, family, and birth control, others because of the church's liberal positions on social justice issues—the academic "old guard" could neither ignore nor stop what soon began to happen within philosophy, theology, history and literature departments—just as they could not stop what was appearing nightly on TV or daily on college notice boards.[7]

Pre-Vatican II Jesuits trained in Roman Catholic neo-scholastic theology, seminary-trained Lutheran faculty members, and Oxford-educated Episcopal ethicists could not remain deaf or "sit on the fence" to their younger colleagues' calls for the integration of schools in America's South, for action about Africa's poverty, medical rights for those with AIDS, the evils of apartheid in South Africa, or land reform in Latin America. Many of these educators (as I found when I took part in conferences, visited, studied, and taught at Jesuit universities in the USA) were conservatives and card-carrying Republicans (rather than Democrats like their parents and grandparents); they found little "positive" in the revolutions swirling around them. They were angry about being passed over by younger colleagues who put publishing ahead of teaching; they were offended when they observed a lack of respect towards themselves or what they held dear—whether the Jesuit robe, devotion to Mary, or the English language.

At the heart of numerous departmental and professional squabbles on American university campuses (the majority resembled those C. P. Snow describes in his novels about English academic life) was the fact that many of those hired to conduct courses in history, psychology, and biomedical or sexual ethics during the 1970s–1980s not only had life experiences quite different from their older colleagues, but they had completed college degrees in departments where the faculty, students, and programs of study were quite different from those where the older faculty members had studied. And to add to the differences, the "new hires" had also (in a lot of cases) completed degrees in sociology, philosophy, psychology, physics, literature, and history, as well as in philosophy or theology, history or literature.

This new generation of faculty members brought beliefs, knowledge and insights to their courses that were frequently quite different from the "old guard." Furthermore, many of these "new" instructors had studied in Europe not simply in regional Catholic institutions; they had read Karl Barth and Emil Brunner, Karl Rahner and Josef Fuchs. Many were married and were not vowed members of religious orders. As a result, they had quite different priorities, including spending quality time with their families, seeking family leave, and spending limited time on campus—especially on nights and weekends. Further, as a large number of the "old guard" found—and resented because it was contrary to their visions of religious life—many of their younger Jesuit or Dominican colleagues also had ambitions quite different from theirs, not to mention radically different understandings of community, obedience, and poverty.

For all of these reasons (as well as others that I might have overlooked), this new generation of college and university faculty brought to their classes at St. Louis University, Boston College, Seattle University, and Detroit Mercy—to name just a few places— approaches and methods, sympathies and goals, quite different from the older teachers of theology or religious studies at these schools.[8] And as departmental conflicts surfaced and professors took different sides on the Vietnam War, the abortion issue, capital punishment, birth control, or the morality of homosexuality, university presidents had to ask themselves, "How we gonna' keep 'em teaching the Bible, Luther, and Aquinas after they've read Karl Barth?"

While "conservatives" (laity and clergy) visited parish liturgies to take notes about homilies, write to local bishops, and send reports to Rome, "liberals" who secured positions as department chairs and college deans were not slow to "clean house" by quietly "retiring" older faculty members whose beliefs and teaching styles were "out of date," and replacing them with instructors with backgrounds, values, and visions similar to their own. Passing theological "litmus tests," something that had been rare prior to WWII, became widespread across America.[9]

Progressively, Catholic colleges and universities came to experience what Harvard, Yale, Princeton, and Cornell experienced during the nineteenth century, when "secular democrats" on faculties—men who believed in limitless progress through science and reason—fought pitched battles against academics committed to preserving a "classical Christian consciousness."[10] As a reaction (quite understandable), the members of the "older" generation sought to protect themselves by forming their own associations, hiring only those who thought like them, and were (or seemed to be) strongly committed to "Catholic" values. Consequently, as the battle lines became fixed, religious women and men (Jesuits, Franciscans, Sisters of Charity) often sought to reside and teach in institutions where they felt "safe" and "at home."

Institutions like the Franciscan University in Steubenville, Ohio, became in time "beacons" of what Catholic colleges should be like, and drew national support from "conservatives," while schools such as Boston College and Seattle University–where during the 1970s every graduate student in religious studies had to take a course in creative puppetry—attracted "liberals" and "progressives." While I know of no theology or philosophy departments that provided parallel programs in which students took courses on Karl Rahner—while others took programs in which Rahner was "taboo" (such separate programs did happen in some state schools over Marxist writers, and post-modernists)—on the "inside" students quickly got to know whom to take and whom not to take among faculty members; while academic advisers (both old and young) steered cohorts of students toward colleagues who thought as they did about politics, economics, history, or Christ's humanity and divinity, the authority of conscience, and the role of women in the Church of the future.

There were other powerful forces for change in Roman Catholic theology at work as well during these years. One was an increased interest in the academic study of the Bible, and its use in ethics.[11] Another was new research about the historical Jesus.[12] Also, there was a renewed (if much smaller) interest in patristic writers (Cassian, Origen, Maximus, Ambrose, Augustine),[13] as well as in medieval scholars such as the Celtic monks who produced the Penitentials,[14] those who composed and spread the codes of courtly love, or those who developed the "just war" theories. There was a new interest in the life and writing of Peter Lombard, Aquinas, Scotus, Francis and Clare, Julian of Norwich, Hildegard of Bingen, Teresa of Avila, Catherine of Siena, Meister Eckhart, and John of the Cross.[15]

The power of the next force should not be judged on the basis of the small number of courses taught today in colleges and parishes throughout America: **Vatican II**. It is impossible to underestimate the worldwide impact on all Christian communities caused by John XXIII's election as pope, his announcement of the Second Vatican Council, the preparations, worldwide consultations, and open debates during the Council's sessions (1962–1965). The Catholic Church—everywhere—is different today because of the changes resulting from the ongoing implementation of the Council's decisions and the study of its documents, with their calls not only for the renewal of the Church's liturgy and law, religious and married life, but also for the reform of Catholic moral theology.[16]

As George V. Lobo states, "All of the efforts of these pioneers [Catholic theologians, for example, Bernard Haring, Joseph Fuchs, Karl Rahner, and Yves Congar] were crowned by the teaching of the Second Vatican Council, especially in its Pastoral Constitution on the

Church in the Modern World, *Gaudium et Spes*. The Council asked for renewal, and in specific areas, itself provided the orientations."[17]

The Second Council of the Vatican was the most important event in the history of the Christian Church in many centuries (it was much more important than Vatican I). And the changes it set in motion will continue for decades to come, as its recommendations about ecumenism, liturgy, education, religious life, and the role of the laity in the Church in the modern world continue (if slowly) to work their way through the Catholic Church and other Christian communities that have ongoing dialogues with the Vatican or with local Catholic communities.

Nobody who knows the years since WWII can ignore the waves of social and moral upheaval (turbulent and unpredictable) brought about by forces from outside the U.S. Catholic Church, as the Eisenhower years (prim, proper, and boring), gave way to the 1960s. Attitudes were changed throughout America as a result of the election of JFK and his assassination, and by LBJ's efforts to win the war against hunger, spread civil rights, and finish the war in Vietnam. Then, there were the worldwide debates within the Catholic Church surrounding birth control and the publication of Paul VI's *Humanae Vitae* in October 1968. Lutheran, Calvinist, and Catholic leaders in Europe faced their own storms as university students were encouraged by their professors and cultural heroes to devour Jean Paul Sartre's writings, Simon de Beauvoir's *The Second Sex*, and Albert Camus's *La Chute (The Fall), Le Mythe de Sisyphe (The Myth of Sisyphus), La Peste (The Plague),* and *L'Etranger (The Outsider).*

In England, America, Canada, and Australia, the "death of God" movement in theology, Bishop John A.T. Robinson's *Honest to God,* Harvey Cox's *The Secular City,* and Joseph Fletcher's *Situation Ethics* caused their own storms. Then there were Betty Friedan's *The Feminine Mystique,* Germain Greer's *The Female Eunuch,* Mary Daly's *The Church and the Second Sex,* and Kate Millet's *Sexual Politics.* The rise of *Cosmopolitan* and the coming of *Playboy,* publications that swept across college campuses and city bookstores, rose to the top of best-selling lists and turned authors into international celebrities.[18]

And of course, there was the thunder and lightning across the whole world because of the spread of TV, the music of the 60s (Elvis, The Beatles, The Stones), and the movies that broke new ground in terms of style, language, and sexual content ("Easy Rider," "The

Graduate," "Who's Afraid of Virginia Woolf?," "The Seven Samurai," "The Silence," "Manhattan," "Some Like It Hot," and "A Clockwork Orange")—all of which brought sweeping changes in social attitudes, dating customs, and dress codes for work and play.[19]

The Janus-Face of U.S. Roman Catholic Ethics: Open and Closed to the World

Roman Catholic moral theology could not remain idle in the face of history's calls to take a leadership role and address the century's changing attitudes toward feminists' calls for voting rights, for safe and legalized abortion, and for birth control education and research; it could not ignore the worldwide debates about euthanasia, IVF, the spread of AIDS, workers' rights, and the brutality of the Korean War and later the Vietnam War. However, the many calls for change brought as many calls for steadfastness to the past and loyalty to tradition—and began what Peter Steinfels calls the "trench warfare" between "traditionalists" and "progressives" within the U.S. Catholic Church.[20]

Just as the Worker Priest movement in France (it was led by priests and brothers from the Dominican order) had taken Christianity to factories during the 1950s in order to meet the challenges posed by communists,[21] Cesar Chavez, Dorothy Day, and other leaders of the Catholic Worker Movement began to challenge priests and lay leaders to stand in solidarity with the working class: with those toiling in New York's sweat shops or employed as seasonal vegetable and fruit pickers in California.[22] During the 1960s–1970s, Martin Luther King, Jr. forced every Christian in American to look segregation in the face and to take a stand for or against changes in civil rights. At the same time, those working in Christian ethics at U.S. colleges and universities were encouraged by their colleagues in Canada, Ireland, and Australia to take up the fight against apartheid in South Africa; to oppose "white Australia" policies; to pressure governments to improve the lives of native and aboriginal peoples; and to play active roles on behalf of gays and lesbians and the disadvantaged children sent without their parents' knowledge from Northern Ireland, Britain, Wales, and Scotland to orphanages and foster homes in Canada and Australia following WWII.

As the decades passed, both Catholic and Protestant ethics (academic, scholastic, clergy-centered) was progressively forced to leave its ivory tower and face the bustle of the marketplace, not simply because of the compelling force of the issues themselves, but also because of other forces: internal pressures and institutional directives. Protestant thinking, on the one hand, was pressured by the Social Gospel Movement that began at the end of the U.S. Civil War and lasted until WWI, spurred principally by the writing of Walter Rauschenbusch (1861–1918).[23] At the same time, Catholic theology saw major shifts in its traditional focus on individual morality and personal spirituality following the publication of Leo XIII's *Rerum Novarum* (1891), and forty years later with Pius XI's *Quadragesimo Anno* (1931), both of which argued against socialism and *laissez faire* capitalism, and in support of workers' rights, living wages, and safe working conditions. Both of these encyclicals emphasized activities foreign to leading Victorian Church leaders like John Henry Newman, who believed that the Church was a religious institution whose mission was to save souls—not to be involved in ending dock strikes.[24]

Both Leo XIII and Pius XI defended the Church's right to play an active role in politics; they encouraged clergy and lay leaders to organize study groups and to set up political organizations in parishes and universities in order to combat the rise of capitalism and communism, and to protect the rights of laborers, millions of whom were being consumed in the fires of the coal, auto, steel, railroad, textile, and farm industries. Their encyclicals were largely responsible for the rise of Catholic-led federations of workers and the creation of political parties in Italy and Germany; for efforts to build strong coalitions to oppose Hitler's National Socialists who grew at an alarming rate in Catholic areas of Germany during the early 1930s.[25]

These encyclicals laid the foundations as well for a number of more recent major papal statements that addressed later social issues: John XXIII's *Mater et Magistra* (1961) and *Pacem in Terris* (1963); Paul VI's *Populorum Progressio* (1967) and John Paul II's *Laborem Exercens* (1981), *Sollicitudo Rei Socialis* (1987), and *Centesimus Annus* (1991).[26]

U.S. Catholic Church's Struggles for Renewal: The Rocks and Hard Places

After starting as a "foreign" church for Irish, Italian, Polish and German immigrants, there is evidence that by the 1950s–1960s Roman Catholicism had become both the most powerful and the most vigorous religion within the United States.[27] While as late as 1955,

European critics saw U.S. Catholic theology as characterized by "spiritual and intellectual infantilism,"[28] American Catholic magazines regularly featured essays indicating how U.S. Catholicism had come of age. Consequently, they stated that the U.S. Catholic Church should take its proper place in the life of the universal church. Authors like John L. Murphy, writing in *The Catholic World,* for example, argued "the American Church must take a more active part in the work of adapting the Church to modern life."[29]

Concerned by such remarks, and the dramatic decline in vocations to the priesthood and religious life, as well as in active participation by U.S. Catholics in liturgical and parish activities (without any real change in their loyalties), the U.S. Catholic Church began to experience a number of orchestrated efforts—from the Vatican and from within the local Catholic hierarchy—to bring back "the good old days."[30] While some bishops appreciated Karl Rahner's image of the church in the twenty-first century as the "church of the diaspora"—smaller, less privileged, less powerful—and actively worked to restructure their communities in the light of the changing political, social, and economic times, the majority adopted a siege mentality and fought to hold onto the past, their social positions, wealth, and authority.[31]

We have already mentioned Paul VI's *Humanae Vitae.*[32] We might also mention the Vatican's other (less memorable) statements on morality, such as its "Declaration on Sexual Issues" in 1975, and its "Declaration on Euthanasia" in 1980. Besides using such encyclicals as *Redemptor Hominis* (1979) and *Solicitudo rei socialis* (1988) as useful tools to reshape Catholic thought in a number of key ethical areas, in 1993 Pope John Paul II issued another important, if little-read, encyclical on Catholic moral theology, *Veritatis Splendor,* the first extensive analysis of the foundations of morality undertaken by a pope. The document is an inspiring (if confusing) essay that builds upon the pope's years as a teacher of moral theology, as well as his statements on practical and theoretical subjects in the field, but is spoiled by its overlapping goals—to provide a scripturally sound basis (using Jesus as the model of obedience to God's will) for the Church's morality; to examine a number of current controversies; and also to undertake (needlessly, I believe) "a police action in an ongoing war that the Holy see is waging with some of its best minds and most devoted members," to quote one well-placed U.S. critic.[33]

More recently, in 1994 the Vatican published a more significant work with lasting implications for the Church's life and faith: the first new catechism in more than 400 years, *The Catechism of the Catholic Church*, whose Part III, "Life in Christ," provides a summary of Catholic moral teaching described by Pope John Paul II as a "sure norm for teaching the faith." The catechism reflects some of the changes that have taken place in the church's understanding of theology, ethics, and the Christian life since the publication of the *Catechism of the Council of Trent*. However, this new "reference text" does not embody many of the developments that have taken place in adult education, psychology, sociology, literature, or theology since WWII, as well-placed and balanced critics have demonstrated.[34]

Whitehead once said, "A clash of doctrines is not a disaster; it is an opportunity." However, U.S. Catholic leaders, lay or clerical, have not made the most of the "opportunity" since Vatican II for renewing the Church's spirituality, ethics, or social teaching. Lacking trust in their colleagues (or the movement of the Holy Spirit) and bent upon preserving as much as possible of the status quo, those who saw themselves as "saviors" of U.S. Catholicism found "dangers" everywhere. Having little interest in developments in psychology or education, such people did not appreciate that millions of U.S. Catholics had been encouraged as a result of their high school and college educations to see that the "normal" process of maturation means moving from dependency toward self-directedness and independence, trusting and valuing their own experience, and fostering learning environments and education processes based upon respect for the individual learner and regard for the competency of each.[35]

These would-be "guardians" of the U.S. Church, its theology, liturgy, and hierarchy, further failed to recognize that American Catholics have always been a people of many different "tastes" and "stripes"—that being Irish, German, Italian, and Polish, they have never been cultural or spiritual conformists, and that ethnic diversity has been a trademark of American Catholicism—points central to two recent studies on Catholics in America.[36]

Prompted by ultramontanists who saw "dissent" where they might have seen independence, "indifference" where they might have seen tolerance, "immorality" where they might have seen self-expression, various Vatican departments gave special instructions to U.S. bishops throughout the 1970s–1980s, in order to rein in "suspect" theologians, and to curb "worrying" pastoral customs and what they saw as "controversial" doctrinal and ethical opinions.[37] Following some years when the Vatican actually encouraged local liturgical, canonical, and pastoral experimentations, the Vatican's Cardinal Ratzinger sent directives to bishops to tighten up Marriage Tribunals (too many annulments were being given).[38]

The cardinal prefects of other Vatican "congregations" ordered local bishops and religious superiors to restore a number of pre-Vatican II practices: they demanded that some customs and traditions (clerical dress, daily recitation of the rosary, *summum silentium*) be restored in seminaries; they stopped some liturgical practices (parish penance services before Easter and Christmas); they advised superiors of religious women that some form of "habit" (religious dress) was mandatory in public; and they set up procedures to remove instructors, counselors, and textbooks from seminaries. Nostalgic for "the good old days" when seminaries were sylvan heritages staffed by docile sisters and packed with adolescent students dressed in biretta and soutane, like Groucho Marx, bishops across 08A adopted the position, "Whatever it is, I'm against it."

Finally, while expressing his support for the decisions taken at Vatican II, Pope John Paul II openly opposed liberation theology on more than one visit to Latin America, and explicitly prohibited clergy from associating with all socialist groups and from assuming leadership roles in politics or government.[39] Then, of course, there was the Vatican's effort to impose the *mandatum*.[40]

Between 1966 and 1988, the U.S. bishops issued 188 official statements and letters, more than half of which were devoted to social justice issues, Jay P. Dolan tells us in the course of his recent history of the American Catholic Church.[41] During these years, particularly during the 1980s–1990s, both the Vatican and local "conservatives" were hard at work trying to change other aspects of U.S. Catholic life and thought. Fearing the secularization of U.S. Catholics, their loss of identity, and their accommodation to changing social values—as the majority of Americans ceased to support collectivist influences in favor of pluralism and respect for ethnicity and diversity—U.S. bishops were encouraged to take action against Dignity, a national organization of gay and lesbian Catholics. Local bishops, encouraged by the Vatican, warned Catholics who belonged to pro-choice groups, and to the progressive U.S. Catholic organization Call to Action (that included several bishops among its members) that they faced excommunication if they did not resign.

In some dioceses (Omaha, Lincoln), bishops went so far as to tell Catholic teenagers that they could not retain their memberships in civic organizations like the Camp Fire Girls. At the same time (to be fair), the Vatican excommunicated the leader of the Church's ultra-right wing, Archbishop Lefavre, who had a strong following within the United States. The Vatican also proscribed the public use of pre-Vatican II liturgical customs; it closed seminaries and religious houses associated with the archbishop.

One hundred years ago, during the closing years of the nineteenth century, Pope Leo XIII took action against "Americanism," because of the theology of Isaac Hecker (1819–1888), founder of the Paulists, and because Baltimore's James Cardinal Gibbons had praised America's separation of church and state, and St. Paul's Archbishop John Ireland had encouraged the establishment of state schools, eulogized the Republic, supported the Knights of Labor, and initiated programs to instill American values in Irish, Italian, Polish, and other immigrant communities. During the 1980s–1990s, the Vatican and its local supporters again undertook a number of special measures to change the tone and thinking of the U.S. Church, because of new concerns about the American Church's independent spirit and liberal leadership, the decline in vocations to the priesthood and religious life, the lessening support for Catholic schools, and what they found in books like James Kavanaugh's *A Modern Priest Looks at His Outdated Church* that caused a sensation when published in 1967.

Some examples: following a General Congregation in 1974–5, Paul VI vetoed the changes that had been passed to the Constitutions and Rules of the Society of Jesus (Jesuits).[42] Then, after using its authority to quash the lifetime election of the charismatic Pedro Arupe as General of the Society, the Vatican (with the support of Jesuits fearful of the future) directly limited a number of the Society's initiates within the U.S. that focused on spirituality, education, justice, and peace. At the same time, the Vatican threw its support behind local "conservative" institutions (Pope John XXIII Center for Health Care Ethics, Braintree, MA; Pope John Paul II Center for Marriage and the Family, Washington, DC); it sponsored the rise of right-wing organizations such as Opus Dei, and the Legionaries of Christ (both of which have begun to play increasingly stronger roles in high school and college education).[43] Cardinals associated with Vatican Congregations as well as with the local "fundamentalist" wing actively supported the Fellowship of Catholic Scholars that was founded by American "traditionalists" who promoted ultramontanist theologians (for example, Janet Smith, Germain Grisez, William E. May, and Joseph Boyle).

Further, the Vatican actively sought the support of conservative Catholics to establish endowed chairs in Catholic studies at U.S. universities, and invited the powerful fraternal order, The Knights of Columbus, to underwrite papal visits, to cover the Vatican's occasional budget shortfalls, and to be a leading player in the Vatican's fight against abortion. Bishops, afraid of "secular" universities, have resorted to seeking financial support to establish institutions such as Ave Maria University located in Naples, Florida, where the "riches of the Catholic intellectual tradition" will be persuasively passed on to a future generations of "neo-conservatives" by instructors eager to disseminate the insights of "loyal" Catholic thinkers, whether medieval or modern.

All of these actions against progressives and institutional renewal were taken ironically while the Vatican was dealing with serious internal problems that were weakening the Church's moral authority and damaging its status in the world community. First, there was the nasty "gossip" surrounding the "sudden death" of Pope John Paul I on September 28, 1978, after only 33 days in office.[44] Then there was the international scandal and legal investigation following the "suicide" death of Roberto Calvi (found hanging under London's Blackfriars Bridge in June, 1982), the collapse of Milan's Banco Ambrosiano— called by the *New York Times* the greatest financial scandal of the twentieth century—and the reckless financial behavior of Chicago-born Archbishop Paul Marcinkus, Pope Paul VI's special advisor and banking expert.[45]

Third, throughout the 70s, 80s, and 90s there was the Vatican's largely unsuccessful defense of Pope Pius XII's dealings with Hitler during the 1930s that led to the centralization of the Vatican's power at the expense of the German Catholic bishops, and its unsuccessful efforts to justify the pope's silence in the face of the slaughter of millions of Jews in Europe (as well as thousands in Italy) during WWII—failures in character and deceptions in practice that Garry Wills sees as reasons for the laity's widespread inability to trust the papacy.[46] Finally, the U.S. Church's present scandals surrounding its treatment of known pedophile priests—and the Vatican's passivity (was it knowing collusion and cover-up?)—have further undermined the Catholic Church's moral authority, as seen in the widespread reaction to recent Vatican statements on ethical issues.[47]

Many will be familiar with Clifford Geertz's central hypothesis, namely, that communities share, perpetuate, and develop knowledge about and attitudes toward life and death primarily through frameworks and cultural narratives, and these great "stories" (myths, legends), each with its master image or central metaphor that is told and repeated to the family and clan, enable us to interpret our experience, fears, and doubts, and to understand what it means to be human. Many will be supportive of Michael Polanyi's opinions about narratives and the biblical narratives: his view that the search for truth is a progressive task undertaken within the context of one's community and culture, and that while there is "objectivity" to truth, it always involves personal affirmation and cultural narratives—in particular the great cultural narratives that are "heuristic," because they enable us to discover new ways to interpret reality and to keep discovering more and more about ourselves and our worlds.

Since WWII, the American Catholic community has devoted little energy to prayerful reflection on its great cultural narratives, to deepening its understanding of itself and its world. While its leaders have participated in biennial "board meetings" and put their names to numerous "statements" (most of which are unknown to the laity and scarcely read by clergy), scant effort has been made to assist Catholics to become more self-aware, or adequately able to appreciate their place in time. This failure in large part explains the lack of identity at all levels of the U.S. Church, and this explains the community's moral shifts during the last fifty years and its embarrassing lack of commitment to the story of God's love in Jesus, without which it is impossible (according to Polanyi) to break out of the human condition, to work against self-centeredness, and to break through rival, but less authentic, frameworks of thought.[48]

The U.S. Catholic community (it is really a loose aggregate of many distinct and diverse communities) has experienced great (stressful, unpredicted) change since WWII for another reason: As U.S. Catholics ceased to be immigrants in a foreign land (they are now close to 65 million and about 25% of the U.S. population)—and (as mentioned above) they became better educated than their parents and grandparents, more affluent, and more at home at the top of their professions, running multinational corporations, directing the armed forces, and playing key roles in state and national politics—an increasingly larger number has left the Democratic Party to become registered Republicans.[49] Whether located in metropolitan centers such as Chicago and New York, or living in rural towns like Grand Island, Nebraska or Emmetsburg, Iowa, U.S. Catholics both lay and clerical have progressively put moral issues such as abortion ahead of economic issues such as wages and jobs. Led by bishops quite different from men like Archbishop Hughes or Archbishop Ireland, they have witnessed the death of the family farm without protest, while being encouraged to become activists against gay and lesbian marriage.

Moreover, on the global front, rather than supporting the UN's worldwide efforts to destroy the scourges of AIDS, TB, and polio, the current leaders of the U.S. Church, influenced by the Vatican diplomats, have voiced their opposition to programs involving condoms. They have repeated pseudo-scientific reports about the ineffectiveness of condoms to prevent AIDS-infected sperm; they have thrown themselves into alliances with ultra-conservative religious groups and agencies that are dogmatically committed to abstinence-only methods of AIDS prevention. Not surprisingly, while Catholics throughout Europe have developed sex education programs that are comprehensive and reasonable, respectful of women, and realistic about responsible parenthood, U.S. Catholics find themselves residing in states where legislation prevents HMOs and medical insurance companies (BlueCross/Blue Shield) from offering any coverage for contraceptive services.[50]

Given Ronald Reagan's appeal, the scandals surrounding Bill Clinton's time in the White House, and George Bush's stand on such issues as abortion, tax cuts, vouchers for private schools, as well as John Ashcroft's leadership of the U.S. Justice Department, the trend toward the Republican Party should continue well into the future—to the Vatican's pleasure and the delight of "traditionalist" bishops and lay leaders.[51]

During the last twenty years, while Southern Baptists have experienced internal conflicts and leadership efforts to fire pastors and teachers over such doctrinal issues as the inerrancy of Scripture or the role of women within their communities, all who have followed the U.S. Catholic Church's history will be aware that the Vatican (with the encouragement of its local allies) has overseen the removal of Seattle's Archbishop Raymond Hunthausen, and the demise of bishops like San Francisco's James Quinn, who was a strong advocate for revisiting the Church's decision on birth control, implementing Vatican II's calls for laicising the Church, and making liturgical and theological adaptations in keeping with American culture.[52]

At the same time, in order to slow the pace of theological, liturgical, and pastoral change, the Vatican has supervised the ascendancy of overtly "conservative" bishops to leadership positions within the U.S.

Church.[53] And further, as U.S. bishops have returned to seeing themselves as members of a special caste and class within the Church—as CEO's of complex corporations with large payrolls and huge assets—many have become less like Bishop Dingman (Des Moines), or Spokane's Bishop John Topel, whom *Time* admired at his death for the simplicity of his residence and his down-to-earth lifestyle (in spite of the fact that he was a top math teacher in Montana before becoming Spokane's bishop). In the process, U.S. bishops have fashioned—with the Vatican's blessings—their work habits, homes, and offices (their autos, meals, and liturgical vestments) in the styles of earlier American "princes of the church" such as New York's Joseph Spellman, whose requirements for his visits to Rome's Bernini Bristol Hotel during the 1960s still cause scandal.[54]

During the last twenty years, the American Church has witnessed what European Catholics experienced when the Vatican censured Hans Kung, Bernard Haring, and Edward Schillebeeckx's. First, there was "L'Affaire Curran," as it has been called, the lengthy canonical process that removed Charles Curran from his teaching position at the Catholic University of America. More recently, the Vatican has silenced Matthew Fox, author of *Original Blessing, Creation Spirituality*, and *The Reinvention of Work,* director of the Institute in Culture and Creation Spirituality in Oakland, California, who was dismissed from the Dominicans in 1993. Then, even more recently, Robert Nugent, a priest of the Society of the Divine Savior, was removed from his ministry with gay and lesbian Catholics and their families, and banned from publishing on the morality of homosexuality.[55]

While the U.S. Catholic Church has never been a theologically monolithic organization as outsiders sometimes wrongly think (and the Vatican would like it to be), each of these actions has sent shock waves of different magnitudes through the U.S. Church. Although some Catholics applauded, because they felt that the Church was in serious need of discipline and a return to the days of solemn "high" masses,[56] others (like myself) saw these actions as unjust and high-handed, because we had (and continue to have) nothing but respect for bishops like James Quinn, and colleagues like Charles Curran and Robert Nugent, whose attitudes and opinions reflect the thinking of millions of college-educated, loyal—but discerning—American Catholics.[57]

In spite of the grains of truth contained in Jeffrey Stout's words quoted above (p. 11) and the "trench warfare" that has stifled dialogue and free exchange within the U.S. Catholic Church since Vatican II (to quote again from Peter Steinfels' recent book), a surprisingly large number of Catholic (as well as Protestant and Orthodox) theologians, both lay and clerical, working independently or for agencies such as the World Council of Churches or the U.S. Conference of Catholic Bishops, has valiantly responded with creativity and devotion to "the signs of the times" during the difficult years since WWII.[58] In the process, they have produced an almost countless number of ethical analyses (imperfect and stumbling in some cases, perhaps) that have brought religious ethics to readers of supermarket magazines and learned journals, parish newsletters, city dailies, school textbooks, and learned dictionaries. And they have done this in the face of what I might call "papalism"—the way that the majority of "loyal" U.S. Catholics approach theology and ethics; namely, by simply accepting and promoting the "clear" teaching of the popes—a method that has features in common with Scholasticism (it studied the Church's great thinkers) but is far less critical or comprehensive.[59]

At the same time, a smaller number of theologians, aware of the validity of Einstein's comment, and influenced by the writings of philosophers such as Max Scheler and Martin Heidegger, J. S. Mill and Immanuel Kant, the Protestant and Catholic theologians Karl Barth and Emil Brunner, Bernard Haring and Karl Rahner, for instance, have valiantly and patiently undertaken the labor-intensive task of developing meta-ethical moral theories that seek to be loyal to the confessional tenets of their Lutheran, Catholic, or Calvinist traditions; while, at the same time, updating those traditions in the light of developments in theology, literature, psychology, economics, politics, physics, philosophy, sociology, or other fields that should have significant influence on religious ethics.

Looking at the results of some of these efforts and assessing their strengths and weaknesses will be the focus of this book's next chapter—and its Part II.

Notes:

[1] "Many Roman Catholic philosophers have in recent years declared themselves puzzled and disappointed by the lack of intellectual rigour in moral theology," Vincent MacNamara wrote in 1985. Then he quotes, "'rich mines of fallacious argument and unexamined assumptions'," words from Gerald Hughes, *Authority in Morals: An Essay in Christian Ethics*, Heythrop Monographs, London, 1978, v.

[2] For this poll that compared Iowa attitudes in 2003 with those in 1983, *Des Moines Sunday Register* (June 1, 2003), A1, A4.

[3] The dominant features of current U.S. ethical opinion can be seen in the responses to the U.S. Supreme Court's 2003 decision in *Lawrence et al. v. Texas* that ruled that homosexual acts between adults in the privacy of their home were protected from government intrusion by the Constitution's right to privacy statute. For a sampling of these opinions, *Newsweek* (July 21, 2003), 16, 18.

[4] The publication in June 1977 of the Catholic Theological Society of America's *Human Sexuality: New Directions in American Catholic Thought* caused one such debate. For a snapshot, Richard A. McCormick, *Notes on Moral Theology: 1965 Through* 1980 (Washington: University Press of America, 1981), 737–745. For another view of the society's work, George Weigel, *The Courage To Be Catholic* (New York: Basic Books, 2002)—an apologetic work that emphasizes what the author calls the "culture of dissent" within the U.S. Church, sees the major causes for the Church's recent crises in the lack of fidelity by theologians to the Church's theological traditions, as well as crises in identity and leadership by priests and bishops.

[5] For useful sociological data on the beliefs and practices of U.S. Catholics since Vatican II, Andrew Greeley, "American Catholicism: 1909–1984," *America,* 150 (June 23–30, 1984), 487–492. The conclusions found in Greeley's, *American Catholics Since the Council: An Unauthorized Report* (Chicago: The Thomas More Press, 1985), 207–226, are especially informative on such matters as church attendance following *Humanae Vitae*, the rejection of the Church's sexual teaching, the anger within U.S. Catholic women, and the changed sensibilities of those who were "younger Catholics" when Greeley's data was complied. Concerning the struggles between fundamentalists and liberals within U.S. Protestant communities, Harvey Cox, *Religion in the Secular City: Toward A Postmodern Theology* (New York: Simon and Schuster, 1984), 27–82.

[6] For an important study of the rise of fundamentalist groups within Judaism, Islam, and U.S. Protestantism, Karen Armstrong, *The Battle for God* (New York: Alfred A. Knopf, 2000). For the author's provocative insights into the rise and growth of American fundamentalists, as well as a wealth of data about their doctrinal beliefs and social goals, 309–316, 354–364.

[7] On the subject of the growing alienation of educated Catholics—women in particular—and the special problem this poses for the church's future, Thomas J. Reese, *Inside the Vatican: The Politics and Organization of the Catholic Church* (Cambridge: Harvard University Press, 1996, 5th printing, 2001), 276–277.

[8] Today one finds college faculty who hold multiple terminal degrees in fields such nursing, law, and sociology. In 1992, while teaching at Creighton University, I learned that as many as 28 U.S. Jesuits had completed M.D. degrees, as well as degrees in philosophy and theology, prior to taking final vows or being ordained.

[9] Being "private" institutions, Catholic colleges did not (in their minds) have to take too much notice of EEOC hiring rules, or laws protecting employees from the sharing of "negative" information about previous performance. As well, being "Catholic" did not mean that these institutions were "outstanding" for the compassion they showed toward older faculty members (usually religious women and men) who had toiled for years on tiny salaries and allowances during the heat of the U.S. Catholic Church's "dog days."

[10] On this subject and other more recent battles within academe, Page Smith, *Killing the Spirit: Higher Education in America* (New York: Viking Penquin, 1990.

[11] For an important study on this subject, John R. Donahue, "The Challenge of the Biblical Renewal to Moral Theology," in *Riding Time Like a River: The Catholic Moral Tradition Since Vatican II*, edited by William J. O'Brien (Washington: Georgetown University Press, 1993), 59–80. Also, Thomas W. Ogletree, *The Use of the Bible in Christian Ethics* (Philadelphia: Fortress Press, 1983); Allen Verhey, *The Great Reversal: Ethics and the New Testament* (Grand Rapids: Eerdmans, 1984); *The Use of Scripture in Moral Theology*, Readings in Moral Theology #4, edited by Charles E. Curran and Richard A. McCormick (New York: Paulist Press, 1984); David H. Kelsey, *The Uses of Scripture in Recent Theology* (Philadelphia: Fortress Press, 1985); and the more recent studies, James T. Bretzke, "Scripture: The 'Soul' of Moral Theology?—The Second Stage," *Irish Theological Quarterly*, 60, 4 (1994), 259–271; Tom Deidun, "The Bible and Christian Ethics," in *Christian Ethics: An Introduction*, edited by Bernard Hoose, op.cit., 3–46.

[12] For a recent and valuable study of a key aspect of this work, Brad H. Young, *Jesus, the Jewish Theologian* (Boston: Hendrickson Publishers, 1995). Also, John Fuellenbach, *The Kingdom of God: The Message of Jesus Today* (Maryknoll: Orbis Books, 1995); Michael Cahill, "An Uncertain Jesus: Theological and Scholarly Ambiguities," *Irish Theological Quarterly* 61, 1 (1998), 22–38.

[13] Two major recent works on these figures are, Boniface Ramsey, *Ambrose* (New York: Routledge, 1997), and Andrew Louth, *Maximus the Confessor* (New York: Routledge, 1996).

[14] For an important new study on this subject, Hugh Connolly, *The Irish Penitentials and their Significance for the Sacrament of Penance Today* (Dublin: Four Courts Press, 1995).

[15] The Pontifical Institute of Medieval Studies in Toronto that was directed by Etienne Gilson after 1929 was a leading catalyst for this interest, and its *Medieval Studies* became a major source of interest for historians and theologians. Some illustrations of this heightened interest are: *The Feminine Mystic: Readings from Early Spiritual Writers*, edited by Lynne M. Deming (Cleveland: Pilgrim Press, 1997)—a collection of thirteen writings by medieval women; Grace Jantzen, *Julian of Norwich: Mystic & Theologian*, New Edition (New York: Paulist Press, 2000)—discusses Julian's life, feminist theology, and use of the image of "Christ as mother"; Renate Craine, *Hildegard: Prophet of the Cosmic Christ* (New York: Crossroad, 1997), provides a useful introduction to the saint's theology, music, and healing methods; Regine Pernoud, *Hildegard of Bingen* (London: Marlowe, 1998), provides context for Hildegard's life and relevance for today; Fiona Maddocks, *Hildegard of Bingen: The Woman of Her Age* (New York: Doubleday, 2001)—examines Hildegard's visions and music in the context of her role in twelfth century Germany's cultural, scientific, and religious revolutions. Also, the significant studies, Marcia L. Colish, *Medieval Foundations of the Western Intellectual Tradition [400–1400]* (New Haven: Yale University Press, 1997); Alexander Broadie, *The Shadow of Scotus: Philosophy and Faith in Pre-Reformation Scotland* (Edinburgh: T & T Clarke, 1995).

[16] For insightful comments on the Council, J. Philip Wogaman, *Christian Ethics: A Historical Introduction* (Louisville: Westminster/John Knox Press, 1993), 237–247; Frederick J. Cwiekowski, "Vatican Council II," *The New Dictionary of Catholic Social Thought*, edited by Judith A. Dwyer (Collegeville: Liturgical Press, 1994), 962–974.

[17] George V. Lobo, *Guide to Christian Living: A New Compendium of Moral Theology* (Westminster: Christian Classics, 1985), 12.

[18] Cultural historians note that Friedan, Greer, Millet, Brown, Daly, and others have changed the world of Western women and their context forever, a fact that still goes unappreciated by Catholic bishops, Southern Baptist preachers, and Missouri Synod pastors.

[19] A survey of opinions published in *The Tablet*, (England) *America (U.S.A)*, and *The Furrow* (Ireland) will reveal both the conservative reactions to these forces, as well as the responses of those who advocated the urgent need to rethink the Church's traditional positions on premarital sex, common law marriages, divorce, the lawfulness of marriages involving impotent persons, and adapting canon law to suit the marriage customs of Pacific island peoples.

[20] Peter Steinfels, *A People Adrift: Crisis in the U.S. Roman Catholic Church* (New York: Simon & Schuster, 2003), at 353.

[21] On this subject, Oscar Cole Arnal, "Worker Priests," in *The New Dictionary of Catholic Social Thought,* edited by Judith A. Dwyer (Collegeville: Liturgical Press), 1994), 1002–1003.

[22] On this subject, June O'Connor, "The, Catholic Worker," in *The New Dictionary of Catholic Social Thought*, op. cit., 128–130. Also, Robert Coles, *Dorothy Day: A Radical Devotion*. Radcliffe Biography Series (Reading: Addison-Wesley Publishing Company, 1987).

[23] On the Social Gospel Movement in Europe and America, J. Philip Wogaman, *Christian Ethics: An Historical Introduction* (Louisville: Westminster/John Knox Press, 1993), 194–208.

[24] While his fellow convert from Anglicanism, Westminster's Edward Cardinal Manning, took a leading role in settling labor disputes, this was Newman's position, and it explains why he did not play any public role in English public affairs or enter into debates about Britain's wars or the condition of its industrial cities and its workers.

[25] On the background and influence of these papal documents on twentieth century Catholic political activities, John T. Pawlikowski, "Catholic Social Teaching in the Catechism," in *Ethics and The Catechism of the Catholic Church*, edited by Michael E. Allsopp (Scranton: University of Scranton Press, 1999), 131–152; Stephen J. Pope, "Rerum Novarum," in *The New Dictionary of Catholic Social Thought*, op. cit., 828–844; Marie J. Giblin, "Quadragesimo Anno," in *The New Dictionary of Catholic Social Thought*, ibid., 802–813.

[26] On these documents, and Catholic social teaching in general, David M. Byers, editor, *Justice in the Marketplace: Collected Statements of the Vatican and the United States Bishops on Economic Policy (1891–1984)*, (Washington: U.S.CC Publications, 1985); Oliver F. Williams, "Capitalism," *The New Dictionary of Catholic Social Thought*, 111–123; John T. Pawlikowski, "Catholic Social Teaching in the Catechism," in *Ethics and the Catechism of the Catholic Church*, edited by Michael E. Allsopp (Scranton: University of Scranton Press, 1999), 131–152.

[27] On this subject, Charles H. Morris, *American Catholic: The Saints and Sinners who Built America's Most Powerful Church* (New York: Random House, 1997). Besides short biographies of New York's John Hughes and Boston's William O'Connell, Morris looks at the a wide range of Catholic leaders in parish and regional communities

in Nebraska, Illinois, Michigan, and New Jersey, as he describes how the Catholic Church became the dominant cultural force in twentieth century U.S.A.

[28] For this view of U.S. Catholic theology, John T. McGreevy, *Catholicism and American Freedom: A History* (New York: W.W. Norton & Company, 2003), 196.

[29] As quoted by John Lukacs in his magisterial work, *Outgrowing Democracy: A History of the United States in the Twentieth Century* (Garden City: Doubleday & Company, 1984), 351. This same spirit is visible throughout Francis J. Lally's *The Catholic Church in a Changing America* (Boston: Little, Brown and Company, 1962). Example: "... there is no place in the world where the Catholic Church is stronger than here in a land where less than two hundred years ago it was under edict" (23).

[30] Large-selling international magazines such as *Time* and *Newsweek* following the style of Andrew Greeley's reports on the faith-life of U.S. Catholics seemed to revel in the fact that U.S. Catholics were upset with Rome, and that they disagreed with the Vatican on birth control, abortion, divorce, and the ordination of women to the priesthood. That, by the late 70s, the U.S. Church had begun to experience a new flowering of faith and a new confidence about being Catholic seems to have been missed by the media—and the Vatican. On the state of the U.S. Church during the late 70s, George Gallup, Jr. and David Poling, *The Search for America's Faith* (Nashville: Abingdon, 1980), esp. 57–78.

[31] On this subject, Thomas J. Reese, *Inside the Vatican*, op. cit., 282.

[32] For a valuable account of this conflict, seen through the eyes of the John Ford, SJ, who began his career as a futuristic moral theologian, but who became progressively reactionary over the morality of birth control and was bypassed by the younger generation of Catholic ethicists, including John T. Noonan and Dan Callahan, John T. McGreevy, op. cit., 216–249. For quite a different reading of this event, H.W. Crocker, *Triumph: The Power and the Glory of the Catholic Church—A 2,000 Year History* (New York: Three Rivers Press, 2001), 414–419. The same author, whose work has been praised by Notre Dame University's Ralph McInerny, defends Pope Pius XII's papacy, his dealings with Hitler, and his efforts on behalf of Europe's Jews, and lauds the twentieth century church for its "sense of historic certainty" without any discussion of the century's theological debates, or Vatican II's numerous calls for structural, liturgical, and theological renewal.

[33] From Clifford Stevens, "A Matter of Credibility," one of just a large number of responses by U.S. theologians published in *Veritatis Splendor: American Responses,* edited by Michael E. Allsopp and John J. O'Keefe (Kansas City: Sheed & Ward, 1995).

[34] For analyses and commentaries on the part of the catechism that deals with morality, *Ethics and the Catechism of the Catholic Church*, edited by Michael E. Allsopp (Scranton: University of Scranton Press, 1999).

[35] These concepts are central to the writings of the most respected authority in the field of adult education, Malcolm Knowles. They are also inherent to the thinking of the widely influential U.S. psychologist Carl Rogers.

[36] Jay P. Dolan, *In Search of An American Catholicism: A History of Religion & Culture in Tension* (New York: Oxford University Press, 2002), and Thomas Day, *Why Catholics Can't Sing: The Culture of Catholicism and the Triumph of Bad Taste* (New York: Crossroad, 1990).

[37] Examples: The Vatican was concerned about some of the ethical statements on mortal sin, sexuality, and the "fundamental option," for instance, that appeared in the

so-called *Dutch Catechism* (1965). It was worried, in the late 60s, about the Canadian bishops' position on the authority of conscience, especially about its right to dissent from Paul VI's teaching in *Humanae Vitae*. *Hans Kung's Infallible?* caused consternation when published in 1970, on the occasion of 100th anniversary of Vatican I's decree on papal infallibility. Quite recently, the Vatican has shown concern about some of the pastoral practices accepted by the Church's bishops, clergy, and laity in Australia. This, in part, explains the recent appointment of Archbishop George Pell as Archbishop of Sydney, following the retirement of Edward Cardinal Clancy.

[38] On the personal role of Pope John Paul II in the decision to tighten the rules for granting annulments, Jonathan Kwitny, *Man of the Century: The Life and Times of Pope John Paul II* (New York: Henry Holt and Company, 1997), 382.

[39] The Vatican's policy led to the resignation of the U.S. Jesuit Robert Drinan from the U.S. Senate.

[40] For a history and analysis of the *mandatum*, "Theologians, Catholic Higher Education, and the *Mandatum*: A Report by the Ad Hoc Committee on the *Mandatum*," Catholic Theological Society of America (September 2000).

[41] Jay P. Dolan, *In Search of An American Catholicism: A History of Religion & Culture in Tension*, op.cit., 201.

[42] On this subject, J.C.H. Aveling, *The Jesuits* (New York: Stein and Day, 1982), 359–363, and "The Modern Jesuit Dilemma," on the years following the death of Jean-Baptiste Janssens, and the generalship of Pedro Arrupe, the battles between conservative and liberal Jesuits in Europe, United States, and Latin America, 364–371.

[43] On the rise of Opus Dei within the Church, its goals and mission, Michael Walsh, *Opus Dei: An Investigation into the Secret Society Struggling for Power within the Roman Catholic Church* (New York: HarperCollins, English edition, 1988,1st U.S. edition, 1992).

[44] On this subject, David A. Yallop, *In God's Name: An Investigation into the Murder of Pope John Paul 1* (New York: Bantam Books,1984). While sensationalizing some of the data, this book has high praise from Morris West and Andrew Greeley, and was on the *New York Times* bestseller list for more than 4 months.

[45] On this second subject, the disturbing analysis by the British investigative reporter Rupert Cornwell, *God's Banker* (New York: Dodd, Mead & Company, 1984). Another recent book that provides another disturbing portrait of the Vatican by examining such subjects as the Vatican's financial turnaround since the 1930s following the Lateran Treaty, its dealings with the National Socialists, the Banco Ambrosiano scandal, and the Vatican's gifts from drug traffickers based in Gdansk, Poland, is Paul L. Williams, *The Vatican Exposed: Money, Murder, and the Mafia* (Amherst: Prometheus Books, 2003).

[46] I use "generally unsuccessful defense" because, as the twenty-first century begins, the educated world (certainly in the United States) still looks upon the pope's efforts as weak and self-serving, in spite of several separate invitations to scholars to examine the Vatican's archives, several separate Vatican reports, and the publication of the pope's secret communiqués and other diplomatic initiatives. On the subject of the Catholic laity's distrust of the papacy, Garry Wills, *Papal Sin: Structures of Deceit* (New York: Doubleday, 2000).

[47] The response of Iowans to the July 2003 papal statement about gay marriage is typical of national sentiment: "How dare the Catholic Church talk to us about

morality after it took no action against hundreds of pedophile priests and knowingly allowed them to remain in office!"

[48] On these subjects, Clifford Geertz, *The Interpretation of Cultures* (New York: Basic Books, 1973), 52, 89; Michael Polanyi, *Personal Knowledge* (Chicago: University of Chicago Press, 1958), 198–199. Also, Polanyi's essays "Beyond Nihilism," and "The Message of the Hungarian Revolution," in *Knowing and Being*, edited by Marjorie Greene (Chicago: University of Chicago Press, 1969), 3–23, 24–39; Roger G. Betsworth, *Social Ethics: An Examination of American Moral Traditions* (Louisville: John Knox Press, 1990)—a book that has no parallel (as far as I know) within Catholic circles.

[49] "In the years since the Vatican Council, American Catholics have surged ahead of their white Protestant counterparts on almost every available measure of educational and occupational and economic achievement," Andrew Greeley writes in *American Catholics Since the Council*, op. cit., 208.

[50] This was something I learned quite by accident after consulting with a health insurance expert who writes policies in South Dakota and Iowa. Further research showed that, as I might have expected, most medical systems associated with the U.S. Catholic Church exclude all coverage of birth control services and medications from their group plans—regardless of the religious affiliations or personal beliefs. Ironically, Viagra is covered—with a physician's prescription!

[51] This shift toward the right and toward the Republican Party seems inevitable (I believe) unless Catholic teenagers who are being educated today in high schools (not in private preps) become displeased with the Bush administration's plans that favor big business, promote school prayer, fight gay rights and euthanasia in states like Oregon, resist gun control, support voucher programs for Catholic schools—not to mention the Republican Party's plans to combat illegal immigration, turn back decades of legislation written to protect the nation's parks and wildlife areas, to cut support for farmers, rural arts and library programs, as well as billions in (unrestricted) U.S. foreign aid.

[52] In 1981, after the U.S. Catholic bishops expressed their collective support for nuclear disarmament, Archbishop Hunthausen said that he would withhold that part of his federal income tax that was going for military purposes. Was he removed for this action—in particular—that was known to rile the White House, as well as conservative Catholics in Seattle, the home of the Boeing Corporation, one of the world's biggest defense contractors? Concerning Pope John Paul II's negative attitude toward Archbishop Quinn for his remarks during the 1980 synod of bishops, Jonathan Kwitney, op. cit., 374–375.

[53] Just a few examples that come immediately to mind are: Archbishop Donald W. Wuerl (Pittsburgh), Archbishop Eldon Curtis (Omaha), Bernard Cardinal Law (Boston), Bishop John Sheets, SJ (South Bend), Bishop Robert Carlson (Sioux Falls), Bishop Blaise Cupich (Rapid City), Archbishop John C. Favalora (Miami), Archbishop John F. Donoghue (Atlanta), Bishop Fabian Bruskewitz (Lincoln, NE), Archbishop Raymond Burke (St. Louis), Bishop John C. Nienstedt (New Ulm, MN), Bishop Michael Sheridan (Colorado Springs), and Bishop John Nevins (Venice, FL). Some of these bishops have made it clear to clergy and laity in their dioceses that they will focus on three issues during their time as bishops: vocations, foreign missions, and abortion—decisions that mean that they will not be focusing on issues that matter

to those Catholics who live in America's rural areas facing severe drought and the death of the family farm, or in urban centers suffering from housing shortages, drug problems, unsafe schools, and high unemployment. The difference between the concerns of many of today's bishops and those who led the fight on behalf of civil rights and migrant workers can be seen from comparing the contents of diocesan papers published during the last 25 years, or what one finds today in diocesan papers *The National Catholic Reporter, Commonweal,* or *The Catholic Worker.*

[54] Throughout America, the St. Vincent de Paul Society's lay leaders have taken over the task of looking after the local poor, while the clergy have assumed leadership roles in liturgical matters—a separation of duties that has weakened, not strengthened the clergy's visibility and respect.

[55] For an example of Nugent's sensitive and insightful pastoral and theological writing, Michael E. Allsopp, *Ethics and the Catechism of the Catholic Church* (Scranton: University of Scranton Press, 1999), 109–130.

[56] There is little doubt that a large number of Catholics became concerned about changes in Catholic liturgy and theology, as well as in the Church's implementation of Vatican II due to what one reads in books like Dietrich von Hildebrand's *The Trojan Horse in the City of God: The Catholic Crisis Explained* (Manchester: Sophia Institute Press, 1st printing, 1967; reprinted and enlarged 1993).

[57] U.S. Catholics are not in favor of abortion, nor do they think that homosexual acts are moral. However, the great majority is quite tolerant. Consequently, Catholics think that others are entitled to hold opinions on abortion different from theirs, and that gays and lesbians should be left alone—so long as their behavior does not harm others, especially minors.

[58] Peter Steinfels, *A People Adrift: Crisis in the U.S. Roman Catholic Church,* ibid., 353. One of the central themes of this book is that both liberals and conservatives must share the guilt for the infighting and bitterness–that must be brought to an end (as Chicago's Cardinal Bernadin tried to do before his death) as it carries out a thorough transformation of itself—before it suffers "irreversible decline."

[59] From a study of episcopal statements, personal communications with bishops, and a careful review of studies in "conservative" Catholic publications, it is hard to deny that "papalism" as I term it, is seen as the right and proper way for all Catholics to become educated in Catholicism and to make "authentic" Catholic moral decisions.

Chapter II

Christian Ethics and the New Century: Its Current Health, Opportunities for Renewal

He who begins by loving Christianity better than truth will proceed by loving his own sect or church better than Christianity and end in loving himself better than all.
Samuel Taylor Coleridge
Aids to Reflection

Christian ethics must arise from the gospel of Jesus Christ. Otherwise it could not be *Christian* ethics.
Oliver O'Donovan
Resurrection and Moral Order

The Christianity of our age and civilization approves of society as it now is, with its prison-cells, its factories, its houses of infamy, its parliaments; but as for the doctrine of Jesus, which is opposed to modern society, it is only empty words.
Leo Tolstoy
My Religion

T.S. Eliot's choruses from "The Rock," contain the perceptive lines, "and the Church must be forever building, and always decaying, and always being restored." The truth of this observation is borne out by the results of a national study about religion in America published in 1980: the data showed a new flowering of faith and confidence among U.S. Catholics only 10–15 years after the Catholic Church in the United States hit rock bottom![1]

While the survey indicated that a larger number of church members living in New York, Chicago, Los Angeles, and Seattle were more inclined to disagree with the official church than those who described themselves as "Catholics" back in the early 1960s, many more Catholics stated they were less inclined to leave the church (ibid., 59–60). The study revealed a number of other surprising results that once again proved the prophets of doom and gloom were quite wrong. First, by 1980 the number of Catholics aged 18–29 attending mass had risen 10% in the two years since 1979 (ibid., 58–59). Second, with Catholics comprising 28% of the national population, large numbers said they wanted more ecumenical activities, more opportunities to study the Bible, better sermons, and more uplifting liturgical celebrations. The "good news for U.S. Catholics" was "good news for all Christians," the authors of the survey George Gallup, Jr. and David Poling stated (ibid., 57).

Christian Ethics Today: A Health Status Report

As this new century unfolds, Catholic moral theology, and in particular its "Anglo-American" expression, reflect the condition of the "world" Church and the Catholic Church in the United States: they are both in *relatively* healthy condition. Their condition can be measured in terms of the worldwide changes in the number of state-funded and church-sponsored university departments and endowed chairs devoted to theology and religious studies, and the rise and fall in the number (and quality) of undergraduate and graduate degrees in religious ethics.

How strong the discipline is can be assessed (to some degree) by: (a) the noticeable increase in the number of academic and pastoral journals that have come to life during the last fifty years (not to mention the websites) that have an express interest in Christian morality; and (b) the healthy growth in the memberships of such organizations as the American Academy of Religion, the Society for Biblical Literature (AAR, SBL), the Catholic Theological Society of America, the College Theology Society, the National Catholic Education Association, the various national societies devoted to moral theology, and the U.S.-based Society for Christian Ethics, whose annual meetings bring together teachers and writers from every continent for three or four days of workshops, paper sessions, reunions, job interviews, and lively breakfast discussions with authors of the latest books.

When I look back now over the half-century, recalling meetings with John Connery, Bernard Haring, Karl Rahner, Teilhard de Chardin,

Yves Congar, Charles Curran, Enda McDonagh, James Gustafson, Joseph Fletcher, Paul Ramsey, Richard McCormick, and Edouard Hamel, and remember the contents of Haring's *The Law of Christ*, Gustafson's *Ethics from a Theocentric Perspective*, Rahner's *Theological Investigations*, Lonergan's *Method in Theology*, and Richard McCormick's *Notes on Moral Theology*, I feel genuine admiration and pride in the achievements that have been made.

Today—because of Vatican II, the ecumenical movement, and the devoted leadership of pastors, lay and religious teachers, as well the influence of these authors—books dealing with Protestant and Catholic ethics, the textbooks being used in high schools and colleges, and the essays appearing in popular magazines such as *America*, *Commonweal*, *U.S. Catholic* show a healthy response to the Council's explicit recommendation that "special attention needs to be given to the development of moral theology. Its scientific exposition should be more thoroughly nourished by spiritual teaching. It should show the nobility of the Christian vocation of the faithful, and their obligation to bring forth fruit in charity for the life of the world" (*Optatum Totius*, 16).

Catholic moral theology is more rigorous, more impressive, than it was in the 1950s–1960s. It is less preoccupied with sin. The focus of its books are less on individual happiness and more concerned with social well-being; they contain far less Church law, features that became entrenched in Roman Catholics ethics texts for reasons that John Mahoney explains in his remarks about the influence of auricular confession on the development of the Church's ethics.[2] Catholic moral theology is also less rationalistic, more modest and tentative; it shows a much keener appreciation of the Bible's place in Catholic life.[3]

While authors strive for holism, conscious efforts have been made to separate (where useful) "moral theology" from such related areas as canon law, social teaching, spirituality, and books dealing with Catholic political theory.[4]

While it is true, as David Ford says: "Churches often do not have an atmosphere conducive to eager learning of the faith or its implications," forty years after the close of Vatican II, millions of Catholics have felt the positive influence of a number of religious movements and specific approaches in Christian ethics.[5] Whether old or young, university educated or not, they have been inspired by theories that are *theocentric* or *Christocentric* in their way of describing the Christian life and resolving current issues in environmental, health care, and military ethics. Together with Protestants in Europe, America, and the Pacific, Catholics have seen changes in their ethical visions due to the rise of *feminist* moral theories, and those that flow out of *liberation* theologies. There has been renewed interest as well in *virtue ethics*, *evangelical ethics*, and *narrative* ethics.

Some Catholic authors still retain a firm (shall I call it "excessive") loyalty toward the *natural law* approach to morality, it is true. However, others are united in the conviction (as I am) that the Church's ethics, whether dealing with biomedical or business morality, should be *theocentric* (focused on God's saving work in Christ), *Christocentric* (a way of life flowing from the Christian's being-in-Christ), *ecclesial* (guided by the "people of God," communal, and showing concern for community), *biblical* (accepting that God's word, as found in Scripture, is authoritative in matters of faith and morality), *sacramental* (emphasizing the divine dimensions of the Christian life), *ecclesial* (it is associated with the church, and brings life and order to the church) and *personal* (it focuses on the human person).

Hundreds of millions of Catholics living in Canada, America, Australia, Ireland, France, Spain, and Germany, furthermore, are convinced that when the Church's bishops and pastors speak on current issues of today, they must speak *positively*, and *constructively* using the language and thought patterns of their audiences, whether religious educators or cardiac physicians. Christian ethics—they affirm—must be *eucharistic* (filled with a spirit of thanksgiving), *hopeful,* and *liberational* (an emphasis on overcoming the barriers of injustice and oppression). It must be a *communicative* ethic—one that actively listens to those who have been marginalized, the oppressed, and those normally ignored when fact-finding is undertaken and decisions are being made, as Sharon Welch has emphasized in her *Feminist Ethics of Risk.*[6]

At the same time, when I remember Einstein's words, and associate them with what Douglas McArthur said about "Old soldiers..." during his farewell address at the U.S. Military Academy, West Point, NY, my feelings become a little sad and bitter: It is hard not to be moved by the needless suffering that has been caused to Catholics young and old, because, like some "old soldiers," a number of "old" and "worn out" notions in Catholic moral theology have taken far too long to fade away.[7]

As the twenty-first century begins, Catholic moral theology, as seen in high school and college textbooks and peer-reviewed essays published in magazines such as *U.S. Catholic* or *Theological Studies*, is still excessively rationalistic. All too frequently the theology wars with adversaries no longer a threat, or embodies dated understandings of human psychology, biology or economics. Sadly, too much Catholic moral theology is myopic, sexist, and paternalistic. Forty years after Vatican II, too many Catholic authors and pastors, as well as those responsible for *The Catechism of the Catholic Church*, still adhere to neo-Scholasticism's worn out concepts of moral norms and ethical truth; they are entrenched against widely accepted developments in linguistics and philosophy that correspond more closely with reality by emphasizing the contingency of moral knowledge and the historicity of ethical discourse.

Disturbed by many of the social changes brought about since WWII through the feminist movement, the access of millions to higher education, and the advances in medical science, Catholic pastors and authors seek to restrict individual decision-making and limit personal autonomy. They rail against Liberalism; they see "dangers" every-where; they are determined to oppose whatever is new or modern—in thought, fashion, or custom.

Rather than supporting the twentieth century's turn toward the individual and adjusting to the research of those who have re-exam-ined the Church's understanding of sin, its teaching on conscience, individuality, and creativity in moral decision-making, too many Catholic writers still resist these developments. Instead of listening eagerly to the doctrinal and ethical beliefs of educated Jewish, Hindu, or Islamic scholars in the spirit of Nietzsche's remark, "There is my truth; now tell me yours," the majority of U.S. Catholic bishops and clergy still stress the importance of an adolescent obedience to the Church's magisterium; they exaggerate the spiritual value associated with self-sacrifice and the importance of bending one's mind and will to the Church's moral teaching, regardless of the promptings of one's heart or the judgments of one's head. Clearly, they prefer to admit to their ranks adult "altar boys"—something one sees in the way future priests are depicted in diocesan newspapers.[8] When their idiosyncrati-cally expressed and antiquated arguments fail to persuade, they resort to threats and sanctions.[9]

For reasons that we will see, much that is called "fundamental" Roman Catholic moral theology (the part that deals with basic, foun-dational issues) still lacks sufficient rigor to impress contemporary scientists and philosophers; it is still insufficiently theological to merit the respect of Protestant and Catholic theologians trained in Scripture, linguistics, and contemporary psychology. While written 25 years ago, Gerard J. Hughes's words still ring true: "Theologians, and moral theologians in particular, have all too often supposed that there is a specifically theological method, leading to a specifically theological ethics, which justified them in paying little heed to moral philosophy, or, indeed, to the philosophical problems underlying theology itself."[10]

When I look back at how Bernard Haring's and Karl Rahner's renewal efforts were received by many of their colleagues, I am reminded of the remark President Carter's mother, Lillian Carter, once made: "Sometimes when I look at my children, I say to myself, 'Lillian, you should have stayed a virgin.' " In too many countries, the Catholic Church has been devastated by the unwillingness of Catholic leaders to think as John XXIII did. Generations of inspiring and involved young adults have been lost to Catholicism because of bishops' conscious opposition to bringing their faith-communities into the modern world, as well as their general resistance to the social and cultural changes sweeping across nations. In Ireland, for instance, Catholic bishops have been too slow to move the Church into the twentieth century. They have failed to realize that Catholics are no longer second-class citizens living in a land occupied by foreigners and ruled by harsh penal laws. Consequently, the clergy and the Christian Brothers are paying high prices for being insensitive as pastors and harsh as high school teachers—for educating generations of talented Irish boys and girls who went to school in the years after WWII to believe that they should not rise above their fathers; to think that having Protestant friends or aspiring to wealth would lead them astray; that "sex" and "drink" were the worst of evils.[11]

How many of us who spent half our lives in schools run by the Presentation Sisters, Christian Brothers, or Jesuits can say of any of our teachers what the journalist and broadcaster, Edward R. Murrow said of his speech teacher, Ida Anderson: "She taught me to love good books, good music, and gave me the only sense of values I have. She knows me better than any person in the world. The part of me that is decent, that wants to do something, is the part she created. I owe the ability to live to her ...."[12]

Likewise, Catholic bishops in Latin America have seen millions leave the Church and join Protestant communities, because they were too slow to rethink the Church's spirituality and ethics, and to remove errors (false beliefs, worn-out notions) leftover from the years of

European conquest and foreign domination: namely, a worldview and morality in which Catholics would please God and gain eternal life by living lives of private and public devotion to Jesus' passion—practicing pious devotions that focused on Mary's miraculous powers, her purity, and sinlessness, and committing themselves not to lives of political activity, economic reform, or education, but to submitting themselves to God's will and servilely accepting lives of poverty.

Too many Latin American Catholics have been brought up in a spirituality of excessive sadness; they knew little about God's saving work in Christ, that they were born to be "eucharistic" people, destined by God to be blessed forever (as Luther's catechism correctly says in its answer to the question, "Why did God make us?").

As fair-minded assessments of the *Catechism of the Catholic Church* show, the Catholic Church's "official" moral theology in 2002–2003 is still excessively rational and authoritarian; it seeks to persuade from fear rather than from friendship. In spite of some exceptions, there are still too many jeremiads in Catholic ethics, as seen when a person reads John Paul II's *Veritatis Splendor*, and pastoral statements in the areas of biomedical and sexual ethics published in recent years by U.S. bishops.[13]

"How to attest in truth to God and to all else in relation to God," remains theology's all-encompassing question today as in the past, David Ford notes.[14] Far too many Protestant and Catholic books used in U.S. college and parish theology and ethics courses are still exclusively Euro-centered in answering this question, however. Rather than extolling New Testament values and virtues, or looking at issues from the point of view of the defeated or the marginalized, Catholic social teaching still suffers from the influence of Charlemagne's rise to power within the western Church. It is still seriously distorted by the ascendancy of military virtues and values that pushed aside New Testament ones.[15]

Catholic social teaching still bears too many signs of the fact that medieval popes, bishops, and abbots were both religious leaders and political powers, who were regularly forced to exert their military and political might to protect their property, and who consequently convened synods and issued laws—not to preach Jesus' message of simplicity and peace, but to justify aggressive and defensive wars, the conquest of a rival's lands, or the brutality of capital punishment, torture, and slavery.[16] Consequently, as this century begins, the Church's "just war" theory is not just seriously out-of-date; it is too beholden to power, politics, and modern warfare—and the Catholic Church's "peace talk," unlike those who represent the Society of Friends, lacks credibility.

"Force is as pitiless to the person who possesses it, or thinks he does, as it is to its victims; the second it crushes, the first it intoxicates," Simone Weil wrote in the first year of WWII.[17] However, few U.S. Catholics see anything out of place with the large number of ROTC programs associated with U.S. Catholic colleges and universities, or the Church's strong involvement in the military services. Anecdotal evidence leads me to believe, moreover, that it is still easier to get a bishop to relieve a priest from his diocese to serve as a military chaplain than to serve as a college professor or hospital chaplain. Sadly, too many otherwise peace-loving men and women have graduated from U.S. Catholic institutions (as well as those in Australia, France, Germany, Chile, and Argentina) only to resemble what the mother of one of Lieutenant Calley's comrades said about her son who had killed women, children and babies at My Lai: "I sent them a good boy and they made him a murderer."[18]

The playwright, Jerry Sterner, author of the hit *Other People's Money*, once said, "If you know how people feel about money, that's more revealing than any other single thing I know, including sleeping with them."[19] A generation or two ago, U.S. Catholics were as generous as their Protestant neighbors, and thought nothing of sharing their wealth, time, and talents whenever "sister" or "father" asked them. They might not have tithed, but they gave to parish schools and built magnificent cathedrals in the prairies; they made sure the local clergy had "nice" places to live, ate well, and drove "the right sort of cars." Today, however, Catholic social teaching rarely deals with labor issues, family wages, or the Church's support for unions and cooperatives. The majority of college-educated Catholics are fiscal conservatives, people who vote "pro-life," but at the same time are opposed to any increases in income or property tax rates or to fully funding federal programs such as Head Start or statewide immunization programs for infants.

Catholic thinking in the areas of economics and labor still fights battles that have ended long ago, and ignores the implications of the rise of global business and the special problems caused by multinational corporations whose profits sometimes exceed the annual budgets of African nations. Catholic hospitals and universities might be listed as "not-for-profit" institutions for tax purposes, but they are run along the same lines as any secular "big business." And does the University of Notre Dame or Boston College invest in ways that reflect their "Catholic" heritage? Do U.S. Catholic leaders embody the simplicity and poverty of Jesus who had nowhere to lay his head or bread to eat? I think not. Tolstoy's criticisms of organized Christianity— European and American–are still valid!

Sadly, after a promising start during the years immediately following Vatican II, the Catholic Church has again reverted to legalism, titles, and honors. Following some years when Catholic communities were leaders in grassroots ecumenical activities, both separatism and triumphalism have reappeared. Church leaders have forgotten Yves Congar's prophetic words: "In a world that has become, or has become again, purely 'worldly,' the Church finds herself forced, if she would still be anything at all, to be simply the Church, witness to the Gospel and the kingdom of God, through Jesus Christ and in view of him. This is what men need; this is what they expect of her ... that she be less *of* the world and more *in* the world; that she be simply the Church of Jesus Christ, the conscience of men in the light of the Gospel, but that she be this with her whole heart."[20]

Catholic medical ethics, at least in its U.S. published form, seems to be in a healthy state due to the efforts of organizations such as the Catholic Health Association, the leadership of Georgetown's Andre Hellegers and Edmund Pellegrino, the editorial work of *The Linacre Quarterly's* John Mullooly, and the influence of *Theological Studies*, *Louvain Studies*, *Christian Bioethics*, books like John T. Noonan's *The Morality of Abortion* (1970), Kevin O'Rourke and Benedict Ashley's, *Health Care Ethics* (1977), and Richard McCormick's *Health and Medicine in the Catholic Tradition* (1984)—not to mention the influence of Paul Ramsey, Joseph Fletcher, Gilbert Meilander, and James Gustafson.

However, administrators of facilities sponsored by the Church, as well as nurses and physicians working in U.S. health care centers (whom I have surveyed) find the Church's positions on in vitro fertilization, sterilization, birth control, abortion, and withholding nutrition and hydration both unconvincing and un-nuanced. Too many physicians and nurses educated in Jesuit institutions, in particular those of an older, but still powerful generation, still resolve all questions about care and treatment in terms of "ordinary" and "extraordinary" means—and sometimes without addressing any other consideration, neither the patient's nor the community's "best interests."

Catholic medical ethics might exhibit more signs of renewal than some other areas of moral theology, but it is still far from what the Church needs—and today's Catholics deserve. "Integrity" might be a significant "value." However, integrity can be seriously over valued in a Christian ethic, especially in the hands of a person like Sydney Biddle Barrows, the "Mayflower Madam," who justified herself with the retort, "I ran the wrong kind of business, but I did it with integrity."[21]

Thirty years ago, Gregory Baum said that Roman Catholic sexual ethics had nothing to offer the modern world, especially younger married women and men who had college educations, or older Catholics who were past their childbearing years. The narrowness and banality of Catholic sexual ethics reflects the intelligence of the U.S. politician Dan Quayle, who said publicly, "If we don't succeed, we run the risk of failure."[22]

The last fifty years have seen some progress in Catholic thinking due to the positive influence of movements like Marriage Encounter, the writings of Lisa Sowle Cahill,[23] John Giles Milhaven, and the English layman Jack Dominian.[24] The Church's unbending commitment to an outdated teleological sexual morality and to a reactionary neo-Scholastic understanding of "natural law" ethics, however, has led not only to insisting that Catholics still embrace misguided views about human reason and moral norms, but also that they accept gross distortions about women, human relationships, sexuality, and marriage.[25] Today's French, Dutch, or German Catholic women might not be like the actor Debbie Reynolds who "thought of sex as a duty, not a pleasure." But (from my research) there are still very few U.S. high school or college classes that deal seriously or maturely with this important area of life.

When these defects are combined with the Church's unwillingness to listen to the voices of women, not to mention its heavy-handed control of moral theology, its paternalism towards the laity, and its patriarchal approach to Catholics under thirty, there is an obvious and urgent need for the Catholic Church to take new directions in this area of its ethics, as Kevin T. Kelly has argued.[26] The rise of neo-conservative bishops to policy-making roles within the Catholic Church in Australia and the United States means that seminaries will revert to pre-Vatican II practices and programs, and clergy, consequently, will be less well-prepared to provide sexual education or counseling to adolescents and engaged or married couples.[27]

"The renewal of moral theology has but begun," Enda McDonagh said in 1972.[28] Thirty years later, it is still in its beginning stages. In spite of some advances—some general support at the Church's grass-roots level—the work of renewal is still far from complete; much still needs to be done.

Why?

There are a number of major hurdles to all renewal efforts. Putting together a moral theory that honors the past and does justice to the present is a hazardous task. Although a theologian teaching today has John Henry Newman as a guide, describing how progress takes place in theology and philosophy, or in the academic study of history and psychology is far from easy, as the model is complex—it is not like the blossoming of a rose, nor the formation of a mountain. Since a change in the Church's thought sometimes begins its life in much the same way as a salmon begins its life's journey in a small mountain stream, it is almost impossible to know if it will develop the strength to swim upstream against rivers of thought as powerful as the Nile.

Furthermore, the Christian church is conservative by nature. Social, institutional, political, economic, cultural, and aesthetic processes are also at work to affect the success or failure of an ethical movement or theory in much the same way as these forces influence movements in art, music, and literature. The history of Christendom shows that the guardians of the Catholic Church's theology—its moral theology in particular—are resistant to innovation.

Roman Catholic Ethics: Opportunities for Further Renewal

As the twenty-first century begins, there are definite opportunities for further renewal, however. Many Catholics living today see that just as the Church's theologians were open to important developments in theology and science in past centuries, theologians, as well as some bishops with leadership authority in the Church, now appreciate that Catholic moral theology should be sensitive to current developments in contemporary thinking about the role of women and the authority of conscience, for example—as well as to advances in the natural and social sciences that have broken new ground in fields like genetics, sociology, and cosmology.[29]

According to a schema proposed by Jurgen Habermas, our post-modern world has been sectored like an orange into three frequently antagonistic spheres: one is primarily "expressive"; another is dominated by "cognitive-instrumental rationality"; the third is committed to "moral-practical rationality." Habermas (along with a growing number of theologians and political and religious leaders around the world) sees that the character of life within these spheres needs to change, and that the three spheres must be integrated and differently coordinated, so that they constitute a just and fulfilling society. They realize the necessity of assisting individuals and nations to achieve integration and personal and cultural identity—to escape alienation, self-destruction, and the upheavals of ceaseless civil strife.

To achieve these goals, a growing number of authors are interested in building contemporary moral theories guided by reliable research into ethics, literature and human behavior, and based on the Church's living insights into the sources which directed the Christian church in the first centuries: the ethical framework of the Hebrew society as described in the Torah and Jesus' teachings; the moral teaching of the secular world with particular attention to the ethics developed by Greek and Roman philosophers (as well as medieval and modern moralists); the words, deeds and example of Jesus as seen in his life and ministry as preserved and expressed in the Church's prayers and liturgical texts, its theological tomes and saints' lives, its conciliar decrees and stained glass.

Appalled that so many years after Vatican II, the U.S. Catholic Church still lacks a respected national radio and TV network, these same leaders realize that if Catholicism's great intellectual and spiritual heritage is to be appreciated, then they must support these renewal efforts.

In spite of the current scandals among the U.S. clergy that have undermined the Church's moral authority and weakened its social and political (not to mention its financial) status, lay and religious educators working in Catholic schools and supervising RCIA programs are aware that the Church's ethics should not be closed to the work of other religious traditions; that Catholic pastors should be engaged not only in active dialogue with other Christians, but with all persons of good will. As Jesuit theologian George V. Lobo sees it, "Just as the Gospel message was expressed in Aristotelian terms by St. Thomas, there should also be a similar possibility of expressing it in Hindu terms. For this we have still to go a long way. Indian Christians would need to be much more familiar with the Gospel message and Hindu thought, and at the same time liberated from a Western problematic which is also becoming increasingly difficult."[30]

Besides these positive signs in favor of the success of further renewal efforts in Catholic moral theology, there is another reason to be hopeful: there are bishops throughout the Church (as well as bishops and pastors to be) who have heard Einstein and Huston Smith, and who are willing to cautiously incorporate recent insights from the study of history, psychology, Scripture, and Christian spirituality into their pastoral statements on sexual, business, social, and environmental ethics. There are bishops, active in organizations like the Catholic Theological Society of America and others, who are willing to consult leading ethicists when they wish to speak about euthanasia or the morality of letting die seriously handicapped adults such as Nancy Cruzan.[31]

Finally, there are bishops soon to be in leadership positions in Australia, France, Germany, Italy, Canada, and America (not to mention India, Kenya, and Uganda) who see that renewal in ethics need not mean secularization, and change need not lead to loss of Catholic identity or a decline in vocations to the priesthood or religious life— but that active involvement in ecumenical activities, whether local or at the level of the World Council of Churches, can lead to stronger, not weaker, faith communities.

These bishops and parish leaders know that the Church's moral theology should contain a stronger sense of the presence of the Holy Spirit in the Christian's daily life,[32] a greater sense of hope, and a deeper appreciation of the changes brought about by Jesus' incarnation, life, death, and resurrection, features that Oliver O'Donovan, Regius Professor of Moral and Pastoral Theology, University of Oxford, has emphasized.[33] Because the Church is now more settled today than it was in the 1960s, and there are leaders who have Pope John XXIII's vision, I believe that the "signs of the times" are such that a moral theory that builds upon the Church's moral tradition, as well as recent insights into moral laws, moral development, and the human person, has greater hope of support and success than in the 1980s–1990s.

The time is right for a Christian ethic of responsibilities. However, before presenting this theory, it will be useful to look at some of the renewal efforts that have taken place, and at the dominant approaches and theories in contemporary Christian ethics. After examining recent efforts by leading Protestant and Catholic writers to bring the Church's medical, business, and sexual moral teaching into the twentieth century, we will be in a better position to discuss how to take the renewal into this century with an ethic that embodies the strengths of the Catholic Church's intellectual tradition, its insights into God's self-revelation in Christ, and its contemporary respect for the human person, the rights of conscience, and the dignity of all persons of good will.

Notes:

[1] On this subject, George V. Lobo, "The Renewal of Moral Theology," op. cit., 14–22; Vincent McNamara, "Moral Life, Christian," in *New Dictionary of Catholic Social Thought*, op. cit., 635–650, esp. 644–650.

[2] John Mahoney, *The Making of Moral Theology: A Study of the Roman Catholic Tradition* (Oxford: Clarendon Press, 1987), 1–37.

[3] On the features that characterize (or should characterize) the discipline in the year 2000, Richard A. McCormick, "Tradition in Tradition," in *Riding Time Like a River: The Catholic Moral Tradition Since Vatican II*, edited by William J. O'Brien, op. cit., 17–33. Almost forty years ago, Enda McDonagh argued for similar changes in "Moral Theology: The Need for Renewal," in *Moral Theology Renewed: Papers of the Maynooth Union Summer School 1964*, edited by Enda McDonagh (Dublin: Gill and Son, 1965), 13–30.

[4] While this separation might lead to problems similar to those that occurred when moral theology was a discipline set apart from dogmatic theology and the study of Scripture, the nine chapter course in General Moral Theology proposed by Enda McDonagh is appealing. For this essay, Enda McDonagh, "Teaching Moral Theology Today," in *Invitation and Response: Essays in Christian Moral Theology*, op. cit., 183–200.

[5] For this observation, David F. Ford, editor, *The Modern Theologians: An Introduction to Christian Theology in the Twentieth Century*, 2nd edition (Malden: Blackwell, 2001), 725.

[6] Sharon D. Welch, *A Feminist Ethic of Risk* (Minneapolis: Fortress Press, 1990), 123ff.

[7] To mention just a few examples: the pain caused to converts to the Catholic Church who were thereby prohibited from taking part in funerals or weddings of family members as late as the 1970s in Australia; the strictly enforced prohibition against burying those who had committed suicide; the excommunication of parents who sent their children to state schools in Australia as late as the 1970s; the pain caused to children who broke their fasts and were prevented as a result from receiving their First Communion with classmates (as happened in the case of a school friend during the 1950s). And, of course, there were all the mortal sins associated with adolescent sexuality, and, in the case of priests, with the celebration of Mass and the recitation of the Divine Office.

[8] The U.S. medical, legal, and military professions present sales and marketing "images" of those being educated to join their ranks that are quite different than those used by the U.S. Catholic Church to recruit and attract priests. However, given the life-long commitments, knowledge, and skills required to be an effective pastor in a U.S. parish, I find the dominant image of the diocesan priest quite disturbing.

[9] This is obvious in the actions of those U.S. bishops who have refused to give the Eucharist to elected officials who are pro-choice, or to any who support pro-choice candidates in state or federal elections. In spite of the archbishop of St. Louis' protestations that his

decisions are neither "partisan" nor "unjust," a careful analysis of the letter he sent to concerned Catholics in June, and his essay in *America* (June 21–28, 2004) both show a patriarchal spirit, and a reading of Catholic theology one associates with the Spanish Inquisition—in particular when he states that "a politician who supports abortion legislation steps outside of communion with the Church."

[10] Gerard J. Hughes, *Authority in Morals: An Essay in Christian Ethics* (Washington: Georgetown University Press, 1978), 124.

[11] For a comprehensive study of the Irish Church today, D. Vincent Twomey, *The End of Irish Catholicism?* (Dublin: Veritas, 2003).

[12] This quote can be found in John Whitcomb and Claire Whitcomb, *Great American Anecdotes* (New York: William Morrow, 1993), 239.

[13] For a sample of U.S. criticism, *Ethics and the Catechism of the Catholic Church*, edited by Michael E. Allsopp (Scranton: University of Scranton Press, 1999).

[14] David F. Ford, editor, *The Modern Theologians*, op. cit., 721–722.

[15] For an important study of the power of such organized groups within medieval Christianity, Michael Walsh, *Warriors of the Lord: The Military Orders of Christendom* (Grand Rapids: Eerdmans Publishing Company, 2003).

[16] On these and related subjects, James Reston, Jr., *The Last Apocalypse: Europe at the Year 1000* (New York: Doubleday, 1998); Kevin Madigan, "The Parish in the Year 1000," in "The Parish in the Year 1000," Special Issue, *Chicago Studies*, 37, 3 (December 1998), 233–244; Michael E. Allsopp, "Culture & The New Europe: Hilaire Belloc's *Crisis of Our Civilization* Reconsidered," *Informationes Theologiae Europae* (Frankfurt: Peter Lang, 1996), 135–144.

[17] These words are contained in her essay, "The Iliad or The Poem of Force," as found in *Simone Weil, An Anthology*, edited and introduced by Sian Miles (London: Virgo Press, 1986), 182–215, at 191.

[18] John Whitcomb and Claire Whitcomb, op. cit., 104.

[19] ibid., 31.

[20] Yves Congar, *Power and Poverty in the Church* (Baltimore: Helicon, 1965), 137. U.S. bishops would do well to spend a retreat reflecting on Congar's words, "It is a fact that at a time when the whole 'mystique' of the Church stresses love of the poor, and even poverty, when the Church is almost everywhere truly poor, even sometimes in real need, yet she has the appearance of wealth, and (in a word) of privilege, or pretensions in that direction. This harms both herself and the cause for whose service she was made, and which she does truly desire to serve" (13).

[21] John Whitcomb and Claire Whitcomb, op. cit., 101.

[22] John Whitcomb and Claire Whitcomb, ibid., 122.

[23] An important contribution by this theologian is Lisa Sowle Cahill, "Catholic Sexual Ethics and the Dignity of the Person: A Double Message," *Theological Studies* 50 (1989), 120–150.

[24] Dominian, a gifted psychiatrist, is best known for his contributions to *The Tablet* (London). However, some of his essays, distinctive for their grasp of dynamic psychology and their relevancy, are found in *Affirming the Human Personality: Psychological Essays in Christian Living* (Huntington: Our Sunday Visitor, 1975).

[25] For a short, balanced study that examines some of the major gaps that exist between theory and the 20th century reality of marriage, Cathy Molloy, *Marriage: Theology and Reality* (Dublin: Columba Press, 1996).

[26] Besides what he has written in his *New Directions in Moral Theology* (1994), as well as in his frequent essays in *The Month* (London); Kevin T. Kelly, *New Directions in Sexual Ethics: Moral Theology and the Challenge of AIDS* (London: Geoffrey Chapman, 1998).

One must admire the Catholic authors who have spent the years since Vatican II renewing the Church's sexual ethics. Such work requires Job's patience, and Moses' determination. During the 1970s, after publishing a study on "Pamphlets for Teenagers: Some Causes for Concern," in the *Australasian Catholic Record*, the national director of the Catholic Truth Society wrote me a letter in which he said that my study had done "irreparable harm" to the Catholic youth of Australia. A few years later, after publishing essays on Rahner's ethics and Newman's understanding of the authority of conscience (there was complete silence), I wrote what I thought was a middle-of-the-road analysis of a pastoral statement that the Australian Bishops Conference had made on birth control, only to find that a colleague wrote in a national priests' publication that I was the bishops' "lackey" and that my study had tried to "make bricks out of straw."

[27] For insights into life within Australia's leading seminary during the 1950s–1960s, Chris Geraghty, *The Priest Factory: A Manly Vision of Triumph 1958–1962 and Beyond* (Melbourne: Spectrum Publications, 2003).

[28] Enda McDonagh, *Invitation and Response: Essays in Christian Moral Theology* (New York: Sheed and Ward, 1972), 19.

[29] For a useful study of major changes in so-called "traditional" moral teaching, Bernard Hoose. *Received Wisdom? Reviewing the Role of Tradition in Christian Ethics* (London: Geoffrey Chapman, 1994). Also, Kevin Madigan, "The Parish in the Year 100," *Chicago Studies*, 37, 3 (December 1998), 233–244; Kenan B. Osborne, "Sacramental Life in the Year 1000," *Chicago Studies*, op. cit., 245–256; Michael E. Allsopp, "Christian Morality in the Year 1000: Reconstructions," *Chicago Studies*, op. cit., 280–294.

[30] George V. Lobo, op. cit., 22.

[31] For Richard McCormick's views of a recent bishops statement, "'Moral Considerations' Ill Considered," in *Corrective Vision: Explorations in Moral Theology* (Kansas City: Sheed & Ward, 1994), 225–232, 249.

[32] On this subject, Enda McDonagh, "Teaching Moral Theology Today," op. cit., 183–200.

[33] Oliver O'Donovan, *Resurrection and Moral Order: An Outline for Evangelical Ethics* (Grand Rapids: Eerdmans, 2nd edition, 1994).

Part II

Chapter III

Major Approaches in Christian Ethics: Natural Law Ethics

Since, therefore, the conjugal act is destined primarily by nature for the begetting of children, those who in exercising it deliberately frustrate its natural power and purpose, sin against nature, and commit a deed which is shameful and intrinsically vicious.

> Pope Pius XI
> *Casti Connubii*

Thought can only live on grounds which we adopt in the service of a reality to which we submit.

> Michael Polanyi
> *The Tacit Dimension*

What then does the New Testament effectively provide, in ethics as in doctrine? It yields certain perspectives, patterns and priorities, and it forms the Christian mind which then turns to the examination of contemporary issues—perhaps to apply central New Testament principles more rigorously than any of the New Testament writers.

> J.L. Houlden
> *Ethics and the New Testament*

The moral theory presented in this book has been influenced by ethical theories, ancient and modern; it has been shaped by the strengths and the weaknesses seen to be present in Aristotle's and Aquinas's moral thought, in Kant's, Mill's, and A. J. Ayer's ethics. In order to appreciate what will be said in the third part of this book on such subjects as morality and moral rules, moral development, and the authorities that should guide Christians as they wrestle with life's dilemmas, it will be useful to look briefly at the moral theories that have been dominant within twentieth century Christian ethics, have shaped the renewal in Catholic moral theology since WWII, and colored key aspects of the ethic being presented in this book.

Due to my own work in Christian ethics since the 1970s, as well as those "accidents of life" which, as James Gustafson remarks, add to the "fabric" that makes up a person's existential self, political, cultural, and religious affiliations, Part II of this book will examine four modern approaches in Christian ethics: renewed "natural law" theory; liberation theology; the feminist approach in Christian ethics; and theocentric ethics. Each of these approaches embodies conscious efforts to renew Christian ethics; each has been a significant cross-fertilizing catalyst within the discipline—and each has colored what is contained in the final chapters of this book.

Natural Law Ethics: History and Background

Because, as the American historian John Jay Chapman has wisely written, "We must never expect to find in a dogma the explanation of the system which props it up," in order to better understand the philo-sophical and theological underpinnings of the "natural law" approach within Christian ethics and the recent debates among Protestants and Catholics about the validity of the approach as a genuinely "theological" ethic, it is necessary to examine something of the tradition's history.[1]

The majority of Catholic moral theories that were articulated during the last two hundred years by Jesuits and Dominicans, Redemptorists and Franciscans (authors from these religious orders wrote almost all Catholic ethics text books) stood clearly within the "natural law" tradition that has its roots in Greek and Roman philoso-phy: the writings of Aristotle, Cicero, Galen, and Marcus Aurelius. From earliest times, Christian writers (as we see in Paul's Letter to the Romans 2:14ff.) were attracted to features within Stoicism, with its emphasis on calmness in the face of life's trials, the importance of courage, and the governing authority of a God-given law inscribed in the hearts of Jews and Gentiles alike.

Many Christians were impressed by the books of Galen, the second father of medicine, because they argued that physiological structures possessed inherent purposes, and that these were the basis for good health and right living—ideas (Galen derived from earlier Greek philosophers) that are still strong today, not only in neo-Scholastic Roman Catholic morality, but also in Oriental medicine.

John Scotus Erigena, a ninth century Celtic monk who played a key role in the molding of medieval thought, was one of the first scholars to make a distinction between *auctoritas* (Scripture) and *ratio* (reason), and to teach that while Scripture is still the main source of our knowledge of God, it is the duty of reason, illuminated by the Spirit, to use its powers to investigate and expound the data supplied by Scripture. During the eleventh century, Anselm was able to gain wide support within Christendom for the position that reason had a right to inquire into revealed truths, not in the sense that we acquire the knowledge of faith through rational reasoning, but because it is reprehensible not to make any effort to understand what we believe. Anselm's influence led to programs of study within the monasteries that had spread throughout Europe based upon the principles *Credo ut intelligam* (I believe in order to understand), and *Fides quaerens intellectum* (Faith seeking understanding). Later, with the introduction of all of Aristotle's works into Europe in the twelfth and thirteenth centuries, reason blended with earlier Stoic themes to generate a powerful philosophico-religious synthesis called Scholasticism.

Over the centuries, different aspects of Roman, Greek, and early Christian thought attracted separate attention. The Stoic belief in a divine spark in the soul became a central theme in the writings of the German Dominican mystic Meister Eckhart (1260–1327). During the same century, Thomas Aquinas (1225–1274) shows a knowledge of the Stoic and the Aristotelian emphases, as well as the tradition that saw "natural law" embodied in what the medieval scholars called the *ius gentium* (the laws of nations). Aquinas creatively incorporated some of these notions into his complex moral theory that, while showing the strong influence of Augustine and Aristotle, does not ignore the importance of Scripture, the Holy Spirit, or Jesus' command to love one's neighbor.

Aquinas's ethics gives a central place to the role of the will (as well as reason), the importance of the theological virtues (faith, hope, love), and the moral virtues (prudence, justice, fortitude, temperance), as well as imitating Jesus' poverty and simplicity in the Christian life (two of the marks of the Dominicans that attracted him to join that order rather than accepting his parents plans that he become a Cistercian monk).[2]

Given Aquinas's influence on Roman Catholic theology, and the use of the concept of *ius gentium* within the development and codification of the Western Church's legal system, the "natural law" approach dominated the Church's ethics for centuries, especially its social teaching and its sexual ethics. Following the Reformation, with its concerns about the powers of reason, man's sinfulness, and the authority of the Bible in matters of faith and morals, the Catholic Church put even greater stress on reason's powers and "natural law" morality. It distanced itself from the Bible, the Reformers' emphasis on the authority of conscience, and the centrality of moral sentiments; justification (Catholic theologians argued) was not achieved simply by God's gift of faith, and the priesthood did not extent to all the faithful. Catholic moral theology strengthened the place of ecclesiastical authority; it fought individualism and liberalism by stressing communal responsibilities (weekly worship was added to church regulations); it resisted democracy by tightening central control (in the appointment of bishops, production of catechisms, and codification of canon law).

With the Enlightenment, there was additional support for the approach throughout Europe, because natural law morality was "scientific" in its method, emphasized reason's powers, and firmly held that humans possessed the native ability to discover God's laws by an analysis of the nature inherent in rational creatures. Due to the wide influence of Christian Wolff (1679–1754), whose system of philosophy was taught in the majority of German universities during the second half of the eighteenth century, Catholic thought took on an even stronger confidence in the powers of reason, and Wolff's disciples extended Aristotle and Aquinas to the point where they argued that Christians were able to obtain objective and universally valid knowledge about God's plans and purposes through reflection on the nature of created sub-systems: for instance, the human reproductive system.[3]

During the last fifty years, Catholic theologians have been divided in their support for the natural law approach, however. On one side there has been Jacques Maritain (1882–1973), a major figure in the revival in interest in Thomism, who sought to relate Aquinas to the times in which he lived and to twentieth century philosophical controversies. *Man and the State* (1947), in which Maritain argues that there are truths about the social order that all people can recognize, embodies the French Catholic philosopher's experiences working on behalf of the United Nations, and his efforts to assist in the drafting of the UN's Universal Declaration of Human Rights. *The Person and the Common Good* (1946), a book that has influenced Personalism in Catholic philosophy and theology, opposed totalitarian and socialist philosophies, arguing that the person has an "end" which transcends both social and political goods.

Three other important Catholic philosophers who supported natural law morality during the twentieth century and kept it central in Catholic thought were: Etienne Gilson (b. 1884), a professor of medieval philosophy at the Sorbonne during the 1920s, and later Director of the Pontifical Institute of Medieval Studies in Toronto, a highly successful center that was responsible in large part for the revival in interest in the Middle Ages as mentioned above; Dom Odo Lottin, a Benedictine monk of the monastery of Maria Lac in Belgium, who undertook thorough study of the sources of Aquinas' writings, and showed their keen reliance on Scripture, Jesus' "Sermon on the Mount," and their emphasis on the primacy of charity. The third scholar was the English Jesuit historian Frederick Copleston, whose individual works on Aquinas, as well as his multi-volume history of philosophy, were widely read throughout the English-speaking academic world.

On the other hand, for reasons mentioned in the previous chapter, there have been a number of important Catholic philosophers and theologians, including Bernard Haring, Hans Urs von Balthasar, Karl Rahner, and Enda McDonagh, who have seriously questioned the usefulness and validity of the "natural law" approach in Christian ethics. This summary and critique of a highly influential exposition of natural law morality by a writer who has left significant marks upon the Church's moral thinking (as well as my own ethic) will allow current readers to judge the approach for themselves: to assess its strengths and weaknesses, to understand why Protestant and Catholic writers have argued (as I will) that as the Church responds to Vatican II's call for renewal and speaks to contemporary people, it should not build its morality on the natural law but on a different foundation—one that is more Christian and more theological.

Richard A. McCormick's Renewed Natural Law Ethics: Tradition in Transition

One of the best examples of an impressive effort to update the natural law approach in Catholic moral theology can be seen in the writings of Richard A. McCormick, SJ, one of the last century's most important Catholic theologians. Trained in the "classic" tradition of Roman Catholic ethics, McCormick's critiques of colleagues' essays, as well as his own frequent studies in biomedical ethics, as well as on such subjects as the distinctiveness of Christian ethics and the role of Scripture and tradition in Catholic moral theology, show that the U.S. Jesuit was much more open to the arguments of colleagues about the defects in the Catholic Church's ethics than more traditional natural law ethicists such as William E. May.

However, by his own admission, McCormick's writings show that, while he progressively made important changes in his ethical approach,[4] nevertheless he remained loyal to the natural law tradition to the end of his life—in spite of the difficulties some Protestant and Catholic authors (such as myself) saw in this approach—and McCormick's personal formulation.[5]

McCormick's contributions to "Notes in Moral Theology," published in *Theological Studies,* indicate that he deeply respected many of the insights contained in the ethics of his Protestant and Catholic colleagues. For example, McCormick admired Paul Ramsey; he engaged in a lively exchange with Joseph Fletcher about criteria central to making treatment decisions in the case of handicapped newborns. Within his reviews of current work in moral theology, he frequently praised Norbert Rigali's essays on the place of Christ in Christian ethics, although he was not able to support either Rigali's existentialism or his stand on the distinctiveness of Christian morality.[6]

While Karl Rahner's essays in moral theology do not seem to have played a crucial role in the early stages of the formation of McCormick's ethic, Rahner's thought seems to have moved McCormick later in his career toward seeing morality in terms of individual choices and unique situations, and to accepting Ignatius Loyola's process for making life-choices: namely, discernment.[7]

McCormick's studies reveal further that although (as we will see) he came to appreciate a number of important insights into the nature of morality proposed by Protestant and Catholics who were not supportive of the natural law approach to morality, he always remained closer to Joseph Fuchs than to James Gustafson—more at home with the contributions of Margaret Farley and Lisa Sowle Cahill than with the work of the liberation theologians Leonardo Boff and Gustavo Gutierrez.

McCormick worked hard to unite religious and secular values, but as Lisa Cahill observes (and I fully agree) "does not so clearly demonstrate the functional significance for ethics of his theology, precisely as Christian."[8] McCormick strove to build an ethics that was Christocentric, personalist, ecumenical, and inductive in its method of formulating principles and making moral decisions.[9] The Bible does have an important place in McCormick's mature moral method. However, McCormick's essays show (on the one hand) that although he was able to accept J.S. Houlden's position on the way that the New Testament shapes morality, he was unable to accept all of the implications of Stanley Hauerwas's "narrative" approach to Christian ethics—it went too far;[10] and that (on the other hand) he was unable to support the use of Scripture (or papal teaching) advocated by Protestant and Catholic "fundamentalists"—it did not go far enough.[11]

In spite of his respect for the role of Scripture in Christian ethics and his close acquaintance with Protestant theologians such as Paul Ramsey, James Gustafson, and Jim Childress, McCormick was never able to accept an ethical approach such as that advocated by the New York Protestant theologian Andrew R. Osborn: "Christian ethics believes, therefore, that in the lives and the teaching of the prophets of Israel, in the life and teaching of Jesus, and in the lives and teaching of his disciples, there is to be found a unique and authoritative statement and exemplification of the principles underlying conduct. Its method is to use the principles discovered from these sources as standards whereby to judge and interpret the facts which it has discovered from its observation of life and its analysis of the process of history."[12] For McCormick, as Cahill says, "The revelation in Jesus Christ discloses the coherence of these [natural] values in God, friendship with whom is the destiny to which persons are invited. This revelation does not, however, generate distinct moral norms which supersede those discernible by reason" (Cahill, art. cit., 399).

McCormick's frequent statements about the role (as he saw it) of Christian stories (Jesus' life, Jonah) in Christian morality are instructive. "Theological work in the past decade or so has rejected the notion that the sources of faith are a thesaurus of answers," McCormick wrote in 1989 in one of his frequent essays on "Theology and Bioethics."[13] "Rather they should be viewed above all as narratives, as a story. From a story come perspectives, themes, insights, not always or chiefly direct action guides. The story is the source from which the Christian construes the world theologically. In other words, it is the vehicle for discovering and communicating this new meaning" (ibid., 138). The Christian story does influence the Church's sexual and biomedical ethics; it shapes the Christian's dispositions, imagination, and values (ibid., 140). The story forms the basis for a "new light" that directs the individual towards solutions that are fully human. In other words, Scripture and tradition comprise the foundations for the Church's self-understanding. Aided by the Spirit, they enable the believer to see with the eyes of faith, to become (as Vincent MacNamara puts it), "people who see things in a particular way, because they are particular sorts of people."[14]

Further, because of what is contained in their story, Christians possess distinctive, faith-filled insights into life, death, warfare, and sexuality, and these insights (drawn from revelation) determine how they see "the facts of life, and what among them are the most prominent and relevant facts" (McCormick, "Theology and Ethics," ibid.,10). However, rather than making decisions directly on the basis of such considerations as the Bible, Christ's compassion, or the care that should be shown to "images of God" (as Allen Verhey has done in writing about euthanasia), McCormick consistently looks at these issues in terms of his updated natural law approach, and he resolves these problems in terms of reason's faith-informed assessments of the human person's purpose, dignity, and well-being.

Reason informed by faith as it reflects upon the human person provides Christians with insights into the way they or others should behave, McCormick maintains throughout his mature essays.[15] The Bible is a normative source of light and a definite inspiration for human reason. Scripture's words (commands, parables) should not be employed, however, to provide contemporary Christian physicians with immediate norms that can be immediately used to decide whether or not it is right to withdraw nutrition and hydration from a comatose adult who has been rushed to an ICU in Chicago. For McCormick, Christian moral decisions about life and death should be settled in terms of rational constructs: benefits and burdens, by reflection on the goals of medicine and the futility of a medical procedure.[16]

Christians should study Scripture, as well as Augustine's *Confessions,* and Aquinas's *Summa Theologiae,* according to McCormick. They should read these works, however, not to find answers to contemporary questions in the fields of biomedical or sexual ethics, but to learn lessons from writings that have colored centuries of Christian consciousness and moral behavior, and in the process their minds will be protected, disposed, and directed.[17] McCormick could not support any moral method in which Scripture's norms were used directly to resolve contemporary ethical problems. In McCormick's mind, Christian ethics is a *rational* discipline, not a religious enterprise (in the sense that a Christian's moral decisions are grounded in religious sentiments); it is a *science* that can stand alongside psychology and sociology. Christian ethics uses logic and has strict rules for verifying its conclusions.

The lessons that a Christian physician gleans from the Book of Job, Jesus' parables, and the Church's teaching on heaven and hell should inform his reason. But a physician facing decisions about a child's life or death should use his reasoning powers to make medical decisions that are competent and in keeping with U.S. law and the Church's insights into the goals of medicine, the duties of physicians, and the dignity of the human person. While guided by Bible and Church, reason should use all of its powers to make rationally defensible judgments that can be articulated to others, whether believers or not, and justified according to empirical criteria, both formal and material.[18] All moral decisions, in McCormick's eyes, involve choices— "the preference of some values over others and may be evaluated by an intelligent perception of their objective hierarchical relations (*ordo bonorum*)." And morally "good" acts are those that realize the highest available good in a given situation.[19]

From beginning to end, McCormick's ethic stands firm on the positions that "right reason" will guide a fair-minded person to the same moral conclusions as "revealed morality," and there is no such animal as a "Christian" justice characteristically different from "Aristotle's" justice.

McCormick's Theory: A Sympathetic Critique

While Catholic and contemporary, McCormick's ethical theory is identical with Kant's on one key point: there is no practical difference between the principles of valid religious (Christian, Jewish, Muslim) ethics and valid philosophical (Aristotelian, Utilitarian) ethics. The reason? God and humans have to obey the same rational principles; reason has the ability to lead humans to these principles.[20] Consequently, in McCormick's eyes, the fact that a newborn lacks the "potential for human relationships" provides the key "theological" principle that physicians and nurses should use to decide correctly whether or not they should treat that infant.[21]

On the basis of such insights that are fundamental to all natural law theories, one belief remained central to McCormick's moral approach throughout his life: Jesus' morality adds nothing over and above human morality, because Jesus taught nothing more than a form of humanism grounded in rationally cogent insights into the human person. Christian ethics and human morality are, therefore, identical. Here McCormick's thought is no different from William May's or the Catholic apologist, J.D. Conway's.[22]

There are several other difficulties for those (like myself) who have sought to provide a more conspicuously "theological" ethics when they look at McCormick's moral theory. First, his central aphorism, "Reason informed by faith," is too limiting. A person makes moral decisions not only by using reason, but also by putting his moral imagination, his conscience, and all of his affective and intuitive powers to work. Or as Paul Quay puts it, "the whole person is involved in every free act as both agent and object."[23] Second, while an improvement on William May's ethical theory, McCormick's focus on the person is again too restrictive. Morality involves social structures as well as persons; it is concerned with long-term considerations that have community implications, as well as short-term implications for individuals. Concentrating on a defective newborn's "potential for human relationships" does give some place to the newborn's parents and siblings: his or her immediate and future affective or romantic associations. However, the criterion does not embrace wider networks and social fabrics. It does not justify itself, nor does it explain its "moral" basis—exactly how this potential becomes the basis for what Christians "ought" to do.[24]

Further, by focusing on the "person," McCormick's approach fails to adequately appreciate that ethics is about people in history, about historical consciousness, and moral reflection in time.[25] Although he recognized that a person's awareness of values involved the heart as well as the head, nevertheless McCormick's moral theory overemphasized objectivity and rationality, the calculation and assessment of values and goods. His theory reflects the "individualism" that dominates U.S. culture and philosophy. It fails to appreciate Sharon Welch's insights into the "communicative" nature of sound moral decision-making, and liberation theology's emphases on the "social" nature of each person.

McCormick's thought shows too little appreciation, as well, for Freud's insights into human behavior, in particular, the role of the unconscious and the superego, and while McCormick had reasons not to support Freud's contention that "biology is destiny," he does not show an adequate awareness of the role that gender (the X chromosome in females) plays in the formation of morality and in making personal moral decisions.[26] While respectful of feminist insights, the U.S. Jesuit's own ethic does not support an ethics of care (Nel Noddings)— nor does it embrace the central features of Sharon Welch's ethic of risk (as we will see).

In spite of his impressive efforts to move beyond his classical training, at no point in his writing does McCormick exhibit a sense of unity and harmony in his vision of the human person equal to what we find in Teilhard de Chardin's descriptions of humans: for instance, what we find in Teilhard's words, "Beings endowed with self-awareness become, precisely in virtue of that bending back upon themselves, immediately capable of rising into a new sphere of existence: in truth another world is born. Abstract thought, logic, reasoned choice and invention, mathematics, art, the exact computation of space and time, the dreams and anxieties of love: all these activities of the inner life are simply the bubbling up of the newly-formed life-centre as it explodes upon itself."[27]

McCormick was never able to develop the cosmic sweep that both James Gustafson and Teilhard did, and to recognize that "For one who sees the universe in the guise of a laborious communal ascent towards the summit of consciousness, life, far from seeming blind, hard, or despicable, becomes charged with gravity, with responsibilities, with new relationships" (ibid., 106).

Nor did McCormick succeed in incorporating an eschatological dimension into his moral theory. It is true that in his listing of doctrines central to ethics, he appreciated this part of Catholicism, without lapsing into the excesses of those who have embraced the "left behind" vision of Christianity, or the Pentecostals who are preoccupied with "the Rapture." Making bioethical decisions in terms of "benefits or burdens" or a newborn's potentiality prescinds from the significance of God's here-and-now actions—aspects that are not missing in liberation theology's focus on the exodus or James Gustafson's "theocentric" ethical theory that consistently asks, "How is this action in keeping with what we discern the Almighty is here and now calling U.S. to do?"

In spite of repeated essays and debates, McCormick never came to accept that Christian moral norms as found in the Decalogue or in Jesus' Sermon on the Mount, for instance, should play a direct role in formulating Catholic ethical principles, or that a person needs to know or understand the Christian "story" in order to arrive at morally correct

decisions in sexual or biomedical ethics. In McCormick's opinion, as
expressed in his comments on Stanley Hauerwas's moral theory, while
Christian ethics is influenced by Jesus' moral teaching and the Christian
story (it is "shaped" by the Bible's images and cultural metaphors), the
Church's teaching about taking life or keeping promises can be (and
should be) separated from that story and its metaphors.

In this, McCormick was convinced that Christian ethics is
autonomous.[28] As already indicated, he was also unmovable in his
belief that rational morality at its best is the same as Jesus' moral teaching—that there is nothing unique or distinctive about Christian ethics.
He found it intolerable that human justice and Christian justice
could be substantially different.

Finally, when it comes to his decision-making method,
McCormick's preference for a "moderate teleology" rather than a
deontological approach, for construing right moral decisions in terms
of their conformity to what McCormick termed the *ordo bonorum*
rather than in terms of W.D. Ross' world of *prima facie* duties (the
approach central to the moral theory being developed in this book) is
understandable (in view of McCormick's scholastic background), yet
at the same time somewhat arbitrary.

Clearly, some of McCormick's other positions are rather arbitrary
as well. Surely, some of Jesus' norms have their place in resolving contemporary ethical issues, and Christian ethics would not be *Christian*
(as Hauerwas contends) if its position on forgiveness, for example,
were separated from Jesus' example. Further, while it fits McCormick's
natural law position, should Christian ethics make the claim that
authentic moral principles are no different from rationally sound
ethical principles, or that its framework and principles stand upon foundations that are intelligible to "right thinking" moral philosophers? I
think not. Ayn Rand thought that Jesus' love command simply created
confusion and dependence, that it was rationally foolish and
unhealthy—and Rand is not alone in her judgments.[29] Further, in his
use of such constructs as "benefits and burdens" or "potential for
human relationships" as the guiding principles for resolving dilemmas
in biomedical ethics, McCormick abandons theology for philosophy.
He puts efficiency ahead of doctrine.[30] Surely, the picture of marriage
as illustrated within the Bible transcends rational thinking on human
relationships.

Besides the difficulties he found in Hauerwas's ethics, McCormick
was not able to support James Gustafon's theocentric ethics either, as

it rejected the place of natural law in religious ethics and gave too little place to Jesus. McCormick saw two additional problems (as he believed) in Gustafson's understanding of morality: First, Gustafson ground morality in religious "responses" (awe, reverence, compassion that are essentially affective). Second, Gustafson held that individual decisions about what God is calling humans to be and become are inherently affective "perceptions" (intuitions, feelings) rather than rational judgments about human dignity, potentiality, or purpose.[31]

Taking a firm stand against both of these friends and colleagues, McCormick consistently taught that the Church's position on abortion, for instance, is intelligible in its own right—and that to make sense, it requires neither the support of the Christian story nor a focus on God's purposes and designs for the whole of creation.[32] Furthermore, while McCormick does not support either "natural law's" (Stoic) position that humans possess inherent moral principles from birth, or David Hume's conviction that all healthy (normal) humans know that an action such as cruelly beating an animal is wrong, because all of them experience negative "feelings" or "sentiments" about such an action when they observe it, the U.S. Jesuit was firmly convinced that some behavior (e.g. rape) is objectively and universally immoral because all *rational* people see/know that it is seriously abusive of women and a violation of their basic rights ("goods") regardless of the Christian or Muslim story.

Here again, McCormick reveals the limits of his ability or willingness to appreciate the contingency and facticity of moral knowledge—features, as we will see, that are central to contemporary research into moral decision-making and moral norms. He was not able to accept that all natural law theories contain views of morality and moral laws that have become dated by advances in research into moral decision-making. More seriously, McCormick did not see that all natural law theories are grounded upon assumptions that undermine the uniqueness of God's saving work in Christ, and seriously weaken the place of Christ, his life, and work in the ongoing history of salvation.[33]

There is another major difficulty associated with McCormick's mature approach to morality. Although he did set out the religious doctrines central to an authentic Christian ethic—and in that sense proposed a "doctrinal" rather than a "scriptural" moral theory[34]— McCormick's method of resolving bioethical dilemmas (Cruzan case, IVF) distances itself too much from doctrines and religious authorities. Nowhere does McCormick advance a "Resurrection ethics" as Oliver

O'Donovan does; nowhere does he solve moral problems by direct reference to Jesus' cosmic incarnation. His ethic cannot be called a Eucharistic moral theory. Rather, while the Christian moral agent might be subjectively affected by Christ's cosmic presence or uplifted by his or her appreciation of God's saving work in Jesus—and throughout history—it is an infant's "potential for human relationships" that provides the "material" justification whether it should live or die. Nothing essentially theological, but the rationally assessed and economically calculated "benefits or burdens" provide the key to maintaining or withdrawing nutrition and hydration.

McCormick's greatest contribution to natural law ethics, according to Lisa Sowle Cahill, is "to tie it more realistically to human experience and to individual and communal discretion …. His distinctive position on the relation between faith and ethics affirms the ability of reason reflecting on experience to grasp essential moral obligations, but also much more self-consciously sets reasonable reflection within a life-perspective shaped by faith."[35]

McCormick's ethic is open, engaging, and contemporary. Like William May's exposition, his approach makes it possible to reach both those who have no religion and those who possess religious convictions quite different from Christianity's. McCormick's approach does not divide communities on the basis of religion, nor does it separate itself from contemporary society. Like Aquinas's ethic, McCormick's "mixed deontology" leaves much to discuss, in particular his basic convictions: (a) that laws, ends, and potentialities associated with the human person are the basis of morality; (b) that faith-informed reason can establish objective, universal norms of "essential" morality, as well as make reliable "individual" decisions from its applications of norms associated with the human person; and (c) that this "natural" morality is identical with the fundamentals of Christian (i.e. Bible) morality.

The U.S. Catholic Church owes much to Richard McCormick's life's work, his public lectures, classroom courses at Georgetown and Notre Dame, and his frequent essays in *America* and *Theological Studies*. In many ways, my own moral theory (as seen in the second part of this book) embraces McCormick's criticisms of Catholic moral theology as it was taught during the first half of the century. Reason—together with religious sentiments—should inform faith; Christian faith should inform the whole person; and the person should form an important part of reflection on moral norms. However, my approach, while standing clearly in the Catholic tradition, separates itself (as we will see) from McCormick's moral theory on a number of key issues.[36] *The morality developed in the second part of this book is a deontological ethic of general and particular responsibilities that are personally discerned from a prayerful and informed cyclical process of (a) examining the Church's and one's own understanding of God's redeeming work in Christ's life, and Christian moral teaching, and (b) applying this understanding to one's own or another's future or past actions viewed in the light of their positive and negative implications for communities or networks of communities. It is a "doctrinal" rather than a "natural" moral theory.*

Before looking at this approach in some detail, however, it will be useful to examine several other recent efforts by Catholics and Protestants to develop Christian ethical theories that are not dependent on the natural law, but are expressly built upon specifically different foundations—God, Scripture, women's experience. Each of these approaches has support within the Church; each has been an important influence upon the moral theory being presented in this book.

Notes:

[1] As quoted by Page Smith in his *Killing The Spirit: Higher Education in America* (New York: Viking Penguin, 1990), v.

[2] On the place of Scripture in Aquinas' thought, Michael M. Waldstein, "On Scripture" in the *Summa Theologiae*," *The Aquinas Review*, 1, 1 (1994), 73–94.

[3] On this subject, George V. Lobo, *Guide to Christian Living: A New Compendium of Moral Theology* (Maryland: Westminster, 1985), 168–198; Enda McDonagh, "The Natural Law and The Law of Christ," in *Invitation and Response: Essays in Christian Moral Theology* (New York: Sheed and Ward, 1972), 22–37, 201; Joseph Fuchs, *Natural Law* (Dublin: Gill and Son, 1965), and "Natural Law" in *New Dictionary of Catholic Social Thought*, edited by Judith A. Dwyer (Collegeville: Liturgical Press, 1994), 669–675; James Gustafson, *Protestant and Roman Catholic Ethics* (Chicago: University of Chicago Press, 1978), 6–12; Gerard J. Hughes, "Natural Law" in *Christian Ethics: An Introduction*, edited by Bernard Hoose (London: Cassell, 1998), 47–56; and the important statements by N. H. G. Robinson throughout *The Groundwork of Christian Ethics* (London: Collins, 1971).

[4] On this subject, "Self-Assessment and Self-Indictment," and "How My Mind Has Changed," in Richard A. McCormick, *Corrective Vision: Exploration in Moral Theology* (Kansas City: Sheed & Ward, 1994), 40–45, 46–54.

[5] For these reasons, and in spite of its modern developments, the U.S. Jesuit is best seen as a major, if "transitional" theologian, whose moral theory stands between the Catholic Church's neo-Scholastic past and its post-Vatican II future. Another important U.S. Jesuit working within this approach was John Connery, who had a major place in Catholic medical ethics during the 1960s–1980s.

[6] For signs of these differences on birth control, the distinctiveness of Christian ethics, as well as on the human person, Richard A. McCormick, *Notes on Moral Theology: 1965 Through 1980* (Washington: University Press of America, 1981), 429–430, 627–632, 705–708, 812–816. Also, Norbert Rigali, "Christ and Morality," in *The Distinctiveness of Christian Ethics, Readings in Moral Theology #2*, edited by Charles E. Curran and Richard A. McCormick (New York: Paulist Press, 1980), 111–120.

[7] On this subject, Michael E. Allsopp, "Karl Rahner's Formal-Existentialist Ethics: A Study," *Australasian Catholic Record* 50, 2 (April 1973), 113–129; and 50, 3 (October 1973), 331–339. Also McCormick's essay on "Discernment in Ethics: What Does It Mean?" in Richard A. McCormick, *Corrective Vision: Explorations in Moral Theology* (Kansas City: Sheed & Ward, 1994), 55–68.

[8] Lisa Sowle Cahill, "Within Shouting Distance: Paul Ramsey and Richard McCormick on Method," *Journal of Medicine and Philosophy,* 4 (December 1979), 398–417.

[9] On this subject, Richard A. McCormick, "Moral Theology in the Year 2000," in *Corrective Vision: Explorations in Moral Theology,* op. cit., 23–39, 239–237.

[10] On this subject, Michael E. Allsopp and Edward R. Sunshine, "Speaking Morally: The Thirty Year Debate between Richard A. McCormick and Stanley Hauerwas," *Irish Theological Quarterly,* 63, 1 (1998), 51–64.

[11] In a letter from McCormick shortly before his death, he stated that he did not know how to use Scripture in moral theology—and he did not believe that other Catholics working in the field did either.

[12] Andrew R. Osborn, *Christian Ethics* (London: Oxford University Press, 1940), 11.

[13] "Theology and Bioethics," in McCormick's *Corrective Vision: Explorations in Moral Theology*, op. cit., 133–148, at 138.

[14] Vincent MacNamara, op.cit., 45.

[15] On this subject, Richard A. McCormick, *Corrective Vision,* 140–141. Also, "Natural Law Ethics," in Michael E. Allsopp, *Models of Christian Ethics* (Scranton: University of Scranton Press, 2003), 31–40, at 34–39.

[16] For a more complete expression of his biomedical ethics, Richard A. McCormick, *Health and Medicine in the Catholic Tradition: Tradition in Transition* (New York: Crossroad, 1984).

[17] On these three features and their roles in influencing decisions in biomedical ethics, McCormick, *Corrective Vision: Explorations in Moral Theology,* op. cit., 141–148.

[18] On the subject of "Morality," in *Health and Medicine in the Catholic Tradition*, McCormick writes, "These general reflections constitute the shape of, the informing of, our reasoning as we deliberate about the more concrete problems of biomedicine. Especially the duty to preserve life. They do not replace reasoning, but moral reasoning ought to be compatible with them." op. cit., 54.

[19]Cahill, art cit., 401.

[20] Kant deals with this subject in his *Critique of Judgment* (1790).

[21] Exactly how this principle relates to Christian doctrine, or is derived from it, McCormick nowhere explains, except in passing remarks about the goals of medicine, the irrationality of using "futile" medical treatments, making decisions on the basis of judgments about procedures being "ordinary" or "extraordinary" means.

[22] McCormick's understanding of natural law—for all its updating—accords with what N. H. G. Robinson says in his summary of the traditional theory's three distinctive

features: (a) the law is derived from the *nature* of man; (b) it is rationally derived without the aid of revelation and is thereby able to command universal assent; (c) it serves as a foundation for the "special requirements" of Christian ethics which are seen as supplemental or as a "second story" built upon the natural law's demands (Robinson, op. cit., 302–307). For McCormick's stand on these subjects, "Does Religious Faith Add to Ethical Perception?" in *Readings in Moral Theology #2*, edited by Charles E. Curran and Richard A. McCormick, SJ (New York: Paulist Press, 1980), 156–173. Also, J. D. Conway, "Natural Law," in *What The Church Teaches* (New York: Harper & Brothers, 1962), 229–239—where one finds a defense of the universality and immutability of natural law, and a summary of its content.

[23] Paul M. Quay, "The Unity and Structure of the Human Act," *Listening* 18, 3 (Fall, 1983), 245–259, at 257.

[24] This was one of the central points raised twenty years ago in a criticism of McCormick's approach to letting newborns live or die, as stated in "Saving Defective Infants: Christian Standards," *The Tablet* (July 21, 1984), 688–689.

[25] This is an important point that exponents of natural law ethics fail to appreciate because of their focus on features inherent to the person, on such material constructs as "benefits and burdens" or "potential for human relationships." Fortunately the rise of Scripture scholars, and professors of literature and history within the discipline has somewhat corrected this emphasis.

[26] For a useful if summary critique of the natural law approach, Lisa Sowle Cahill, "Feminism and Christian Ethics—Moral Theology," in *Freeing Theology: The Essentials of Theology in Feminist Perspective*, Catherine Mowry La Cugna, editor (New York: HarperCollins, 1993), 211–234, esp. 214–218 on feminists & natural law-revision.

[27] Teilhard de Chardin, *Hymn of the Universe* (New York: Harper and Row, 1961), 102.

[28] On the debate about whether or not Christian ethics is "autonomous" or "heteronomous," N. H. G. Robinson, op. cit., 115, 124, 148, 155, 160, 167, 181, 197, 236, 268.

[29] Rand's position is important, as her moral philosophy (objectivism) holds a dominant place not only in Anglo-American political theory, but also within the U.S. business community, in part due to the fact the current chairman of the U.S. Federal Reserve Board, Alan Greenspan, is a leading exponent of Rand's philosophy.

[30] James Gustafson in conversations about McCormick's ethics made it clear that he did not consider McCormick's approach to be "theology"—a stand that I expressed in 1984 when commenting in *The Tablet* (London) on McCormick's approach to letting seriously handicapped newborns die on the basis of their potential for human relationships.

[31] While this might seem a petty difference, whether Christian morality rests upon reason or religious feelings is a major matter. It reflects, on the one hand, the Catholic Church's dependence on Aristotle and Aquinas; on the other hand, the Reformed Church's respect for Augustine, Luther, and Calvin. For Gustafson's position on the nature of religion, *Ethics from a Theocentric Perspective*, I, 119–121.

[32] For McCormick's difficulties with Gustafson's moral theory, "Gustafson's God: Why? What? Where? (Etc.), *Journal of Religious Ethics* 13, 1 (Spring 1985), 53–70.

[33] For a thorough and masterful study of these issues, N. H. G. Robinson, *The Groundwork of Christian Ethics* (London: Collins, 1971).

[34] One example of McCormick's efforts to specify those doctrines central to a Christian ethic can be found in his *Health and Medicine in the Catholic Tradition* (New York: Crossroad, 1984), 30–36, 36–39, 49, 51–62. Also McCormick's "Moral Theology in the Year 2000," and "Theology and Bioethics," in *Corrective Vision: Explorations in Moral Theology* (Kansas City: Sheed & Ward, 1994), 23–39, and 133–148 respectively.

[35] Lisa Sowle Cahill, "Richard A. McCormick: Reason and Faith in Post-Vatican II Catholic Ethics," in *Theological Voices in Medical Ethics,* edited by Allen Verhey and Stephen E. Lammers (Grand Rapids: Eerdmans, 1993), 78–105, at 81–82.

[36] In keeping with James Gustafson's insights into a person's preferences in developing an ethical theory, these differences are due to such special forces as: "an accident of birth and a matter of conscious assent," as well as a body of "religious and theological conviction,"(as James Gustafson describes them); my personal (existential, spiritual, cultural) understanding of the "authentic" foundation of Christian ethics; my own life's-journey (health, temperament, friendships); and my study of John Henry Newman, Gerard Manley Hopkins, Fritz Tillmann, James Gustafson, Bernard Haring, Karl Rahner, Edouard Hamel, Yves Congar, Joseph Fletcher, Carol Gilligan, Paul Ricoeur, Max Scheler, W.D. Ross, J.S. Mill, and Norbert Rigali.

Chapter IV

Major Approaches in Christian Ethics: Liberation Theology

Here is the fundamentally distinctive quality of the Christian ethic, that it is God who works in the Christian both to will and to do of his good pleasure.

N. H. G. Robinson
The Groundwork of Christian Ethics

Every human being, every group attains equity only through a hard struggle against all that masks and alters justice in the human heart.

Pierre Bigo
The Church and the Third World Revolution

For St. Augustine, virtue is "rightly ordered love," which means that virtue is not a balance one gains through avoiding two extremes as if it were the vices that define virtue rather than the other way round. For Augustine, there is a guiding light that corrects our wavering from the true course as we make passage through the world. Put another way, St. Augustine is more Platonic than Aristotelian in his pursuit of virtue.

Marion Montgomery
Virtue and Modern Shadows of Turning

I f there are difficulties with building Christian ethics upon the natural law approach, as we have just seen, it must also be recognized that Protestant and Catholic moral theologians cannot ignore natural morality completely, as N. H. G. Robinson reminds us.[1] The reason: "Christian ethics as a distinct study takes its stand in some sense upon the Christian revelation; and if the revelation of God in Christ addressed men as moral beings, as it seems unquestionably to do, then this revelation itself holds us firmly to natural morality (ibid., 100).

Developing a Christian ethic that stands more firmly on the Christian revelation, while at the same time giving an adequate place to natural morality, the community of moral discourse, and the social issues of particular cultures, have been among the goals of those who have spearheaded the growth of the next approach we will examine: Latin American liberation theology, arguably the dominant movement for renewal in Catholic moral theology since WWII.

"Liberation thought is not an animal without a head moving this way and that way, like a decapitated chicken," writes James G. Ward. "It is a serious intellectual movement urging us to find that which is intelligent and meaningful in *action* which aims always at the enhancement and realization of the dignity of the person in the world."[2] Who can deny that, during the last thirty years, liberation theology has been an impressively powerful, if controversial, force for change? Based upon traditional scriptural and doctrinal themes, the approach (as we will see) is not so much a new way of Christian theology and ethics, as a classic model adapted to special contexts.

More specifically, it is a way of being and doing in the world that challenges Christians to abandon both Capitalist and Marxist idolatries, and calls those who wish to follow Jesus, as well as all people of goodwill, to commit themselves to an alternative moral vision and to a way of living that is Christ-centered, freeing, and focused on building communities of virtue, service, and solidarity. Like the social gospel movement that was on the cutting edge of early twentieth century Protestant Christianity, liberation theology has been a major force in the renewal of Christian ethics in general as the century ended, and of the Catholic moral tradition in particular.

Latin American Liberation Theology: Origins and Emphases

For the benefit of those who have not been involved in courses in Christian ethics in recent years, the following summary of liberation theology will not be out of place; it will also allow readers to make a better evaluation of the strengths and weaknesses of this approach.

"When the term 'liberation theology' burst on the world scene in the 1970s, it was first as an expression of Latin American social Christianity," J. Philip Wogaman writes.[3] Its founders focused upon those who were most oppressed, and they gave special importance to the "preferential option for the poor."[4] Juan Luis Segundo, one of the pioneers of the movement, has described it as "an irreversible thrust in the Christian process of creating a new consciousness and maturity in our faith."[5] Almost immediately after its start, other liberation theologies began to be noticed: black, feminist, environmental, and gay.[6] Like feminists and situationists, each liberation theorist in his or her own distinctive way forms part of a broad grassroots effort which has the goal of developing what Karl Rahner called a community-oriented "dogmatic morality," that is, a personally-meaningful, well-integrated and ecclesially-constructive spirituality in which one tries with the help of God's grace and the support of others more gifted in the Spirit (as well as in the knowledge of history, philosophy, sociology, and psychology) to speak intelligently about God, to grow in wisdom and virtue, and to discern and implement God's will in one's place and time.

In company with Yves Congar—whose *Power and Poverty in the Church* (1965) explained how legalism invaded the Church's ecclesiology with the rise of papal power during the Middle Ages, liberation theology's founders advocated reinstating an understanding of "hierarchy" in terms of serving the welfare of the faithful, and criticized church leaders because of their desire for honours and titles and for forgetting that the Church is the "Mother of the poor."—Latin American theologies of liberation embodied strong reactions against traditional views of seminary and academic ethics; they contained aggressive responses to prevailing social situations.

According to Ricardo Planas, these theologies were shaped by a variety of specific forces: One was a mass-based education program developed in rural Brazil by Paulo Freire in the 1950s, a highly successful initiative that taught adults to read and to take active control of their lives. Another force was the spread of "basic ecclesial communities" that began in Brazil in the 1960s, a program in which families gathered to listen to Scripture, share their problems, and work toward practical solutions. A third force was the promise of Vatican II, with its emphasis on respect for persons, evangelization, effectively addressing the concerns of the poor, and building a just and peaceful world in cooperation with all people of good will.[7] Marxism was another powerful influence.[8]

Some of liberation theology's difficulties with the Catholic Church grew out of critiques of perceived limitations and shortcomings within the Church's prevailing pastoral theology and catechetical practices. Some of these criticisms: the Catholic Church's long-standing stress on individual salvation in the next world represents a distortion of Jesus' message; the Church does not possess any magical effectiveness where salvation is concerned; there are not two separate orders—a supernatural order outside history and a natural order inside history; the Catholic Church's excessive emphasis on reason, its support for neo-Scholastic expressions of natural law morality, as well as the Church's overt endorsement of reactionary (fascist, totalitarian) political parties in Europe and Latin America, plus its opposition to healthy developments in psychology, literature, and history.

On the constructive side, liberation theologians have tried to give Christian ethics a solid scriptural and doctrinal basis; they have made serious efforts to relate the data of religious knowledge to the findings of the social sciences; and they have attempted to be pastorally responsible, as well as sensitive to the Church's call to evangelization and world peace.[9] Latin American liberation theologians have taken Vatican II's *Gaudium et Spes* seriously. As Charles Curran says, "Liberation theologies begin with the location and experience of the oppressed—the poor, people of colour, and women—and take their subjective strivings for liberation seriously. In this light God is not an objective, detached observer of the human scene but God too is prejudiced and partial—in favour of the oppressed."[10]

Contemporary Christians should applaud Latin American liberation theology's efforts to link salvation and liberation. Like Joseph Fletcher's situation ethics, liberation theology has also emphasized method more than content. According to Segundo, "the one thing that can maintain the liberating character of a theology is not its content but its method" (ibid.,192). As well, the approach has stressed the importance of renewing Roman Catholic theology and the need for an ethics more authentically Christian, scientific, and practical.

Praxis: Its Essential Place in Liberation Ethics

"All theology starts with an act of faith," Gutierrez reminds us.[11] However, it is easy to forget the aphorisms and reform recommendations made by these theologians. The most important expressed the conviction that effective theology (reflection, critical attitude) begins with and results from *praxis,* rather than creed or catechism. For Gustavo Gutierrez, this methodological starting point builds on the premise that

"Only if we start in the realm of practice will we be able to develop a discourse about God that is authentic and respectful."[12] This principle is grounded in an insight basic to monastic pedagogy: first live the Christian life, then reflect; first develop a lifestyle, then speak about God.[13]

This approach to theology insists on the active integration of thought and action (the mutual interaction of theory and practice), because, in its eyes, to be engaged in theology does not mean to seek an exact, library-known familiarity with the writings of Aquinas, Luther, or Calvin, but to be involved in ministry and engaged in the critical interpretation of history in the light of divine revelation. Or, as Berryman says, liberation is both prior to pastoral work and the outgrowth of pastoral work. It is both theory-*for*-praxis and theory-*of*-praxis (ibid., 82).

Praxis, one of the distinctive terms in liberation theology, has generated a variety of meanings, given its place over the centuries in the writings of Aristotle, Hegel, Marx, and Freire. Basically, it means "practice" and "experience." According to Thomas Schubeck, it extends to what sociologist Alfred Schutz calls the world of everyday life, i.e. the practical day-to-day coping of people (farmers, nurses, and soldiers) whose decisions are guided by the maxims of a common wisdom.[14] *Praxis* implies life-history rather than book-knowledge; it means active living rather than armchair analysis: committed action rather than distanced observation; it means concrete, hands-on involvement rather than objective, impartial speculation. While not all *praxis* has the same truth-value, and some cannot be called Christian, for Latin American liberation theologians, *praxis* provides a lens through which one is better able to understand social and political issues—while a people's collective or an individual's personal *praxis* constitute foundational (primary, basic) sources of religious and ethical insight.

Segundo reinforces the importance of *praxis* in liberation theology: "We can only have an authentic faith and do theology in a genuine way when we have committed ourselves to an authentic struggle that opens our eyes to the new possibilities and meaning of God's word" (ibid., 97). It is *praxis* that makes progressive Latin American theology more interested in *being liberative* than in *talking about liberation* (ibid., 9). In the minds of these theologians, theology will have somewhat different responses to its controlling question when done on continents outside Latin America, e.g. Africa, Asia, Europe, and Australia.

However, in Gutierrez's judgment, theology's central question in Latin America today is "How are we to speak of God in the face of the poverty, ignorance, suffering, disease, and death of the innocent?" (ibid., 550).

Liberation Theology's Hermeneutical Circle

Liberation theology has provided Christians with a fruitful way to read Scripture—something lacking in traditional Catholic moral theology. As one looks back on the twentieth century, its wars and its famines, one must admire Segundo and other liberation theologians for their bold criticism of Catholic moral theology for evading the century's problems, and for not addressing the great issues in biology, health, evolution, and social change. One should also admire how they have used sociological tools to assist them in developing methods of dealing with past and present—especially in relating the teaching of Scripture with modern problems through a process they call the *hermeneutic circle*—the continuing change in our interpretation of the Bible which is dictated by the continuing changes in our present day reality, both individual and societal. Hermeneutic means "having to do with interpretation." And the circular nature of this interpretation stems from the fact that each new reality obliges us to interpret the word of God afresh, to change reality accordingly, and then to go back and reinterpret the word of God again, and so on.

Segundo, Boff, and Gutierrez have forced the Catholic Church to take a stand about their belief that God addresses us today as God addressed the Hebrews in the days of Moses: *within concrete events.* They have raised the consciousness of Christians by emphasizing that God's word is incarnated in contemporary history, as it was in the history of the first Christians.[15] In other words, liberation theology and ethics has shaped today's faith by maintaining that God communicates in historical moments; that the Bible contains living *normative* records of these communications within cultural and religious narratives (Genesis story, Fall story, Exodus story); that as we read these stories today they interactively shape and mould, explain and define both past and present divine communications.

The Exodus story provides a prime example of this approach to Scripture.[16] The story was read by the Hebrew people during the time of the Babylonian exile, and used by them to give meaning to their lives; the same story was read later by the first Christian communities, and the narrative provided them with inspiration and understanding about Jesus, his death, and Resurrection; it was read later still by European and American communities (Baptists, blacks), and provided them with insights into God's dealings in their lives and conditions. Unlike Roman Catholic moral theologians teaching prior to WWII who made no reference to this event, liberation theologians argue that the story of the Exodus, when contemplated today by committed Christians living in Latin America, Africa, Asia, or Europe, sheds light upon their efforts to respond to God's will in this time—to see how the living God sides with the oppressed against the pharaohs (the rich, elites, militaries) of "this" world.[17]

This is the circular method in which we should read Scripture, the highest authority and last word in theology—from *praxis* to Bible, from Bible to *praxis*. And in the dynamic learning process we find new insights and solutions; we become different, as we more fully grasp meanings and solutions locked in God's word. "People engaged in a *praxis* confer added meaning to the text, and a faithful reading of the text gives new meaning and direction to their *praxis*," Schubeck writes. "As Gutierrez is fond of saying, we read Scripture—seen as 'the book of life'—from within the context of our own *praxis*, but Scripture also reads us by effecting change in us" (ibid., 131).

From the start, liberation theology taught that theological truth must be grounded in concrete experience, that "black theology," for instance, is grounded like "black music" in "black" experience, and Latin American theology in the experiences of the Latin American peoples, especially in the memories and experiences of the oppressed, for whom liberation, as Wogaman says, can be the deep word about God.[18] The approach contained a morality that emphasized coming to know and work with God and Jesus Christ in relation to one's neighbors—especially the widow, poor, and orphan in one's community. In Alfred Hennelly's estimate, liberation morality is *creative* and *progressive*; it is not an ethics of the licit and illicit, but one suitable for the construction of love.[19] It is essentially *social* and *significative* (it is a sign, light in the world).

The "truth" discovered by liberation theology is not universal or absolute. Rather, as James Cone has argued, such "truth" is relative to its social location.[20] It is like the "truth" contained in Newman's *The Idea of a University* or in Cervantes *Don Quixote*. Consequently, the "truths" about living and acting developed from using liberation theology are different (in shade, sometimes in substance) from those found in both the lived morality and ethical textbooks in the mainstream European or North American Catholic communities (ibid., 95).

Latin liberation theology has learned important lessons from the social sciences. While it has been criticized from its inception for its use of Marxist categories, it has confidently used both Marxist and postmodern approaches to analyze and interpret Scripture and to critique society. Modern sociologists have taught these theologians that although "faith" is an absolute, "theology" (at its best) is always incomplete, its conclusions never able to be universalized, and its concrete doctrines and principles are always relative—because a person's theology (Paul's, Augustine's, Luther's, Tillich's, Welch's, Gustafson's) can never be totally separated from his or her *self, history, culture,* or *ideology*—the person's concrete thought and value system conditioned by his or her life-history.[21] Consequently, in Segundo's judgment, each of us lives in the midst of relativism; and Christian conduct, like non-Christian conduct, is always subject to a "human dose of relativism" (ibid., 175).

This does not mean that we live in chaos, however (ibid., 67). The Church's faith has been incarnated throughout the centuries in successive ideologies (Jewish, Greek, Renaissance, Enlightenment), and while it is impossible to wring out "faith" in its essence—to reduce Christianity to a book or a page of the Bible—it is possible to see in all these successive faith-incarnated ideologies *the road to be traveled* by modern and future Christians (ibid., 181).

Liberation Theology: Specific Concerns

Liberation theologies (Latin, black, feminist) have had major impacts upon Protestant and Catholic ethicists. Early in the 1970s, for instance, the Permanent Council of the French Catholic Bishops said "Christians would be unfaithful to their mission of evangelizing if they did not mobilize effectively to work with all their brothers, believers and nonbelievers, for human liberation, of each person and all persons."[22] However, liberation theology has also had its detractors. Andrew Greeley was an early critic.[23] More recently, the American Protestant theologian, Don S. Browning, has written in support of Luis Segundo's concept of the "hermeneutic circle," as described in *The Liberation of Theology* (1976), and he has expressed sympathy for Segundo's "partiality for the poor" as in some way part of the central message of the Christian faith. Browning believes, nevertheless, that

Segundo is "so attached to this prejudice, which is doubtless born of his experiences with the struggle of Latin American poor, that he is insensitive to aspects of the Scriptures that this precommitment does not grasp."[24]

On the other hand, the Irish Catholic writer, Vincent MacNamara, praises liberation theology and ethics for giving a fresh and powerful impetus to the well-attested Biblical theme that faith works through love. "It has also helped to highlight several related themes," MacNamara notes. "That salvation is not just personal and spiritual but social and institutional; that bringing about liberation from oppressive situations is bringing about God's kingdom; that in the Christian tradition God is father of the poor." At the same time, McNamara questions (as I do) liberation theology's ability to provide answers to today's complex medical, environmental, and economic issues. "But does it enable the Christian to know what to do?" he writes. "Does it, through its interpretation of revelation, give a specific and concrete insight into what is morally required, what God is requiring and enabling us to do?"[25]

J. Philip Wogaman commends liberation theology for four contributions that will likely endure as the second millennium gives way to the third: it has underscored the importance of structural, institutional moral issues; it has brought into the mainstream of Christian thinking the contributions of nineteenth century Marxist and twentieth century social sciences in order to demonstrate the links between "social location" and "moral truth";[26] it has emphasized the full humanity of oppressed people in its efforts to empower, highlight, and give voice to the insights of the marginalized; it has reminded Christians, in particular those who reside in elitist centers of power and privilege, that the moral and spiritual health of the Church is tied to the liberation (education, employment) of all of its members.[27]

As well, Sharon Welch pays tribute to the work of liberation theologians for a number of different reasons: for calling Christians to conversion and repentance; for calling liberal Euro-American theologians to recognize the ways in which the Christian tradition and liberal political and theological traditions of the first world have served to perpetuate various forms of oppression.[28] She does not agree with Dennis McCann's critique of liberation theology, the problems he has with its "revolutionary enthusiasm" and its lack of "criteria for distinguishing limits that summon people to worshipful contemplation rather than political action" (ibid., 109). Welch is sympathetic to liberation theology's emphasis on loyalty and action, joy and integrity (ibid., 110).

Leaving aside the Vatican's concerns about liberation theology and Pope John Paul II's opposition, one of the best-known contemporary American critics of this approach in Christian ethics is Michael Novak, author of *The Spirit of Democratic Capitalism* (1982), "The Quintessential Liberal: John Stuart Mill," in *Freedom with Justice: Catholic Social Thought and Liberal Institutions* (1984), "Democracy and Human Rights," in *Speaking to the Third World: Essays on Democracy and Development*, edited by Peter Berger and Michael Novak (1985), and *Will It Liberate? Questions About Liberation Theology* (1986). And Novak's criticisms deserve special attention.

There is much in Latin American liberation theology to admire, most of all its intellectual ambition, Novak admits (*Will It Liberate?*,2). Theologians should take liberation theology seriously. It asks the right questions. Is has good intentions (ibid., 33). "There can be no question that great revolutions in political economy are necessary in Latin America, if that great and much-blessed continent is to fulfill its full human destiny," Novak writes (ibid., 2). However, Novak is critical of Latin American liberation theology's basic concepts. He disagrees with its image of history and with its sense that the basic law of creation is oppression (ibid., 108–110). It is abstract, vague, and general (ibid., 113). He is most critical of its judgment upon economic activism, commerce, invention, discovery, entrepreneurship, enterprise, and investment—in a word, capitalism (ibid., 3). "Latin American humanism has been hostile to commerce and to economic dynamism, which it considers vulgar, low, of little esteem, and more than a little tainted with evil. Latin American humanism prefers the mode of the aristocratic spirit on the one side, and the simplicity of the rural peasant, on the other. Its basic enlivening vision is feudal ..."(ibid. 3).

Latin America needs a revolution, but it does not need a socialist revolution. This is the central thesis of Novak's book. Latin America needs to throw off its protections for the rich, strip them of their ancient privileges. It needs to move from being pre-capitalist to capitalist (ibid., 5). "It is my hypothesis that the liberal society, built around a capitalist society that promises discovery and entrepreneurship among the poor at the base of society, will succeed more quickly, more thoroughly, and in a more liberating fashion, than the socialist societies so far conceived of by liberation theologians" (ibid., 8–9). Or as he says later, "Nothing so lifts up the poor as the liberation of their own creative economic activities" (ibid., 217)—an opinion supported by all who have been involved in running their own business.

Novak argues (correctly I believe) that Latin America will develop much more quickly under leaders committed to economic, political, civil, religious, and cultural liberties, because "economic liberties give material substance to political and civil liberties, and to intellectual and artistic liberties. To own printing presses—in general, to have autonomy over economic instruments—is an indispensable condition for other liberties, among incarnate creatures such as we" (ibid., 217). He supports Latin American liberals who believe in an economy in which ordinary people will be free to choose and to act and to create without being controlled by "statism" or dominated by socialist secret police (ibid., 254). This criticism has its force.

Latin American Liberation Theology: Moving Communities Toward Freedom

Latin American liberation theology has been a definite force in shaping the ethic presented in this book. The approach has strengthened my convictions about the unhealthy (uncritical, untheological) state of Catholic moral theology, the limitations of neo-Scholasticism, and the urgent need to develop an ethic that is conspicuously religious, as well as philosophically sound in terms of its understanding of morality and moral knowledge, the limits of language, and the contingency of ethical truth. However, during this century, the next generation of liberation theologians will have to argue in favor of biblically rich and economically sound approaches that develop and protect what Novak calls "the three fundamental liberations: freedom in the political order, freedom from poverty, and freedom of conscience, information, and ideas" (ibid., 228).

Since American Protestant and Catholic leaders have become openly critical of liberalism (they have always been contemptuous of socialism), these writers and pastors will be facing uphill tasks as they develop ethical theories that delineate and protect those inalienable rights endowed in each human person by the Creator. No doubt, some will be inspired in their efforts, not only by pressing global needs within Third World countries, those in particular being devastated by AIDS, debt repayments, and genocidal wars, but also by Thomas Jefferson's words, "The God who gave us life gave us liberty."

Liberation theology has its obvious strengths. It is scriptural; it is clear, consistent, and coherent. "Sobrino presents a remarkably consistent vision of the foundation of Christian morality developed from the kingdom of God," Schubeck maintains.[29] "He demonstrates how the imperative (e.g., commit oneself to the poor) arises from a graced encounter with the spirit of Jesus mediated through the Bible, community worship, historical events, and through the poor themselves. His grounding obligation in gratuity respects God's initiative and power, as well as human freedom" (ibid.,197).

The approach avoids some of the problems in evangelical ethics' literal use of Scripture. It is ecclesial, while at the same time affirming that while it is important to look to the Church for guidance, Christians must work through their own wisdom and pursue their own community interests in historical circumstances. Further, while employing the resources of contemporary sciences and humanities in order to better understand and interpret reality and the human condition, at the same time, liberation theology does not claim that reason's moral principles or conclusions are identical with those of God's self-revelation in Christ. Aphorisms such as "The first shall be last, and the last shall be first" (Matthew 19:30), Jesus' "Great Commandment" (Matthew 7:12; Luke 25–28), as well as the parable of the Good Samaritan (Luke 10:29–37), contain ethical norms that few contemporary Anglo-American philosophers—today's right reasoning individual—would support.

Liberation theology is more conservative than Sharon Welch's feminist ethics of risk, although like the latter it strives to allow for the influences of culture and history, while it tries to incorporate the compelling insights of developmental psychology and the findings of research into adult spirituality—features that have been influential on the ethical theory presented in this book. The approach's emphasis on the socially and historically socialized nature of moralilty, on solidarity, the dignity of the poor, and its focus on effecting institutional change (overcoming structural injustice), as well as promoting the personal morality of the members of groups, have been catalysts already—and they will continue to purify and heal.

Liberation theology forces Christian ethics back to its biblical roots; it makes morality a part of daily life. In its basic drive "to make the Word of Life present in a world of oppression, injustice, and death," the approach emphasizes crucial themes (liberation, God's presence with the poor) frequently omitted by moral theories that focus on the *status quo*. Gutierrez's words, "Liberation is at bottom a gift of the Lord," remind us that liberation theology creates moral attitudes and actions that constitute a theological ethic—in spite of its obvious use of the social sciences and its political objectives.[30]

As mentioned already, however, the ethics' usefulness is somewhat limited by the fact that its proponents do not provide a set of explicit first-level or second-level moral standards or principles. In order to make a morally sound decision in the Terri Schiavo case, for instance, a person using Gutierrez's method should (it seems) prayerfully and intelligently employ the biblical theme of Exodus, along with Jesus' teaching about respect for the "widow, the poor, and the orphan" in order to reach a decision about maintaining or removing the feeding tube that is supplying nutrition and hydration vital for Terri to live in her severely impaired ("persistent vegetative" state). Nowhere do liberation theologians present standards such as "quality of life" "best interests," or "sacredness of life" to assist nurse or physician decision-makers. The frequently-used bioethics principle associated with "ordinary and extraordinary means" (it was the basis of the argument used by Georgetown Jesuit ethicist Kevin Wildes to justify stopping Terri's feeding) cannot be found in Gutierrez's writings.

In spite of these limitations, however, because liberation theology actively integrates morality and spirituality, appreciates creativity and autonomy, and has a socially advancing goal, it will have strong appeal to those who see Christ's message in terms of personal integrity and overcoming the chains of social and personal sin. Its emphasis on freedom and its inherent simplicity will always attract.[31]

Notes:

[1] N. H. G. Robinson, *The Groundwork of Christian Ethics*, op. cit., 100.

[2] James G. Ward, "The Context for Liberation Thought," *Listening*, 21, 1 (Winter, 1986), 43–55. Also, Gustavo Gutierrez, "Liberation Theology," *New Dictionary of Catholic Social Thought*, op. cit., 548–553.

[3] J. Philip Wogaman, "Liberation Theology," in *Christian Ethics: A Historical Introduction* (Louisville: Westminster/John Knox: 1993), 248–256, at 248.

[4] On the beginnings of this movement, Phillip Berryman, *Liberation Theology* (Philadelphia, PA: Temple University Press, 1987), 9–28. Also Harvey Cox's valuable essays, "Liberation Theology: The Voices of the Uninvited," and "But Is It Really Theology," in his *Religion in the Secular City: Toward A Postmodern Theology* (New York: Simon and Schuster, 1984), 135–149, 150–158. Also, Donal Dorr, "Poor, Preferential Option for," *New Dictionary of Catholic Thought*, op. cit., 755–759.

[5] Juan Luis Segundo, *The Liberation of Theology* (Maryknoll, NY: Orbis Books, 1976), 3.

[6] For example, James Cone, *A Black Theology of Liberation* (New York: Lippincott, 1970). For the "essence" of feminist theology of liberation, Wogaman, op. cit., 254–256.

[7] On the role of Vatican II in the origins of liberation theology, Leonardo Boff, *When Theology Listens to the Poor* (San Francisco: Harper & Row, 1988), 1–31.

[8] Ricardo Planas, *Liberation Theology: The Political Expression of Religion* (Kansas City: Sheed & Ward, 1986), 3. As J. Philip Wogaman notes, authors such as Jose Miguez Bonino who saw the "unsubstitutable relevance of Marxism" distinguished between Marxism as a method of analysis and Marxism as a philosophy, and they saw that there "could be no Christian capitulation to Marxist atheism" (Wogaman, op. cit., 250–251). This is an important distinction that has been too frequently dismissed by liberation theology's conservative critics. More than one theologian has found much to commend in Marx's analyses and critiques of 19th century capitalism, and such support for Marx's insights should not have been taken to imply that the scholar was either an atheist or a materialist.

[9] From liberation theology's emphasis on "seeing, judging, acting," one also sees signs of the influence of the highly successful Catholic youth movement founded by a Belgium priest Msgr Joseph Cardijn called the Young Catholic Worker (YCW) movement, that was a worldwide force for religious education and social action during the 1950s–1960s.

[10] Charles E. Curran, "Absolute Moral Norms," in *Christian Ethics: An Introduction* (London: Cassell, 1998), 72–83, at 82.

[11] Gustavo Gutierrez, "Liberation Theology," art. cit., 549.

[12] Gustavo Gutierrez, ibid., 549.

[13] For a useful essay on the meaning and critical functions of this term, Roger Haight, "Praxis," *New Dictionary of Catholic Social Thought*, op. cit., 776–777.

[14] Thomas L. Schubeck. *Liberation Ethics: Sources, Models, and Norms* (Minneapolis, MN: Fortress Press, 1993), 39. Also, Berryman, 85–87.

[15] That history rather than nature is the locus of morality, and that God's will is found in the "signs of the times" rather than in ontological structures—is one of the major emphases in liberation theology.

[16] On the place of the Exodus in liberation theology, Norman Lohfink, *Option for the Poor: The Basic Principle of Liberation Theology in the Light of the Bible* (Berkeley: Bible Press, 1987).

[17] On liberation theology's key scriptural themes, Leonardo Boff, Clodovis Boff, *Introducing Liberation Theology* (Maryknoll, NY: Orbis Books, 1987), 43–65.

[18] J. Philip Wogaman, op. cit., 253.

[19] Alfred T. Hennelly, *Theologies in Conflict: The Challenge of Juan Luis Segundo* (Maryknoll, NY: Orbis Books, 1979), 93–94.

[20] James H. Cone, *God of the Oppressed* (New York: Seabury Press, 1975), 17.

[21] An ideology is "any conception that offers a view of the various aspects of life from the standpoint of a specific group in society." On this subject, Berryman, 131–134; Planas, 77–125.

[22] For these words, Richard A. McCormick, *Notes on Moral Theology: 1965–1980* (Washington, D.C.: University Press of America, 1981), 619.

[23] Andrew Greeley, "Theology without Freedom?" *Catholic Chronicle* (November 28, 1975), 5.

[24] Don S. Browning, *A Fundamental Practical Theology: Descriptive and Strategic Proposals* (Minneapolis: Fortress Press, 1991), 66.

[25] Vincent MacNamara, *Faith & Ethics: Recent Roman Catholicism* (Dublin: Gill and MacMillan, 1985), 138. For James Gustafson's criticism of liberation theology, *Ethics from a Theocentric Perspective*, I, ibid., 72–74. Also, George V. Lobo, op. cit., 27–28, 148–149, 315–316, 418, 436; Alfred T. Hennelly, "The Biblical Hermeneutics of Juan Luis Segundo," in *The Use of Scripture in Moral Theology: Readings in Moral Theology #4*, op.cit., 303–320; Anthony J. Tambasco, "A Critical Appraisal of Segundo's Biblical Hermeneutics," ibid., 321–336.

[26] Charles Curran commends liberation theology for this contribution too. Charles E. Curran, "Absolute Moral Norms," in *Christian Ethics: An Introduction*, edited by Bernard Hoose, op. cit., 82.

[27] J. Philip Wogaman, op. cit., 256.

[28] Sharon D. Welch, *A Feminist Ethic of Risk*, op. cit., 104.

[29] Thomas L. Schubeck, , op. cit., 197.

[30] On the specifically "theological" aspects of this approach, Gustavo Gutierrez, "Liberation Theology," *New Dictionary of Catholic Social Thought*, op. cit., 552–553. For useful remarks about "freedom," and Segundo's linking of "sincerity" and "authenticity" with "true freedom," George V. Lobo, *Guide to Christian Living: A New Compendium of Moral Theology*, op. cit.,314–319.

[31] The fact that liberation theology contains so few of the practical principles that have been the standard fare of Catholic medical ethics, for instance, poses serious difficulties for medical and nursing students, I have found. As much as they admire Gutierrez's spirituality, his emphasis on *praxis*, and his practical use of Scripture, they feel too insecure to make life and death decisions simply on the basis of what they find in his theology. In their efforts to free Catholic moral theology from the prison of its past, those who have articulated this approach might have provided I fear an excess of freedom rather than sufficient structure for confident moral decision making by today's business, health care, and political leaders.

Chapter V

Major Approaches in Christian Ethics: Feminist Ethics

Feminists who emphasize the liberation of women have believed that their work of overcoming oppression is an implication of their faith in the Redeemer.

Susan F. Parsons
Christian Ethics: An Introduction

We might think that God wanted simply obedience to a set of rules; whereas He really wants people of a particular sort.

C. S. Lewis
Mere Christianity

A correct understanding of the nature of Christian tradition, whether in the Bible or in later writings, makes it clear that this tradition cannot be ultimately authoritative for our moral reasoning.

Gerard J. Hughes
Authority in Morals

E thical theories that can be accurately termed "feminist" comprise the most forceful movement in contemporary Christian ethics. Powered by a set of beliefs and goals that have already reshaped a number of the basic assumptions and principles within the discipline, feminist ethics now has its own language and literary style; it possesses its own methodological and epistemological rules.

Sharing some of the features we find in situation ethics, casuistry, and liberation ethics, Christian feminism embraces a distinctive approach to moral issues, as well as a unique set of normative principles and operative rules. Like Richard McCormick's and Gustavo Gutierrez's moral theories, this approach has played a significant part in renewing Christian ethics and the Catholic moral tradition—it has shaped features central to the moral theory that will be presented in the final chapters of this book.

Again, because of the importance of this approach, this chapter will provide both statement and critique, an opportunity for readers less familiar with this way of doing ethics to gain a clear understanding of feminist thinking, as well as an adequate assessment of its strengths and weaknesses.

Christian Feminist Ethics: Features

Feminists working in ethics believe that all systems of religious and philosophical ethics, whether Eastern or Western, developed to date to provide guidance about living the "good" life are both distorted and inadequate. Why? Susan Parsons gives a number of reasons: Classic moral theories did not take women, their insights, or experiences into account; some theorists presumed that males alone were moral agents; patriarchal ethicists have viewed women as lesser humans, and confined women to areas of life and work chosen by males.[1] Since they ignore the worth of women (seeing them as either temptresses or irrational), restrict women to nonpolitical, petty, and domestic affairs, and generally omit all reference to women's religious, moral, and spiritual experience, the works of past mainstream ethics must, consequently, be set aside, while at the same time the analysis of contemporary writers needs to undergo major revision.[2]

In order to achieve these goals, feminists working in business, legal, or health care ethics start with critiques. For Harvard's Carol Gilligan, the best-known American writer on women's moral development, psychological research into moral behavior and theories of moral development have largely misunderstood women—their motives and moral commitments, their values and ethical development. Repeatedly, research into moral maturity and decision-making has been built upon male observations about men's behavior, Gilligan argues.[3] Sharon Welch's highly acclaimed *A Feminist Ethic of Risk* (1990) opens with the argument that America's rationally-deduced, male-dominated nuclear weapons policies are classic examples of dangerously flawed thought, and that U.S. foreign policy's confidence in superior economic and military strength has consistently masked immorality as ethics.[4]

For a third feminist writer, Virginia L. Warren, mainstream medical ethics has used a male perspective to frame moral questions and to shape ethical solutions. As well, it has set up debates in ways that have kept women on the defensive.[5] Such ethics seduces women to work within its framework by offering hope for improvement, but only if women do not rock the patriarchal boat too vigorously (ibid., 34). In Warren's view, both the way that bioethics looks at the rightness of actions and how bioethics is done—the process—exhibit male biases and masculine distortions (ibid., 35).

These criticisms of mainstream Protestant and Catholic ethics are central to Eleanor Humes Haney's valuable summary review of feminist critiques of Catholic and Protestant moral theology. What has been called "Judeo-Christian ethics" represents only a part of Christian and human experience—that of men who were usually called to celibacy rather than to marriage, to positions of power rather than to service, to lives as insiders in societies rather than to lonely existences on the margins, according to Haney.[6] "Little of the ethics considered significant by the church and by divinity schools has been written by women, by nonwhites, by the poor, and by those whose expressed sexual orientations that deviated from a heterosexual and marital one"(ibid., 115).[7]

Because of Christian ethics' "parochialism" and "arrogance," feminists working in the field have never felt comfortable doing Christian ethics as it has been done by past scholars. In their minds, they could not simply fill in history's gaps or add women's experiences to the historical record. "For women to go back to some starting point in the past or to some already defined authority is to do little more than think men's thoughts after them," Haney explains (ibid., 116). Therefore, from the start, feminist ethics sought to articulate and make real the visions of women (and men) who shared beliefs and values grounded in women's experience of the "right" and their communal apprehension of the "good." They have been interested in researching early, medieval, and recent feminist visions and voices (ibid., 116).[8] Here we see the basis for the claim that Christian feminist ethics relates to traditional Christian ethics as critique and alternative (ibid., 122).

Two hundred years ago Elizabeth Cady Stanton, Susan B. Anthony, and Lucretia Mott spearheaded nineteenth century efforts to abolish slavery and to advance women's rights throughout the United States.[9] And now, thirty years after Betty Friedan's *Feminine Mystique* (1963), Kate Millett's *Sexual Politics* (1970), Mary Daly's *Radical Feminism* (1973), and Rosemary Radford Ruether's *New Woman/New Earth* (1975), there is obvious pluralism within the feminist movement in general and feminist ethics in particular. "Feminists have understandable reasons both to reject and to promote belief in a common or universal morality," Margaret Farley says.[10]

Black feminist liberation ethics and feminist liberation theology have their own distinctive emphases and interests.[11] However, there are some generally shared methodological principles, common goals, and characteristic emphases within the feminist movement within Anglo-American ethics. The two original streams, one focused on caring, the other on justice, have been brought together by recent feminist writers, e.g. Peta Bowden and Rita C. Manning.[12] The initial insights into human knowledge and decision-making have been developed and strengthened; feminists have actively applied their analyses to areas of life vital to women.[13]

The feminist ethicists' focus on connectedness and context—central to both situation ethics and liberation theology—makes evident other conclusions: the nature of specific relationships is an important element of ethical analysis; an ethics of actions is incomplete when evaluation is done in abstraction from the relationships that exist between the participants and those affected; objective and accurate knowledge result from a patchwork of inherently incomplete perspectives.

Further, as Susan Sherwin writes, "Within feminist ethics, there is widespread criticism of the assumption that the role of ethics is to clarify obligations among individuals who are viewed as paradigmatically equal, independent, rational, and autonomous" (ibid., 21).

And there are other significant differences. "Fair mindedness" is one of the central features of critical thinking as described by contemporary Anglo-American authors, and, like the Comte de Mirabeau, students of critical thinking courses are taught that "Good sense is the absence of every strong passion." However, feminists are inclined to dispute the importance of "fair-mindedness"—in the lives of patient advocates, political leaders, and those desiring to bring about social change in particular. And they are more sympathetic toward the second part of Mirabeau's ironic aphorism: "and only people of strong passion can be great."[14]

Further, questions relating to "subject identity" are of primary importance to feminist philosophers, according to Gill Howie. "If the way in which the identity of the subject is formed is linked to particular earlier events, then the relevance of an analysis of social conditions comes to the fore."[15]

While showing some respect for Alisdair MacIntyre's contributions to ethics, Susan Okin criticizes MacIntyre for his "pervasive elitism" and his "equally pervasive sexism." She argues that MacIntyre's *After Virtue* is a clear case of "false gender neutrality," and that the author's "use of gender-neutral language in the discussion of tradition and societies in which sex differences was a central and determining feature that justified the domination of women continues throughout MacIntyre's recent work." Due to these and other major defects, Okin concludes that most women, "as well as men who have any kind of feminist consciousness, will not find in any of his [MacIntyre's] traditions a rational basis for moral and political action."[16]

Besides the twin emphasis on knowledge's contextuality and the moral significance of specific, unequal relationships, feminist writers have enlarged the discussion of religious morality in important ways. While some (Sharon Welch, for example) have stepped outside of Christianity to develop their theology, the majority have worked within their faith communities to renew and restore theology.[17] Grace Jantzen, for example, has developed a specifically feminist approach to religion;[18] Monika Hellwig has presented Catholicism in terms of an appealing Trinitarian motif that emphasizes the Father as compassion, Jesus as God's self-revelation, and the Spirit as the power of grace to liberate human creativity.[19] A number of feminists have chosen to chronicle their spiritual journeys[20] or to write about Jesus, the early Church, and Christianity's feminine face.[21]

Feminist authors have studied the important interconnections between gender and language.[22] Those with expertise in sacred Scripture and Christian theology have carefully critiqued the symbolism and narratives of the Bible, church documents, and theology in order to expose the distortions and exaggerations that have seriously harmed women, minorities, and marginalized groups. In the process, these writers have alerted millions of Christians to the importance of being sensitive about inclusive language and the use of gender-free speech with regard to God. They have warned against the overuse of imagery drawn from warfare and sport when talking about life, medicine, spirituality, and morality.[23]

Mary Anne Warren has examined the ethical significance of birth.[24] Susan Wendell has provided an outline of a feminist theory of disability that attempts to overcome the entrenched Western understanding of pain, ideal bodies, and control.[25] Other feminists have examined the social and personal causes of anorexia, bulimia, and alcoholism among women, exploring why millions feel that there is something inherently flawed and shameful about the female form, or why so many women experience constant body loathing, self-starvation, and obesity, as Caroline Knapp reports in *Appetites: Why Women Want*.[26] Jennifer Lee Carrell has brought to life women whose contributions to science have been given insufficient attention,[27] while Sandra Day O'Connor has written about her work on the U.S. Supreme Court.[28]

A number of feminist writers with historical interests have undertaken research to recover "lost" women artists, novelists, and political and military heroes; they have resurrected marginalized women (courtesans, lesbians). Others have focused on women as friends, lovers, and competitors in the lives of famous artists, singers, novelists—and theologians.[29] Isabel Allende has written with humor, longing, and stinging criticism about her homeland,[30] while Iris Chang has examined her extended family and ancestors, the Chinese in America, and their contributions to national life, politics, economics, education, and culture.[31]

What one finds today as the twenty-first century begins was evident from the start: Feminists working in ethics have sought to broaden the scope of the field; they have focused attention on "housekeeping" issues, on wildlife and pets, and the environment; and they have emphasized topics pertaining to the oppression of women—subjects on the margins of traditional mainstream ethics.[32] Ecofeminists have proposed new images of creation and reformulations of the relationships between God, humans, and the nonhuman world.[33] A number of feminists have been highly influential in biomedical ethics.[34] Some have looked at how women deal with death and dying; they have found that mothers, spouses, daughters, and companions deal with these events in ways that are quite different from men of both dominant and nondominant cultures.[35]

Others have reexamined the moral significance of birth, sex selection, surrogacy, and ectogenesis.[36] Womanists have challenged liberal societies to reshape their social structures in ways that deal more justly with the family.[37] Catholic and Protestant feminist writers have called upon their communities to rethink their stands on abortion, women in ministry, and homosexuality.[38]

The body plays a significant role in a number of feminist analyses, but one finds little support for classic "natural law" morality.[39] Some writers have been critical of theories that equate ethics with decision-making. Others have argued that ethics should be concerned not only with actions and relationships, but also with questions of character and the development of attitudes of trust within relationships, a theme that has special significance for Annette Baier.[40]

Feminists have rejected the view of human persons as "self-isolating," and have insisted on the need for "a corrective to a liberal philosophy that fails to understand persons as embodied subjects, with essential capacity and need for union with other persons," Margaret Farley states.[41] Rather than a focus on rational self-interest (Ayn Rand) or the patterns and potentialities inherent in human nature (Grisez), womanists have set their sights on developing a social ethics whose final goal is the liberation of oppressed groups from structural injustice.[42] Feminists interested in epistemology have examined issues relating to the role of language in human knowledge and the ways that male and female worldviews influence science, history, and ethics. Defending the position that "the standpoint of the marginalized" provides the correct and most fruitful place to search for "truth" has been another central task.[43] Both the ethics of care (Nel Noddings) and the ethics of justice (Rita Manning) have exhibited strong commitments to social action. As Sharon Welch says, "Marxists are right—love for individuals is not enough. Structural change is required" (ibid., 166).

From what has been stated about feminist ethics' problems with mainstream moral theories, it should not surprise U.S. that feminists have abandoned Mill's "greatest happiness" principle and distanced themselves from Hobbes's egoism. Denise Lardner Carmody, in her best-selling *Virtuous Woman: Reflections on Christian Feminist Ethics* (1992), argues for a number of changes in the Catholic Church's sexual teaching.[44] Further, the paradigms of nurture and friendship embodied in an ethics of "just caring" support concrete action for the liberation of oppressed minorities, as well as historically disadvantaged groups. "They require action by the oppressed themselves and by those in positions of advocacy for the oppressed," Haney writes (ibid., 119). The ethics of justice recognizes the importance of rights, autonomy, and equality. Both approaches emphasize women's interests and issues of special concern to women: e.g. fairer distribution of federal funds for research on mental health, on the impact of pornography, and the links between racism and sexism. "In pursuing feminist ethics, and we must continually raise the question, 'What does it mean for women?'," Susan Sherwin states (ibid., 28).

Honesty and integrity have been major themes in this approach from its beginnings. Caring, both as disposition and as expressed in action, is another important theme. Hope and fidelity-to-being are additional virtues. Annette Baier has employed "appropriate trust" as a concept that effectively bridges an ethics of love and an ethics of duty. Linda A. Bell has advanced an ethics of centering freedom instead of an ethics of care taking—of playfulness instead of control.[45] Starhawk has argued that the basis of ethics is erotic love for the particular, a belief that one finds in Gerard Manley Hopkins's poetry.[46] Marie J. Giblin calls feminist bioethics a "prophetic lens" with which we are able to see more clearly the injustices in the health care system and the possibilities for more caring and just communities.[47]

Approaching the third decade in its modern history, Christian feminism views dimensions of Christ's teaching and life as consistent with and enriching to a feminist ethics, according to Haney (ibid., 23). Christ's teaching on self-sacrifice, however, is a subject of difficulty for some writers—likewise Christ's teaching on the cross, suffering, discipleship, and non-resistance (Farley, 231). "Christianity is prone to an ethics of Christian character, of personal virtue, that is as ahistorical and apolitical in orientation as an unreconstructed ethic of care," Kathryn Tanner observes (ibid., 188). Emily Culpepper, Sharon Welch, and Mary Daly have been critical of classical monotheism and have advocated the creation of multiple images and symbols of the Holy. They have emphasized God's immanence rather than God's transcendence; they have seen divinity within relationships and events. Feminist writers, e.g. Denise Lardner Carmody, have been cautious about Bible morality because of its patriarchal bias and its violence— the "dark side of monotheism" to use Regina Schwartz's phrase.[48]

Because of the limits seen in the theology and ethics of Paul, Augustine, Aquinas, Luther, and Calvin, Elizabeth Fiorenza has put forward a widely influential reconstruction of Christian beginnings, while Rosemary Ruether has developed a distinctive feminist theology. Clearly, Christian feminist ethics cannot be called either "theocentric" or "evangelical." In a valuable study of medieval Christian writers, Eleanor McLaughlin has examined Aquinas' discussion of creation and the Fall, and how later writers saw "that better life through which the woman can in theory escape the natural subordination and inferiority to which she is ordained by her sex"—the monastic life.[49]

Both Protestant and Roman Catholic feminists have challenged traditional ecclesiology and spirituality. They see the need for major changes because of the patriarchal structures and masculine images that impact negatively upon women's roles and functions within family, society, and church. In recent years, Rosemary Chinnici has invited women to transcend the traditional boundaries and to discover their self-worth through a process of re-imaging the church.[50] Sandra Schneiders has put together themes intended to develop a new concept of religious life for women's religious orders.[51] Leanne McCall Tigert has told the stories of gays, lesbians, and bisexuals in the church in order to offer possibilities for healing changes.[52] Kathleen Fischer has presented a new approach to spiritual direction based upon women's experience and their concern for inclusiveness, connectedness, justice, and mutuality.[53]

The Vatican's position on birth control, abortion, and high tech fertility, its unwillingness to use inclusive language in the text of *The Catechism of the Catholic Church*, as well as its refusal to make any concessions on women's ordination, have angered—but not deterred—Catholic feminists.[54] Finally, Haney considers grace not as forgiveness, but as being-at-home-in-the-universe—as living gracefully—to be a rich concept (ibid., 123). Christian feminism has, as we will see, a strong eschatological dimension, too (ibid., 123–24).

Assessing Feminist Ethics: Weighing Its Worth

Contemporary feminist theory at its best is "the most ethically challenging and intellectually sophisticated exposure of the full dilemmas of our pluralistic and ambiguous postmodern moment," according to David Tracy.[55] Consequently, it is not yet possible at this time to make anything like a final assessment of feminist ethics, its methodology or epistemology, or the soundness of its theological or spiritual insights. While the ethic being presented in this book has been shaped by a number of emphases within the feminist movement, it recognizes that the approach has its shortcomings. For instance, some writers (e.g. Tom Beauchamp and James Childress) have pointed out (convincingly) problems in an ethics of care: it falls short in terms of its completeness, explanatory power, and its ability to justify its conclusions; it is undeveloped; it is too contexual and hostile to principles. "Without a broader framework, the ethics of care is too confined to the *private* sphere of intimate relationships and may serve to reinforce an uncritical adherence to traditional social patterns of assigning caretaker roles to women," they write (ibid., 91).

While an ethics of care faces some of the same problems inherent in Joseph Fletcher's ethics, care-like love provides neither explicit rules nor certain guidance when we are faced with complex social or personal issues–it is important to note that recent authors (e.g. Peta Bowden, Rita Manning) have addressed some of the main criticisms and strengthened this approach. In her review study, "Feminist Ethics After Modernity: Towards an Appropriate Universalism," Susan Parsons argues that contrary to what Michael Novak has argued in his critique of liberation theology, liberalism may not furnish the best way for feminist ethics to develop, and other alternatives need to be explored.[56] Feminists and some working in Catholic social ethics have sought, in their own different ways, to address issues central to women of color, the poor, gays, and lesbians.[57]

Four groups have special problems with feminist ethics. First, those who see human knowing as inherently objective and universal, naturally transcending the limits of bodies, genders, contexts, and cultures. Such thinkers must be unsympathetic, indeed hostile, toward the feminist understanding of reasoning and moral decision-making, just as classic Thomists were hostile toward Karl Rahner's theory of personal existentialist knowledge. Second, there are those who are not supportive of a morality based on anything less than rationally sound normative principles. George Sher, for instance, is skeptical about Carol Gilligan's claims to have found male bias in existing moral theories.[58] Sher calls "spurious" the suggestion that women's decisions are "concrete" and "contextual" (ibid., 595). He does not accept Gilligan's observed opposition between personal relationships and impersonal principles. Rational, self-interested Rawlsian contractors would always adjust their principles to protect important personal relationships, Sher argues (ibid., 602). "All things considered, Gilligan's findings seem neither to undermine nor decisively to adjudicate among the familiar options of moral theory. They may edge U.S. in certain theoretical directions, but the movement they compel takes U.S. nowhere near the boundaries of the known territories" (ibid., 604). In Sher's opinion, "The opposition of concrete and abstract, personal and impersonal, duty and care are not recent empirical discoveries.... We have always known that an adequate theory must assign each its proper place" (ibid., 604).[59]

Third, in spite of the religious features found in Christian feminist theories, the approach has been anathema to Christians who believe that the Bible or the Church contain infallible moral teaching that possesses lasting authority over law, science, conscience, and culture. Both conservative Roman Catholics, as well as Evangelicals, find feminist ethics apostate, because of its insistence that Scripture and theology can be subject to serious critique and radical change.

Finally, there are those who consider feminists naive because they give a special place, indeed a privileged truth-value, to women's moral experiences. Feminist ethics has been influential in nursing largely due to the influence of Nel Noddings's *Caring: A Feminine Approach to Ethics and Moral Education* (1984). It has found little support, however, in business, trade, military, sports, legal, or political fields, where either national or group self-interests dominate. One doubts if feminist thinking will ever come to rule on Wall Street or within the Pentagon, whether an ethics of "just care" will control ownership decisions in major league baseball or professional basketball.

Further, the fact that feminists show a preference for the oppressed and minorities—target institutional injustices—means that they have put themselves in conflict with powerful forces that have nothing to gain either from concession or collaboration. Here lies lasting trouble.[60] On the other hand, feminists' concerns about the obvious inequalities within health care in America will find support in some circles. Its prophetic leadership will be welcome, and find a home in communities sensitive to the evils of sexism, racism, and educational and economic deprivations. However, feminist ethics must avoid both the leadership and agenda problems raised by Rene Denfeld in *The New Victorians*, which argues that feminist leaders have become bogged down in extremes and lost touch with reality—that the feminist movement needs a new agenda.[61]

Since feminist ethics does not aspire to becoming a universal moral theory, its humbler and more realistic stance should protect it from competitors with these ambitions—and probably insure its ability to survive and cross-fertilize. Support for women's studies programs and for women's health issues will further protect and strengthen it, again provided feminists can separate themselves from problems surrounding some of these programs: the charge that such programs provide nothing more than opportunities for anti-intellectual male bashing, as Daphne Patai and Noreta Koertge argue.[62]

From my own research and teaching experience, I have found that white Anglo-Saxon males and females educated in America's elite universities find problems with Sharon Welch's appeals to the ethical insights within African-American women's literature. Corporate leaders feel frustrated by decision-making processes like Giblin's and Manning's that go beyond experts and include the "subjugated." American management in health care and in the auto industry has always been highly structured, with sharp divisions between labor and management. To be successful in most management circles, any proposal for change must be practical and efficient, cost-effective and inexpensive—and feminist ethics gives little weight to such concerns. Its calls for greater communication and inclusion fly in the face of shareholder demands for high dividends and smaller payrolls.[63]

In terms of its *Christian* features, feminist ethics must score highly because of its emphasis on "just care" and its concerns for the oppressed. Modern moral theology is being defined above all by a "turn to the oppressed," and to the "otherness" in all who are oppressed, Anne E. Patrick rightly notes, and this must assist feminist ethics' acceptance.[64] In spite of its rejection of Western theology's standard images of God and its reservations about mainstream Christology, feminist ethics is theistic and Christ-centered. Grace and the Spirit have important roles in Welch's moral theory. Catholic feminists, as we have seen, value liturgical celebrations and the church's sacraments and sacramentals, anointings and blessings in particular. However, traditional Christians find feminist ethics' ecclesiology disturbing, its anti-clericalism bitter, and its stress on erotic love somewhat embarrassing. The fact that feminist ethics is a liberation ethics (with Marxist heritage) poses a separate problem.

Feminist Ethics in 2050: A Major Force for Social Change

Feminist ethics is celebrating its adolescence today; its future is full of life, health, and promise. Feminists have only just begun to reinterpret all the theological categories that have informed Catholic social thought—its theological anthropology in particular: its understanding of human persons, female and male.[65] The liberation perspective central to the approach, as well as the legacies of feudal and monarchist worldviews, have a long way to go before Catholic ecclesiology, liturgy, psychology, and ethics are thoroughly revised.[66]

As future writers describe the state of feminist ethics in the year 2050, I believe that they will see a broad movement that has continued to grow during this century, its influence much wider than it was in 2000. Such studies will see (I expect) some acceptance worldwide of feminist ethics' calls for broader and more representative decision-making and more support of its efforts to overcome oppression within church and society. Nurture, caring, hope, and joy will be more central virtues within Christian spirituality. Building upon the foundations laid by Mary Daly, Margaret Farley, Lisa Cahill, Christine Gudorf, Anne E. Patrick, Judith Dwyer, and Elizabeth Johnson, Roman Catholic sexual ethics, the church's social morality, its schools and institutions, its pastoral policies and canon law—in application if not in theory—will bear clearer signs of the saving power of this model of Christian ethics, even if there are still no women bishops in the Catholic Church.

In coming years, feminist thought will have reshaped (with differing results) all other models of theology, life, and ministry. Rather than being described as a new and minor alternative to mainstream theories in biomedical ethics (as it is today), feminist ethics (alongside liberation ethics) will have a major place in all fields of ethics, just as their thoughts will have in the physical and natural sciences.[67] Women's voices, as they articulate feminist visions of life, family, society, and church, will be familiar in law, psychology, sociology, political science, criminology—and theology.

Feminist ethics has been a liberating influence within Catholic moral theology (and a powerful force on the ethic presented in this book): through its emphasis on self-determination and creativity; respecting the rights of all humans (not simply corporate or male rights); the importance of community and communication, solidarity and liberation; and its practical recommendations about revising moral education so that female and male children, adolescents, and adults will achieve moral maturity (emotional, intellectual, character) and develop consciences that are healthy, sensitive, astute—and ethically well-informed.

As women gain stronger footholds in economics and politics, in healthcare and theology, I have no doubt that at all levels feminist thinking will continue to be a leaven within society and the professions, and will bring about healthy and long overdue changes in the Christian understanding of humanity, society, and life-in-the-world. As Gill Howie says, "The future of feminist philosophy ought to be the future of philosophy."[68]

Notes:

[1] For a valuable summary and critique of Aristotle's ethics, Eve Browning Cole, "Women, Slaves, and 'Love of Toil' in Aristotle's Moral Philosophy," in James P.

Sterba, *Ethics: Classical Western Texts in Feminist and Multicultural Perspectives* (New York: Oxford University Press, 2000), 78–87.

[2] Susan F. Parsons, "Feminist Ethics," in *Christian Ethics: An Introduction*, edited by Bernard Hoose, op. cit.,135–148.

[3] Carol Gilligan, *In A Different Voice: Psychological Theory and Women's Development* (Cambridge: Harvard University Press, 1982), 5–23. Also Susan J. Hekman, *Moral Voices, Moral Selves: Carol Gilligan and Feminist Moral Theory* (University Park, PA: Penn State University Press, 1995).

[4] Sharon D. Welch, *A Feminist Ethic of Risk* (Minneapolis, MN: Fortress Press, 1990), 23–47.

[5] Virginia L. Warren, "Feminist Directions in Medical Ethics," in *Feminist Perspectives in Medical Ethics*, edited by Helen Bequaert Holmes and Laura M. Purdy (Bloomington, IN: Indiana University Press, 1992), 32–45.

[6] Eleanor Humes Haney, "What is Feminist Ethics? A Proposal for Continuing Discussion," *Journal of Religious Ethics* 8, 1 (Spring 1980), 115–124.

[7] The feminists' sense of the limitations within Catholic social teaching can be discerned in the following words by Barbara Hogan, "Despite its limitations, Catholic social teaching has formulated some valuable principles regarding conditions for realizing human dignity and some trenchant criticisms of existing social systems. Feminists and others, however, have pointed out that the church does not even apply its own criteria to itself; it does not provide a model of the participation in decision-making that it advocates for society … ." From "Feminism and Catholic Social Teaching," *New Dictionary of Catholic Social Thought*, op. cit., 394–398.

[8] The results of this research have become vast. Some useful examples include: Gale Sigal, *Erotic Dawn-Songs of the Middle Ages: Voicing the Lyric Lady* (Gainesville: University Press of Florida, 1996); Veronica Makowsky, *Susan Glaspell's Century of American Women: A Critical Interpretation of Her Work* (New York: Oxford University Press, 1993); Mary Cullen and Maria Luddy, *Women, Power, and Consciousness in 19th Century Ireland* (Dublin Attic Press, 1995); John Larkins and Bruce Howard, *Sheilas: A Tribute to Australian Women* (Adelaide: Ribgy Limited, 1976). Also the invaluable resource, Mary T. Malone's *Women & Christianity* (Marynoll: Orbis Books), Vol. I The First Thousand Years, 2000; Vol. II 1000 to the Reformation, 2002. The final volume will be published soon.

[9] On this stage of the U.S. feminist movement, J. Philip Wogaman, *Christian Ethics: An Introduction*, op. cit., 186–190.

[10] Margaret A. Farley, "Feminism and Universal Morality" in *Prospects for a Common Morality*, Gene Outka and John P. Reeder, Jr., editors (Princeton, NJ: Princeton University Press, 1993), 170.

[11] On this subject, Katie G. Cannon, "Response," *Journal of Feminist Studies in Religion* 5, 2 (1989), 92ff. Also J. Philip Wogaman on "Feminist Theology of Liberation," op. cit., 254–255.

[12] For a valuable survey of developments in Christian feminist ethics, Kathryn Tanner, "The Care That Does Justice: Recent Writings in Feminist Ethics and Theology," *Journal of Religious Ethics* 24, 1 (Spring 1996), 171–191. Also Lisa Sowle Cahill, "Feminism and Christian Ethics," in Catherine Mowry La Cugna, editor, *Freeing Theology: The Essentials of Theology in Feminist Perspective* (New York: HarperCollins, 1993), 211–234.

[13] The feminist movement can be divided into three historical stages, according to Julia Kristeva. "Rights" were central to the first stage. The distinctiveness of women's experience and women's voices marked the second stage. A concern about ontology, the concepts of "essence" and "identity", as well as the analysis of post-modernist themes, are characteristic of the third and present stage of the movement. On this subject, Julia Kristeva, "Women's Time" in *Feminist Theory: A Critique of Ideology*, edited by N. Keohane, M. Rosaldo, and B. Gelpi (Brighton: Harvester, 1982), 31–53.

[14] The main feature of the "strong-sense critical thinker" is "fair-mindedness," defined as "to strive to treat every viewpoint relevant to a situation in an unbiased, unprejudiced way ... without reference to one's own feelings or selfish interests, or the feelings or selfish interests of one's friends, community, or nation... ." Besides being psychologically impossible, with Mirabeau (and George Bernard Shaw who said something almost the same) one wonders whether such an emphasis really does lead to "truth" or to deeply felt personal goals. On this subject, Richard Paul and Linda Elder, *Critical Thinking: Tools for Taking Charge of Your Learning and Your Life* (Upper Saddle River, NJ: Prentice Hall, 2001), at 4–5.

[15] Gill Howie, "Feminist Philosophy," in *The Future of Philosophy: Towards the 21st Century*, edited by Oliver Leaman (London: Routledge, 1998), 105–119, at 105.

[16] Susan Okin, *Justice, Gender, and the Family* (New York: Basic Books, 1989).

[17] It would be wrong to see in feminists' support for postmodernism, or in their interest in non-Christian religions, what Peter Gay saw in the modern philosophers: namely, a desire to find an alternative to Christianity to satisfy their own needs and those of their worlds. On this subject, Peter Gay, *The Enlightenment: An Interpretation* (New York: Alfred A. Knopf, 1966).

[18] Grace M. Jantzen, *Becoming Divine: Towards a Feminist Philosophy of Religion* (Manchester: Manchester University Press, 1998).

[19] Monika K. Hellwig, *Understanding Catholicism*, 2nd Edition, (New York: Paulist Press, 2002).

[20] One interesting example is Nevada Barr's *Seeking Enlightenment ... Hat by Hat: A Skeptic's Look at Religion* (New York: Putnam, 2003)—that discusses sin, humility, life after death, as well as the author's personal journey from atheism as a teen to the Episcopal Church as a "forty something" adult. Another, though it has less focus on religion, is the memoir by novelist Jane Stern, *Ambulance Girl: How I Saved Myself by Becoming an EMT* (New York: Crown Publishers, 2003).

[21] A major work that integrates all of these features is the new book by Elaine Pagels, *Beyond Belief: The Secret Gospel of Thomas* (New York: Random House, 2003).

[22] On this subject, the recent study by Penelope Eckert and Sally McConnell-Gingert, *Language & Gender* (Cambridge: Cambridge University Press, 2003).

[23] I must acknowledge my own debt to a number of feminist critics and novelists, as well as Jim Childress, for the insights that led me to publish "Of Medicine & Metaphor: Significant Findings from Walker Percy," *Linacre Quarterly*, 60 1 (February 1993), 48–55.

[24] Mary Anne Warren, "The Moral Significance of Birth," in *Feminist Perspectives in Medical Ethics*, edited by Helen Bequaert Holmes and Laura M. Purdy (Bloomington: Indiana University Press, 1992), 199–215.

[25] Susan Wendell, "Toward a Feminist Theory of Disability," in *Feminist Perspectives in Medical Ethics*, op. cit., 63–81.

[26] Caroline Knapp, *Appetites: Why Women Want* (New York: Counterpoint, 2003).

[27] In *The Speckled Monster: A Historical Tale of Battling Smallpox* (New York: Dutton, 2003), Carrell has produced a work of history and fiction that brings together an English aristocrat, Lady Mary Wortley Montagu, and a Boston physician, Zabdiel Boylston, both of whom were pioneers in using inoculations to fight smallpox.

[28] Sandra Day O'Connor, *The Majesty of the Law: Reflections of a Supreme Court Justice*, edited by Craig Joyce (New York: Random House, 2003).

[29] Susan Karant-Nunn and Merry Wiesner-Hanks have done this in their useful book *Luther on Women: A Soucebook* (Cambridge: Cambridge University Press, 2003). Other examples are Pat Hitchcock O'Connell and Laurent Bouzereau, *Alma Hitchcock: The Woman Behind the Man* (Berkeley: University of California Press, 2003).

[30] Isabel Allende, *My Invented Country* (New York: HarperCollins, 2003).

[31] Iris Chang, *The Chinese in America: A Narrative History* (New York: Viking Press, 2003).

[32] A concern for peers, children, and animals is central to Rita C. Manning, *Speaking from the Heart: A Feminist Perspective on Ethics* (Lanham: Rowman & Littlefield, 1992).

[33] On this subject, Elizabeth A. Johnson, *Woman, Earth, and Creator Spirit* (Mahwah, NJ: Paulist Press, 1993); Sallie McFague, *The Body of God: An Ecological Theology* (Minneapolis, MN: Fortress Press, 1993).

[34] On central aspects of this approach in bioethics, cf. *Special Issue: Feminist Perspectives on Bioethics, Kennedy Institute of Ethics Journal* 6, 1 (March 1996).

[35] On these subjects, Joan M. Merdinger, "Women, Death, and Dying," and Juliette S. Silva, "Mexican-American Women: Death and Dying," in *A Cross-Cultural Look at Death, Dying, and Religion,* Joan K. Parry and Angela Shen Ryan, editors (Chicago, IL: Nelson-Hall Publishers, 1995).

[36] For example, Judith Lorber, "Choice, Gift, or Patriarchal Bargain? Women's Consent in In Vitro Fertilization in Male Infertility," in *Feminist Perspectives in Medical Ethics*, op. cit., 169–180; Julien S. Murphy, "Is Pregnancy Necessary? Feminist Concerns about Ectogenesis," ibid., 181–197.

[37] On this subject, Susan Muller Okin. *Justice, Gender, and the Family* (New York, NY: Basic Books, 1989), 23.

[38] On this subject within the Presbyterian Church in America, Sylvia Thorson-Smith, *Reconciling The Broken Silence: The Church in Dialogue on Gay and Lesbian Issues* (Louisville: Presbyterian Publishing House, 1993). Within the U.S. Roman Catholic community, Denise Lardner Carmody, *Virtuous Woman: Reflections on Christia Feminist Ethics* (Maryknoll: Orbis Books, 1992), 97–102,

[39] On this subject, Lisa Sowle Cahill, "Feminism and Christian Ethics—Mora Theology," in *Freeing Theology: The Essentials of Theology in Feminist Perspective* Catherine Mowry La Cugna, editor, op. cit., 214–218—on feminists and natural law.

[40] Annette Baier, "Trust and Antitrust," *Ethics* 96 1986, 231–260.

[41] Margaret A. Farley, "Feminist Ethics," in *The Westminster Dictionary of Christic Ethics*, edited by James Childress and John Macquarrie (London: Westminster, 198(229–231, at 230.

[42] On this subject, in particular, the liberation of women, Susan F. Parsons, "Feminist Ethics," in *Christian Ethics: An Introduction*, edited by Bernard Hoose, op. cit., 135–148.

[43] On this subject, Gill Howie, op. cit., 109–115.

[44] Also on this subject, *Redefining Sexual Ethics*, Susan E. Davies and Eleanor Humes Haney, editors (Cleveland, OH: Pilgrim Press, 1991).

[45] Linda A. Bell, *Rethinking Ethics in the Midst of Violence: A Feminist Approach to Freedom* (Lanham, MD: Rowman & Littlefield, 1993).

[46] Starhawk, *Dreaming the Dark: Magic, Sex and Politics* (Boston, MA: Beacon Press, 1982), 44.

[47] Marie J. Giblin, "The Prophetic Role of Feminist Bioethics," *Horizons* 24, 1 (1997), 37–49.

[48] Regina Schwartz, *The Curse of Cain: The Violent Legacy of Monotheism* (Chicago, IL: University of Chicago Press, 1997).

[49] Eleanor McLaughlin, "Equality of Souls, Inequality of Sexes: Women in Medieval Theology," in James P. Sterba, op. cit., 137–144.

[50] Rosemary Chinnici, *Can Women Re-Image the Church?* (Mahwah, NJ: Paulist Press, 1992).

[51] Sandra M. Schneiders, *Re-Imagining Religious Life Today* (Mahwah, NJ: Paulist Press, 1993).

[52] Leanne McCall Tigert, *Coming Out While Staying In* (Cleveland, OH: United Church Press, 1994).

[53] Kathleen Fischer, *Women at the Well: Feminist Perspectives on Spiritual Direction* (Mahwah, NJ: Paulist Press, 1993).

[54] On this subject, Christine E. Gudorf, "Encountering the Other: The Modern Papacy on Women," in *Feminist Ethics and the Catholic Moral Tradition*, ibid., 66–89.

[55] Quoted by Lisa Sowle Cahill, ibid., 63.

[56] Susan Parsons, "Feminist Ethics After Modernity: Towards an Appropriate Universalism," *Studies in Christian Ethics* 8, 1 (1995), 77–94.

[57] On this subject, Barbara Hogan, "Feminism and Catholic Social Thought," *New Dictionary of Catholic Social Thought*, ibid., 394–398.

[58] George Sher, "Other Voices, Other Rooms? Women's Psychology and Moral Theory" in *Moral Philosophy: Selected Readings*, 2nd edition (Orlando, FL: Harcourt Brace College Publishers, 1996), 593–604.

[59] For other points of criticism, Rosemary Tong, *Feminine and Feminist Ethics*, ibid., 80–107.

[60] For a summary and critique of Nodding's ethics, Rosemarie Tong, ibid., 108–134.

Rene Denfeld, *The New Victorians* (New York, NY: Warner Books, 1995).

Daphne Patai and Noreta Koertge, *Professing Feminism* (New York, NY: Basic Books, 1994).

For a thoughtful analysis of morality in the light of feminist thought and action, James P. Sterba, "The Justification of Morality and the Behavior of Women," in his *Ethics: Classical Western Texts in Feminist and Multicultural Perspectives* (New York: Oxford University Press, 2000), 511–526.

Anne E. Patrick, "The Linguistic Turn and Moral Theology," *Catholic Theological Society of America Proceedings*, 42 (1987), 51.

[65] On this subject, Barbara Hogan, "Feminism and Catholic Social Thought," op. cit., 396.

[66] Feminists such as Christine Gudorf and Lisa Sowle Cahill have seen some successes for their efforts. However, recent U.S. episcopal and papal statements on marriage and sexuality reflect the hard and long road ahead.

[67] The road still to be traveled can be seen, for instance, by the fact that feminist ethics is absent from the index of George V. Lobo's *Guide to Christian Living: A New Compendium of Moral Theology* that was published in 1985, and in some ways is one of the most useful works in its genre.

[68] Gill Howie, op. cit., 119.

Chapter VI

Major Approaches in Christian Ethics: Theocentric Ethics

The benevolence that we know and experience does not warrant the confidence that God's purposes are the fulfillment of my own best interests as I conceive them.... Both Christian piety and Christian theology have had excessive confidence in the divine goodness toward individuals and communities, and toward our species.... But I reject the notion of trust as ultimate confidence that God intends my individual good as the usually inflated and exaggerated terms portray that good.

James Gustafson
Ethics from a Theocentric Perspective

To take Christ away from the sovereign center of the Christian life and to represent it as something self-contained and self-complete is to make nonsense of the Christian life and the Christian ethic.

N.H.G. Robinson
The Groundwork of Christian Ethics

This God is the initiator: He encounters them; they do not encounter him. He begins the dialogue, and he will see it through. This God is profoundly different from them, not their projections or their pet, not the usual mythological creature whose intentions can be read in auguries or who can be controlled by human rituals. This God gives and takes beyond human reasoning and understanding.

Thomas Cahill
The Gift of the Jews

The theocentric approach in Christian ethics—perhaps the most important theological influence on the moral theory presented in this book—belongs to a moral tradition with a long history.

In a sense, all Jewish, Christian, and Muslim moralities are "God-centered." However, some religious moral theories focus more specifically on the deity (God's being, plans, and purposes) rather than on such reference points as natural law, the human person, or sacred Scripture. And in this sense, they are consciously "theocentric."

In this century, Karl Barth developed a specifically theocentric ethic,[1] while Emil Brunner identified moral "goodness" with what God does, and argued that the Christian ethic reveals the Good, the one really and truly Good. "No one has a claim on a man, or on a people, save God alone," Brunner wrote. "And this claim permeates all the relationships of life. It is the only valid norm."[2] More recently, the American theologian John Howard Yoder, best known for his defense of Christian pacifism, has articulated an ethic that flows out of a Barthian vision of God's *kenotic* (self-emptying) way of love and success.[3]

In Roman Catholic circles, Pope John Paul II's morality is clearly theocentric, as we see from the *theological* argument based on a couple's "cooperation with God's creative power," which the pope has presented to demonstrate the Church's stand on contraception.[4]

However, the American Protestant theologian, James Gustafson, Henry R. Luce Professor of Humanities and Comparative Studies at Emory University, prior to his retirement late in the 1990s, is the best-known recent exponent of a consciously and thoroughly "God-centered" moral theory. Gustafson, who stands with Notre Dame's Richard A. McCormick as one of the most prophetic voices in twentieth century moral theology, was one of the first theologians to address medical ethics issues in the 1960s and to write major studies on Roman Catholic and Protestant ethics on the place of Scripture in Christian ethics and the role of the church as a community of moral discourse.[5] While practical and pastoral, Gustafson's most important work deals with moral methodology—with articulating an up-to-date Christian ethical theory—one that is thoroughly religious, because shaped by specifically *religious* affections and *theological* convictions.

Theocentric Ethics: James Gustafson's Approach

Tourists seeking travel directions in Ireland are occasionally told, "Well, I wouldn't go there from here." They are reminded that one's starting point has a major impact on how one reaches one's destination. Gustafon's ethic emphasizes orientation; it also appreciates the importance of perspective, a theme crucial to the climax of the musical *Camelot,* where the wizard Merlin teaches a dejected King Arthur to see things through the eyes of a bird—a skill which dramatically alters Arthur's values and perceptions. Gustafson's theocentric ethic causes similar changes in our orientation and judgment.

Because of convictions central to Protestantism's understanding of creation, culture, the Almighty, and, most of all, of the role of religion in shaping morality,[6] Gustafson's emphasis on "theocentricity" forces U.S. to construe reality in new ways: to think less about individual happiness and more about cosmic good; to discern not what we wish, but what God is calling and empowering U.S. to be and to do; to broaden the focus of morality, and to study the patterns and processes of interdependence (physical, social, cultural) in which humans, animals, and inanimate creatures participate.

Theological ethics develops, according to Gustafson, in a process of selective retrieval of one's traditional ethic, in the recombination and reinterpretation of that ethic's traditional elements and in innovation.[7] On the basis of what we find throughout Gustafson's writings on religious ethics—in particular, his two-volume *Ethics from a Theocentric Perspective* (1994, 1991)—the major features of this moral theory result not only from this methodological procedure, but primarily from deep convictions and reasoned analyses about the shape of Christian morality.[8]

"I was very interested for a number of years in trying to develop methods for Christian ethics that would correct the simplistic moralisms to which Protestantism has been addicted for a long time," Gustafson admitted in 1980.[9] Just as Aquinas's moral theology—innovative and controversial in its own day—took its distinctive form from Thomas's creative reading of Aristotle, Plato, Paul, Cicero, and Augustine, as well as from the goals inherent in Thomas's pastoral concerns (converting Muslims, limiting heresies), Gustafson's theocentric ethic stems from a number of factors: his interest in moral method ("the importance of making the moral arguments of Christianity more rigorous both philosophically and theologically") and a firm belief that "the destiny of the world is not in human hands."

Gustafson's basic tenet—"the primacy of piety, evoked by the powers of the Deity"—shapes his efforts to redirect religious ethics away from its traditional focus on humans to a focus on God. Further, Gustafson's controlling notions that "religion qualifies morality" and that Christian ethics should be "God-centered" rather than "man-centered" are the results of (a) his personal life's journey, (b) his study of the history of ethics, and (c) his religious, pastoral, and personal convictions.

While appreciative of certain features of personalism and the natural law tradition, Gustafson has limited confidence in the power of human reason and in the role of nature to generate a Christian ethics. As Jeffrey Stout says, "Gustafson comes by his stress on human finitude and historicity honestly. It is part and parcel of the ethical heritage of the Reformed tradition that culminates in Schleiermacher and reaches Gustafson through intermediaries such as Ernst Troeltsch and H. Richard Niebuhr" (ibid., 169). In many respects, Gustafson's ethic embodies the tensions described by J. Leslie Dunstan in his summary of the Protestant understanding of the proper relationship between faith and reason: "Man [sic] is to live by faith—faith in God and God's saving action through Jesus Christ."[10] This means that a person will make decisions on "his understanding of God's will for him in that situation." And faith becomes, therefore, an individual's "inner life, granted him by God and informed by God through divine revelation" (93).

Differing from neo-ultramontane Roman Catholicism, this means that a Protestant is "bound to question any form of imposed authority" (94). Quakers, Methodists, Congregationalists, and Anglicans worked out in time their own answers to questions about the way God worked in each person to bring about salvation. They also worked out their own positions about the relation between religious faith and reason. Some communities placed reason above faith; some separated reason from faith; some advocated adjusting the church's doctrines in the light of reason; others "refused to make any adjustments to the findings of the intellectual leaders. That which the Bible and church tradition said about man [sic] was true, and all contradictory statements were false. Of that there could be no mistake, for the Bible was the Word of God, and God did not make known that which was not so" (40).

While in some respects Gustafson can be called a modern liberal theologian, in many ways his theocentric ethic stands squarely in the mainstream of contemporary Protestantism. For example, his ethic embodies the Old Testament revelation of God as the Holy One of Israel, infinitely exalted above all creatures, yet caring for creatures. This God rules and overrules the events of history in justice and mercy. Gustafson supports Bath's theology of the Word. He upholds Protestantism's view of faith not simply as the intellectual acceptance of the revelation of God in Christ, but as a "wholehearted trust in God and His [*sic*] promises, and committal of ourselves to Jesus Christ as Saviour and Lord" (209). The church is the "servant of God's Word" (216), and it is the role of the Church to live in "faithful obedience" to God's purpose. Or as the World Council of Churches said at Evanston in 1955, "Man [*sic*] and all the powers of this world are under the sovereignty of their Maker who calls men [*sic*] in families, societies, nations, and all human groups to responsibilities under Him [*sic*]" (241).

In Gustafson's mind, as seen in his books and essays, to be human means to be situated in nature, history, culture, and society—to have a particular location (ibid., 169). This emphasis on the existential rather than the generic is joined with another significant shift in perspective: Gustafson holds that a *religious* ethic is quite different from a philosophical ethic in which human concerns and values hold ultimate importance. Faithful to its roots in the Reformed tradition's emphasis on God's sovereignty, Gustafson's ethic grounds his theory as Schleiermacher did in the "piety" of a historical (Reformed) community. And he sees "theology" as critical reflection on that tradition and its piety (ibid., 171).

Gustafson distances himself from those Jewish and Christian ethicists who provide moral insights into health care, sexuality, or modern warfare through either a literal reading of Scripture or a reasoned reflection on natural phenomena; he stands by his belief that in *religious* ethics normative rules pertaining to human behavior properly flow from grace-inspired religious convictions about God, the ultimate reality in whom humans live, move, and have their being. In taking this stand, Gustafson departs obviously from Aristotle, Kant, Mill, Fletcher, Richard McCormick, and the majority of Roman Catholics working in social ethics, who have prized "unaided" reason's powers and looked upon human nature as a source of divinely inscribed laws or meanings.

In Gustafson's eyes, the "theological qualifies ethics," when agents take "religious affections" (awe, gratitude, remorse) seriously; when they undertake critically thoughtful reflection on God's nature, purpose, and relations to the world; when theologians creatively integrate these convictions and insights into their theories and decisions about birth control, abortion, the environment, and physician-assisted suicide.[11]

Humans are God's creatures and God's stewards, according to Gustafson; and creaturehood and stewardship mean that we care for ourselves: as individuals, as communities, as institutions, and as species; it means that responding to the wellsprings of our affections, we acknowledge God's sovereignty and we freely act in cooperation with and in the service of God's wider ends and purposes.

While conservative, Gustafson's ethic is, in fact, radical—iconoclastic in several places. His piety puts God, not humanity, at the center (ibid., 173). Further, in a twist that has been criticized by both Protestant and Catholic colleagues, Gustafson does not support the approach (defended by Bernard Brady) which describes morality in terms of human flourishing, and with what it means to be a person (both "being" and "doing").[12] Central to Gustafson's theocentric ethic is the belief that "the salvation of man is not the chief end of God; certainly it is not the exclusive end of God" (*Ethics from a Theocentric Perspective* I, 110). In taking this stand, Gustafson's ethic has little in common with Joseph Fletcher's situation ethics, with its emphasis on Christ's love, and its act-utilitarian approach to moral decision-making.[13]

Gustafson writes: "Human purposes and human conduct have to be evaluated not simply on the basis of considerations derived from reflection about what is good for man. Rather, reflection is needed on how human life is to be related to a moral ordering objective to our species. It may be that the task of ethics is to discern the will of God— a will larger and more comprehensive than an intention for the salvation and well-being of our species, and certainly of individual members of our species" (ibid., 113). Here is a cosmic vision which Gerard Manley Hopkins would have appreciated.[14]

The hallmark of "liberal theology," according to Sharon Welch, is its "intellectual honesty," visible in acknowledging the disparity between the limits of theology and its subject (God), and in exposing the bad faith of those theologians who claim identity between the interpretation of the divine found in Scripture or tradition and the divine itself.[15] Using this criterion, Gustafson's ethic stands clearly within the liberal theological tradition, because central to his moral method is the conviction that, given its orientation and the difficulties inherent in all efforts to grasp God's will, Christian discernment will usually not provide any "certain" answers; and it will be filled with "risks."

With Burton L. Visotzky, author of *The Genesis of Ethics* (1996), Gustafson reminds U.S. that like life, moral dilemmas are often quite messy; that suicide, for example, "is always a tragic moral choice; it is sometimes a misguided choice. But it can be, I believe, a conscientious choice."[16] Indeed, the best Christian decisions will be "tragic" in many circumstances from human points of view (ibid., 113). Discernment is further complicated for another reason: Gustafson (as mentioned already) is convinced that "Religion is basically a matter of the affections, in that rich eighteenth century sense of the term that Jonathan Edwards used; that it is a matter of piety (not piousness or pietism), in the rich sense that both St. Augustine and Calvin affirmed."[17]

Here once more, Gustafson turns his back on the Scholastic emphasis on an exalted reason, and the Enlightenment's confidence in reason's ability to control nature, and to progress steadily toward an always better future. Gustafson's writings draw U.S. back to the Book of Job and to the Bible's understanding of religion—and it recalls to our minds the Bible's central warning: *Humanum est errare.*

As Gustafson moves toward applying his theory in the areas of marriage and family, population and nutrition, biomedical research and medical funding, he takes several additional and important methodological stands that flow from his reflections and revisions of Reformed theology.[18] First, that in morality and religion there are affective as well as cognitive aspects of experience (ibid., 119). As Stout rightly says, "When Gustafson says that piety is affective or prereflective, his point is not that it is noncognitive. To the contrary, he repeatedly insists that we should not draw overly sharp distinctions among the affective, cognitive, and volitional aspects of experience" (ibid., 180). With W. D. Ross, whose analysis of moral experience is crucial to contemporary biomedical ethics (as to the moral theory to be presented later in this book), Gustafson maintains that the "good" is not merely inclined toward or felt; it is also known, and thus there is a cognitive aspect as well (ibid., 119).

Second, Gustafson holds that experiences are "articulated, explained, and given their human meaning through cultures, and cultures are the products of societies and social experiences"—in other words, human experience has a deeply social character (ibid., 120ff). The implication: explanations and meanings, both secular and religious, are socially interpreted and tested (ibid., 124); they are always framed and limited by the boundaries of the particular communities to which they belong (ibid., 125). "Righteousness" has a special meaning for Jews, for example, and "justification" has a distinctive meaning for Lutherans. In Gustafson's eyes, his own religious ethic, like all theologies, belongs to a particular tradition (Reformed), and it possesses linguistic, religious, and cultural features specific to that tradition's social experiences.[19]

When he looks at how human affections and virtues rise and become "religious," Gustafson defends a holism now characteristic of feminist ethicists. His remarks about the "religious" significance of "nonreligious" experiences (in nature, history, culture, society, self) stress unity and integration. Gustafson writes: "The religious affections are human *responses*. They are not acts; in the sense that I choose to respond with delight to a landscape or with remorse to suffering I have caused. Nor, as has been indicated, are the affectivities uniquely religious .... Often affectivities are responses to particular events, but they can become general dispositions to respond to many events" (ibid., 229).

There is nothing of Duns Scotus's hairsplitting here; and the same features are evident throughout Gustafson's summary articulation of Western religion's themes about God (as Creator, Sustainer, Governor, Judge, Redeemer). His comments are built upon the insight that "Respect and awe evoked by nature, history, culture, society, and by our capacities as persons, lead to acknowledgment of the creative powers on which all things depend. God as Creator, remains, in piety, a vivid religious symbol" (ibid., 238). Holism, integration, and harmony are essential, as well, to Gustafson's position on the use of scientific data in theology.

One cannot draw scientific conclusions or hypotheses from theological statements, and theology cannot explain the world scientifically (ibid., 257). Further, one cannot draw theological conclusions deductively from scientific data and theories (ibid., 257). Nevertheless, the sciences do provide some useful support for the religious ethic, which Gustafson is developing—the religious sense of dependence upon powers beyond ourselves, for instance, is supported by data and theories from a number of the sciences (ibid., 260–261). Likewise, physics and biology provide evidence of an order and ordering of natural processes (ibid., 262–263).[20] On the other hand, some traditional affirmations about God are so incongruous with science that they should now be set aside, Gustafson affirms. For instance, that God has full and total foreknowledge of all historical events (ibid., 267); God will come to earth to judge the living and the dead (ibid., 268); God possesses intellect and will (ibid., 270); and God as person (ibid., 271).

Gustafson's Theocentric Ethics: Comment and Critique

When Anglicans are asked to identify the authority by which they make ethical judgments, they usually appeal to three sources: Scripture, tradition, and reason.[21] As readers will have gathered from this synopsis of Gustafson's *magnum opus*, the author takes a creative, independent, and contemporary approach to moral authorities; his ethic solves a number of problems and creates others. In terms of renewing Christian ethics, the Catholic tradition in particular, there are few Anglo-American theologians working in ethics for the last twenty years whose work has not been influenced by James Gustafson, or whose analyses have not been assessed in terms of Gustafson's orientation, understanding of religious morality, ethical truth, or moral methodology. For these reasons, it is important to examine the strengths and weaknesses within this Reformed theologian's theory.

First, unlike John Jefferson Davis and others who develop Evangelical moral theories, Gustafson does not give the Bible a uniquely normative place in his ethic. For Christian ethics, the Bible is the "charter" document. However, God's governance is not revealed to us in its moral details in the Bible.[22] Further, the use of the Scripture to gain insight into God's laws must be in accord with their contributions to theology (ibid., 339).[23] Like Richard Hooker, Gustafson takes the position (supported by this book's moral theory) that Christians in every age must judge to what extent a passage of Scripture is intended to apply to their own situation; that not all the laws of Scripture are to be understood as binding for all time; and that some are manifestly intended for particular times and places, but not forever.[24]

Scripture enjoys a central place in Christian ethics, according to Gustafson. In his judgment, however, Scripture does not stand as an absolute norm of the moral life (a *norma normans non normata*), nor does it control Christian theology, liturgy, or piety. Rather, theology (grounded in one's tradition, but a revision of that tradition in the light of history and reason) controls Scripture—a position that will be difficult to accept for those who view the Bible as God's absolute and always-binding word about right living.[25]

As already implied, tradition and reason play important roles in Gustafson's ethic. However, the Reformed tradition provides "theocentric" ethics with shaping methodological insights into religion and morality without a large body of prefabricated prescriptive norms or rules. That tradition, along with the Bible's images, metaphors, and narratives, colors Gustafson's vision of God and his selection of theological and ethical authors. Thus, Gustafson's analyses of the U.S. military's invasion of Cambodia, for example, and his ordered reflections on health care and environmental issues concentrate on the service of God, the future, and the wider implications of government and research policies.[26]

When Gustafson speaks about marriage and family, his thought is not determined by icons, ancient synods, or patristic tomes (as an Orthodox theologian's might be), but his key question is, "What is God enabling and requiring us to be and to do as participants in the patterns and processes of interdependence in marriage and family life?"[27] Gustafson's reasoned and analytical approach to morality, his desire to make morality rigorous, has its affinities with Anglican morality and with the Roman Catholic moral tradition.

Carefully discerning the physical and cultural patterns and processes is crucial to his theory. It is true that Gustafson says little about the place of intuition in making moral decisions, and nowhere does he dwell upon inner lights or personal revelations. Nor does he write at any length about the role of Holy Spirit or the "moral imagination" in communal or personal decision-making. Nevertheless, the place of reason in his theory can be seen throughout his theocentric ethic: Gustafson gives a major task to logic and orderly analysis; he gives a central place to the findings of the natural and physical sciences in making religious moral judgments.

Clearly, Gustafson is a *twentieth-century* theologian. Nature plays a central role in his ethical theory. Environmental issues are central to his ethic. However, as mentioned already, Gustafson has consciously distanced himself from natural law morality's emphasis on "right reason reflecting on nature." Nature has no absolute authority in his theocentric ethics. Where Catholic moral theology, as seen in Richard A. McCormick's approach, now keeps its eyes fixed on the human person as its primary source of data for making decisions about ethical behavior,[28] Gustafson affirms that moral values and principles are backed by, or grounded in, the patterns and processes of interdependence—but these considerations (rooted in piety) cannot resolve moral questions unless they are related to convictions about what God is calling humans to be and to become—to transcendent, not purely physical or human considerations, whether individual or national.

Where McCormick will be satisfied to settle a moral issue (e.g. letting a comatose patient die) in terms of its "benefits and burdens,"

Gustafson will take the wider perspective. Unlike the neo-Scholastic theologian William E. May, Gustafson does not believe that natural processes provide absolute or immutable laws to which human activity must be conformed. Neither cost benefit analyses nor judgments based on natural teleological processes or functions are crucial to Gustafson's decision-making method.

Jeffrey Stout sees a number of major difficulties with Gustafson's ethic. In Stout's opinion, Gustafson never clearly explains why we should speak about "the powers that bear down upon us" as divine, or what this belief adds to ethics (ibid., 182). Stout believes that Gustafson "has failed to offer compelling arguments—arguments so powerful that any reasonable intellect would be forced to lay down its objections and submit" (ibid., 183). Why add, as Gustafson does, "that there is an Ultimate Order who deserves our ultimate concern?" Stout asks (ibid., 183). "What difference does it make for ethics to place a Mystery at the center once humanity has been displaced?" (ibid., 183). However, while not justified to Stout's liking, for Gustafson, the natural course of events is not necessarily morally or humanly normative in the light of the ends that life and health serve.[29]

And while we should relate all things in a manner appropriate to their relations to God—there are no divinely initiated or infallibly revealed prescriptions of proper actions—we cannot know what we should do from reading directly off the patterns of interdependence of life, because there is no moral blueprint in nature.[30]

Further, while Gustafson gives an important place to *experience* in developing his approach, nevertheless, his theory does not give a central place to the sources of human experience favored by feminists, e.g. women's literature, journals, letters, and diaries.[31] Gustafson does not give women's experience a special place in his ethic, nor does his *magnum opus* draw upon the morality one finds in Dante or Shakespeare, George Eliot or G. M. Hopkins, Flannery O'Connor or Walker Percy, Toni Morrison or Adrienne Rich. Indeed, Gustafson's ethic does not say much about the role of cultural narratives in shaping a community's sense of self and the world, a methodological insight central to Roger Betsworth's *Social Ethics: An Examination of American Moral Traditions* (1990).[32]

Gustafson's view of the classic moral authorities is summarized in the closing words of his ethic: "The task of ethics is to use knowledge and intelligence to discern, under the inexorable conditions of finitude, how we are to relate ourselves and all things in a manner appropriate to our and their relations to God. It is to seek how to participate in nature and society, in history and culture, and in the ordering of ourselves so that human life is in the service of God, the power that brings all things into being, sustains them and bears down on them, and creates the conditions of possibility for newness and renewal. We are fated never to have the certainty we desire in the human condition."[33]

For Gustafson, discerning God's will (active, changing, and contemporary)—not simply assessing individual selfishness or human happiness—is crucial to making correct moral judgments. A theme not easily reconciled with Fletcher's situationism or Mills' utilitarianism where loving one's neighbor is the same as loving God.[34]

These and other issues were central to a series of essays on Gustafson's ethics published in the *Journal of Religious Ethics* in 1985. Stanley Hauerwas concentrated on "Time and History in Theological Ethics," Lisa Sowle Cahill and Richard McCormick focused on Gustafson's theism, while Paul Ramsey authored a thirty-page letter that raised a host of apparent difficulties. Besides these astute observations, there are other methodological problems in Gustafson's ethic: the theory does comment on the place of the faith-community in the formation of morality[35] and recognizes the social aspects of morality.

However, Gustafson does not give a unique place to the Christian church as a moral guide and authoritative teacher. Religious communities shape individual choices and the ethos of cultures, but the morality that these communities foster is "generally not unique, though they may have distinctive religious and theological backings for it."[36] Moreover, *Ethics From a Theocentric Perspective* contains no detailed treatment of the place of the Church's historic or current moral teaching in the formation of an authentic ethic; it is silent, as well, about such subjects as the respect that should be shown to the pastoral statements of Church leaders, synods, or councils.[37] Gustafson believes that "the simpleminded moralism that Protestant churches (more than the Roman Catholic Church) engage in is morally irresponsible...."[38] Here Catholics and Orthodox Christians will find Gustafson's work wanting.

Further, in his efforts to unify the religious and nonreligious, Gustafson has weakened some traditional distinctions, and he has reduced the place of "grace" in the moral life. Prayer and the ritual sacraments are scarcely mentioned. Christ-centered theories of Christian ethics have a history that starts in Paul's Epistles and the Gospels. Gustafson's theory has been criticized for not giving Christ an adequate place in his ethic.[39] "We must think of Christian ethics as the systematic account of human conduct as given over in faith to the overlordship of Christ as containing within himself the whole duty of man," says N. H. G. Robinson.[40]

In such an ethic, Jesus' theocentric piety forms a model for Christians. However, Gustafson does not support such a vision, since, in his mind, Jesus was the bearer of God's revelation, and he came among U.S. to bear witness not to himself, but to God, as John tells U.S. in the prologue of the fourth Gospel. Jesus' person, life, and moral teaching comprise parts, but not the whole, of Christian morality, according to Gustafson.[41] Jesus' cross and the way of the cross are revealing symbols of what is enabled and required of persons who seek to serve and glorify God.[42] However, Gustafson does not ground the material norms of his moral theory on Jesus' life or ethical teaching, nor does he focus his theory on Jesus, the man for others—but on *God's* sovereignty—on *God's* patterns and potentialities—what *God* is calling humans to be and do. For Gustafson, an authentic Christian ethic must be "theocentric" rather than "Christocentric."

While philosophers find Gustafson's religious assumptions and categories wanting, indeed out of place in secular and pluralistic societies (as Richard McCormick argued in his exchanges with Stanley Hauerwas), conservative Christians have been shocked not only by Gustafson's departures from traditional Trinitarian theology, but by his stand on Scripture's authority in ethics. Rather than Aquinas's vision of a gift-giving and beneficent Deity who created all things for human use and benefit, for instance, Gustafson (as we have seen) prefers and proposes a very different God. While there is some support within the Bible and tradition for his position, his understanding of God's nature, creative and saving work, seems both selective and arbitrary.[43]

Conclusion: Calling Christians to Discern God's Patterns of Empowerment

In his important study of the renewal efforts within Catholic moral theology during the years 1940–1980—in particular, the debates between those who sought to develop "autonomous" moral theories and theologians committed to developing an ethic grounded in the Christian faith (in Christ, in "revealed" morality)—Vincent MacNamara concludes his work with the observations that images such as "following," "discipleship," and "response," are important, but they need to be supplemented. In MacNamara's opinion, "The Christian must also situate morality in the overall scheme of the relation of God to the world. For him, morality must, in some way, be referred to the lordship of God. He does not say how he sees things as a Christian unless he says something about the fact of creation and the dependence of all things, including human beings and the whole moral order, on God."[44] Nowhere does MacNamara refer to James's Gustafson's efforts to build a critically viable theocentric ethic—but as we have seen, he might have.

The mild-mannered, quietly spoken scholar's lasting contributions to twentieth century Christian ethics, his revisions of Protestantism's basic tenet of *sola scriptura*, his emphasis on community as the locus of morality and ethical decision-making, as well as his emphasis on piety and God's authority, have left distinctive marks upon Protestant and Catholic ethicists. Courageously addressing both the foundational and applied questions of the times, Gustafson has steered a middle course between neo-Scholastic rationalism and Lutheran pietism.

While striving to provide a central place for the empirical sciences in religious ethics, Gustafson has consistently avoided the "physicalism" and oversimplification found in Catholic medical ethics (such as resolving life and death issues simply by recourse to assessments of medical measures that constitute "ordinary" or "extraordinary" means). And he has done this without embracing Protestant fundamentalism's uncritical use of the Bible.[45] By examining the "received" methods of Lutheran ethics and revising them in the light of Brunner's interest in philosophical and religious ethics, Barth's theocentric theology, and Schliermacher's critiques of Kant's morality, Gustafson has strengthened contemporary religious ethics throughout Protestant, Catholic, and Orthodox communities.

By reminding his readers (as well as those privileged to be his graduate students) that moral truth on this side of the grave must contain the same characteristics of its agents, without at the same time lapsing into cynicism or exaggerating Luther's image of humans as *massa damnata*, Gustafson's writings, whether on the use of Scripture or the person's ability to discern God's patterns and potentialities, are to be admired for their realism and balance, their respect for God's transcendence, and their awareness of human weakness.

Gustafson's common sense acknowledgements that "Christian social ethics must analyze social action in the sociological sense," that it "must be grounded in knowledge of how decisions are made in the centers of social power," and that the "moralist must know the patterns of personal and institutional interrelationships within which he seeks to develop purposive change"—because "Effective moral action depends upon astute and accurate analysis of the social system in general and of the problem situation in particular"—are further signs of his astute powers of perception.[46]

While Jeffrey Stout finds serious limitations in Gustafson's recourse to divine realities, Gustafson's ethic avoids the hubris contained in (what for Gustafson must be) the "false" impression that religious truth approximates mathematical truth, while at the same time defending the fundamental Reformed belief in God's sovereignty and man's dependence on God—not man's self-sufficiency nor the self-justification of individual reason and "good" conscience. Surely, Gustafson is correct in proposing an ethic for Reformed Christians that sees the goal of morality in righteousness rather than in happiness; that takes its orientation in a mature respect for God's plans and purposes rather than in an adolescent regard for personal pleasure.

One must applaud Gustafson for the lessons that he has taught about moral methodology, for his thoughtful efforts to link the human species to other precious (sacred) life-forms, and for his patient attempts to refocus Christian morality away from humans, with their petty goals and narcissistic selfishnesses. However, it is hard to see (from what one reads) exactly what place physicians, economists, or politicians should give to nonhuman ends and values (other aspects of nature) as they struggle with life and death decisions, or how these realities should be taken into full account in developing the specific rules or general principles of Christian moral action. Gustafson does provide U.S. with broad parameters and impressionistic outlines, but little more.[47]

An example: it is reasonably obvious—simply in human terms—that it is immoral for a community to expend limitless resources on weapons of mass destruction. It is more difficult, however, to make this same judgment if one takes into account the possibility (popular in science fiction) that current human weapons are simply "toys" when compared with those developed millions of years ago by alien species, (The Shadows) who will be visiting U.S. some day on missions of conquest! Further, maybe the WCC's (World Council of Churches) experts are able to grasp some sense of what God is enabling and requiring humans to be and to do, but not individual Christian nurses, teachers, and parents—or the base communities within which these people seek to find life and strength.

There is merit in any ethic that forces humans to look beyond themselves and to examine the long-term implications of their behavior and social policies. Christian morality must be different from secular ethics—as Gustafson emphasizes. Reminding Christians to be "theocentric" rather than self-centered will protect them from lapsing into selfishness and blindness; it will preserve God's intended relationships. Gustafson's orientation and emphases, those, in particular, on developing an authentically "religious" ethic, on the limits of theology and human reason, and the importance of holism, narratives, and the historicity of moral truths, have shaped the ethic being presented in this book. And together with W. D. Ross's insights into the nature of morality, the role of intuition, common sense, and *prima facie* responsibilities, Gustafson's insights and arguments have been the most influential influences on the moral theory found here—for reasons that we will immediately explain in the following chapters.

Notes:

[1] Karl Barth, *Church Dogmatics*, III/4 (Edinburgh: T&T Clark, 1961), 351–56. For an important work on Barth, which sets out to show that Barth's ethics of reconciliation is grounded in the Christian story that unites temporal-historical reality with God's temporal eternal nature, John Webster, *Barth's Ethics of Reconciliation* (New York: Cambridge University Press, 1995).

[2] Emil Brunner, *The Divine Imperative* (London: Lutterworth, 1937), 53,54, 59.

[3] John Howard Yoder, *The Politics of Jesus* (Grand Rapids: Eerdmans, 1972). Two examples of theocentric ethics applied to other areas of life are: Richard A. Young, *Healing The Earth: A Theocentric Perspective on Environmental Problems and Their Solutions* (Nashville: Broadman & Holman, 1994); Stephen H. Webb, *The Gifting God: A Trinitarian Ethics of Excess* (New York: Oxford University Press, 1996).

[4] Pope John Paul II, "Christian Vocation of Spouses May Demand Even Heroism," *L'Osservatore Romano,* (October 10, 1983), 7, 16. For a thorough survey of the Pope's thought, Edward Vacek, "John Paul II and Cooperation with God," *The Annual of the Society of Christian Ethics,* edited by Dianne M. Yeager (1990), 81–107.

[5] For Gustafson's positions on these subjects, *Can Ethics Be Christian?* (Chicago: University of Chicago Press, 1975); "The Changing Use of the Bible in Christian Ethics," in *Religion,* edited by Paul Ramsey (Englewood Cliffs: Prentice-Hall, 1965), and "The Place of Scripture in Christian Ethics: A Methodological Study," in Gustafson's *Theology and Christian Ethics* (Chicago: University of Chicago Press, 1974)—both reprinted in *The Use of Scripture in Moral Theology: Readings in Moral Theology #4,* edited by Charles E. Curran and Richard A. McCormick (New York: Paulist Press, 1984), 133–150, 151–177; James Gustafson, *Varieties of Moral Discourse: Prophetic, Narrative, Ethical, and Policy* (Grand Rapids: Calvin College: 1988); James Gustafson, *A Sense of the Divine* (Cleveland: Pilgrim Press, 1994). Also on the latter subject, Bernard V. Brady, *The Moral Bond of Community: Justice and*

Discourse in Christian Morality (Washington: Georgetown University Press, 1998), x-xi, 3–5, 5–7, 7–11, 11–17.

[6] James M. Gustafson, *Can Ethics Be Christian?* (Chicago: University of Chicago Press, 1975).

[7] These words are taken from Jeffrey Stout, *Ethics After Babel: The Languages of Morals and Their Discontents* (Boston: Beacon Press, 1988), 169.

[8] Gustafson, *Ethics*, I, 87–113. For a useful list of Gustafson's publications, "Bibliography of the Writings of James Gustafson, 1951–84," *Journal of Religious Ethics* (JRE) 13, 1 (Spring 1985), 101–112.

[9] In James M. Gustafson, "A Theocentric Interpretation of Life," *The Christian Century*, Vol. xcvii, 25 (July 30–August 6, 1980), 754–760.

[10] J. Leslie Dunstan, editor, Protestantism, *Great Religions of Modern Man* (New York: George Braziller, 1962).

[11] On this aspect of Gustafson's approach, Allen Verhey, "On James M. Gustafson: Can Medical Ethics Be Christian? in *Theological Voices in Medical Ethics*, edited by Allen Verhey and Stephen E. Lammers (Grand Rapids, MI: Eerdmans, 1993), 30–56, at 31–39.

[12] Bernard V. Brady, *The Moral Bond of Community: Justice and Discourse in Christian Morality* (Washington, D.C.: Georgetown University Press, 1998), 75–77.

[13] On this subject, Michael E. Allsopp, "Joseph Fletcher's Situation Ethics: 25 Years after the Storm," *Irish Theological Quarterly*, 56, 3 (Summer 1990), 170–190.

[14] On Hopkins' theocentric moral vision, Michael E. Allsopp, "G. M. Hopkins, Narrative, and the Heart of Morality: Exposition & Critique," *Irish Theological Quarterly*, 60, 4 (1994), 287–307.

[15] On this subject, Sharon D. Welch, *A Feminist Ethic of Risk* (Minneapolis: Fortress Press, 1990), 105.

[16] *Ethics*, II, 215.

[17] James Gustafson, "A Theocentric Interpretation of Life," *The Christian Century*, op. cit., 758.

[18] For Gustafson's reflections on environmental ethics, James M. Gustafson, *A Sense of the Divine: The Natural Environment from a Theocentric Perspective* (Cleveland: Pilgrim Press, 1994).

[19] While some will fear the implications of this point, those who have any knowledge of Irish culture and history will acknowledge its validity and soundness.

[20] For a more recent statement on the role of science in theology, James M. Gustafson, *Intersections: Science, Theology, and Ethics* (Cleveland: Pilgrim Press, 1996).

[21] Earl H. Brill, *The Christian Moral Vision*, The Church Teaching Series, #6 (New York: Seabury Press, 1979), 12.

[22] On the different understandings of the term "charter" in the writings of recent Protestant and Roman Catholic authors, Gustafson's "The Changing Use of the Bible in Christian Ethics," op. cit., 133ff. For Gustafson's own position, "The Place of Scripture in Christian Ethics: A Methodological Study," op. cit., 151–177—in which it is argued that Scripture alone is never the final court of appeal for Christian ethics, but the Bible provides the basic orientation toward particular judgments, because "the vocation of the Christian community is to discern what God is enabling and requiring man [*sic*] to be and to do in particular natural, historical, and social circumstances" (176). Like Richard McCormick, Gustafson holds that "Scripture deeply informs these

judgments ... but it does not by itself determine what they ought to be. That determination is done by persons and communities as finite moral agents responsible to God" (176).

[23] Obviously, Scripture does not have the formative role in Gustafson's ethic as it does in liberation theology's approaches to morality and to moral development.

[24] ibid., 153.

[25] The role of Scripture in Christian ethics has been a subject of major concern in recent years. For an important analysis of the issue, one more conservative than Gustafson's, yet influenced by his writing, Allen Verhey, *The Great Reversal: Ethics and the New Testament* (Grand Rapids: Eerdmans, 1984). Also, Michael E. Allsopp, "The Role of Sacred Scripture in Richard A. McCormick's Ethics," *Chicago Studies*, 35 (August 1996), 185–196.

[26] For Gustafson's comments and analyses of the Cambodian invasion, his use of Scripture etc., "The Place of Scripture in Christian Ethics: A Methodical Study," op. cit., 154–159, 168–174, 175–177. For some insights into Gustafson's understanding of biomedical ethics and its languages, his "Moral Discourse about Medicine: A Variety of Forms," *Journal of Medicine and Philosophy* 15 (1990), 125–142.

[27] *Ethics*, II, 153.

[28] For Gustafson's own analysis of the relationship between his ethic and Aquinas's, *Ethics*, II, 42–64.

[29] *Ethics*, II, 273.

[30] ibid., 275. From several conversations with Gustafson, it is clear that he understands McCormick's ethic, and he respects the natural law approach—but he does not consider either to be "theological."

[31] On this subject, Michael E. Allsopp, "Feminist Ethics at Thirty: A Retrospective," *Explorations* 16, 4 (Summer 1998), 5–28.

[32] Without wishing to be unfair, Gustafson's theory exhibits a somewhat limited view of the role of the liberal arts (painting, poetry, stories, plays) as valuable sources of knowledge for Christians seeking solutions to today's moral problems. It is more scientific than humanistic.

[33] *Ethics*, II, 322.

[34] On the relationship between Gustafson's theory and utilitarianism, *Ethics*, II, 100–116.

[35] *Ethics*, II, 316–319.

[36] ibid., 317.

[37] For a somewhat different position about Gustafson's view of the role of the church, Martin L. Cook, "Reflections on James Gustafson's Theological-Ethical Method," *The Annual of the Society of Christian Ethics*, 17 (1997), 13–17.

[38] *Ethics*, II, 318.

[39] This is central to Richard McCormick's essay, "Gustafson's God: Why? What? Where (Etc.), *JRE* 13, 1 (Spring 1985), 53–70.

[40] N. H. G. Robinson, *The Groundwork of Christian Ethics*, op. cit., 266.

[41] ibid., 22.

[42] ibid., 22.

[43] For Gustafson's reply to these criticisms, "A Response to Critics," *JRE* 13, 2, (Fall 1985), 185–209. Also: *Christian Ethics: An Introduction*, edited by Bernard Hoose, 27–28,28–29; Bernard V. Brady, *The Moral Bond of Community: Justice and*

Discourse in Christian Morality (Washington: Georgetown University Press, 1998), x-xi, 13–14, 51, 80, 128; Jeffrey Stout, *Ethics After Babel: The Languages of Morals and Their Discontents* (Boston: Beacon Press, 1988), 167–188.

[44] Vincent MacNamara, *Faith & Ethics: Recent Roman Catholicism* (Dublin: Gill and Macmillan Ltd, 1985), 199. Also, Vincent MacNamara, "Moral Life, Christian," in *New Dictionary of Catholic Social Thought*, op. cit., 635–650.

[45] For a useful study that provides valuable insights into Gustafson's position on the use of Scripture, Tom Deidun, "The Bible and Christian ethics," in *Christian Ethics: An Introduction*, edited by Bernard Hoose (London: Cassell, 1998), 3–46.

[46] James Gustafson, "Christian Ethics and Social policy," in *Faith and Ethics: The Theology of H. Richard Niebuhr*, edited by Paul Ramsey (New York: Harper, 1957), 126ff.

[47] This is evident, for instance, when Gustafson deals with biomedical research funding, *Ethics*, II, 253–277.

Part III

Chapter VII

A Christian Ethic of Responsibilities: Ethics, Unifying Metaphor

There is only one ultimate and invariable duty, and its formula is "Thou shalt love thy neighbour as thyself." How to do this is another question, but this is the whole of moral duty.

William Temple
Mens Creatrix

The climax of history, which does not bring history to a close, but makes known in its meaning and the victorious finality of its goal within history itself, is the cross, the death, and the resurrection of Jesus in one. Here God's "Yes" to the world and the world's to God becomes historical, unambiguous, and irrevocable.

Karl Rahner
The Cross: The World's Salvation

Every Christian is called to follow Christ in some form, even though his way of life cannot be the same as that of the disciples of that day. The imitation of Christ always demands concrete realization, whether we live in the world or in a cloister, whether we serve in the world as priests or as laymen.

Rudolf Schnackenburg
Christian Existence in the New Testament

The moral theory developed in these chapters has been shaped by classic, medieval, and twentieth century discussions about philosophical and religious ethics. The approach springs from the desire to articulate a contemporary Christian ethic that is methodologically stronger than Richard McCormick's and Gustavo Gutierrez's, and one more responsive to the critiques of feminist writers, as well as the writings of Protestant and Catholic ethicists such as Stanley Hauerwas, William Barclay, Paul Ramsey, Charles Curran, Norbert Rigali, Bernard Haring, Yves Congar, Louis Janssens, Edouard Hamel, and Hans Urs von Balthasar. The ethic bears, as well, the positive effects of a thirty-year association with Ignatian spirituality, Newman's theology, and G. M. Hopkins's poetry.

It is difficult, of course, to know what books, teachers, or colleagues have shaped one's worldview or powers of evaluation. However, the theory's *holistic* description of moral reasoning (a feature, as we have seen, of late twentieth century ethics) is indebted to Bernard Lonergan's *Insight,* Daniel Maguire's *The Moral Choice,* Rita Manning's *Speaking from the Heart: A Feminist Perspective on Ethics,* and in a special way to Sidney Callahan's *In Good Conscience: Reason and Emotion in Moral Decision-Making.* The theory's stand on the roles that metaphors and language play in moral development has been colored by Heidegger's essays on language, Gabriel Marcel's *Creative Fidelity* (1964), and Paul Ricoeur's *The Symbolism of Evil* (1967); by continuous contacts with Gerard Manley Hopkins's poetry and Walker Percy's novels and philosophical books; by returning regularly (and happily) to Herbert McCabe's *What is Ethics All About?* and the reworking of his best seller *Law, Love, and Language,* that contains such hard-to-forget statements as "Ethics is just the study of human behaviour in so far as it is a piece of communication, in so far as it says something or fails to say something."[1]

This theory is sensitive to the emphasis on realism and the practical nature of ethics that is central to Aristotle's *Nicomachean Ethics,* Aquinas's moral theory, as well as to Joseph Fletcher's calls during the 1960s–1970s for a moral method that is authentically Christian and can be used by today's busy nurses, soldiers, and business leaders. Twentieth century developments in moral philosophy, linguistics, and sociology and the opinions of Richard Rorty, A. J. Ayer, Richard Brandt, Michel Foucault, Max Scheler, Lawrence Kohlberg, and James Rachels have played roles in what this theory says about ethical rules, values, and moral language (its contingency, facticity, and ambiguity), as well as what this ethic has to say about consequences, the mind's creativity, and the ground of ethics.

The theory developed here shows signs of the positive influence of other writers: Gabriel Marcel's *Homo Viator;* Karl Rahner's efforts to develop an existentialist ethics compatible with Catholic theology and philosophy; Newman's essays on the authority of conscience and the role of the laity within the Church; and the development of Christian doctrine. N. H. G. Robinson's *The Groundwork of Christian Ethics*, first read with enthusiasm in the early 1970s, still impresses because of its scholarship, balance, and masterful grasp of issues still dividing Protestant and Catholic ethicists who are working to strengthen Christian ethics. Other more general influences include: feminist ethics' emphasis on the importance of memory, the role of culture, gender, and an agent's point-of-view in moral decision-making; and liberation theology's criticisms of academic moral theology, its stress of *praxis*, Scripture, the place of the Church's vivifying doctrines, its emphasis on the importance of social change, the concerns of the oppressed, and the wisdom contained in the life-experiences of the marginalized, the lonely, and the forgotten.

As readers will quickly realize, the conviction that Christian ethics should be developed within a theocentric perspective comes (on the one hand) from the recent awareness of the limitations within in the Catholic Church's long-held natural law tradition; and (on the other hand) from the persuasive power of James Gustafson's writings read in the light of Vatican II's calls for the renewal of the Catholic Church's moral theology, plus the positive results of postconciliar efforts by scholars like Haring, Congar, and von Balthasar to strengthen Catholic moral theology's biblical foundations, to improve its vision of the Christian life, its regard for the environment, its acceptance of religious liberty, and its understanding of the primacy of charity.

The most important influence on the development of many features of this theory is Sir William David Ross, Oxford scholar and public administrator, twentieth century translator of Aristotle's *Nicomachean Ethics*, creative critic of Kant's ethics and G. E. Moore's writings, author of *The Right and the Good*, and *The Foundations of Ethics*.[2] This Christian ethic of responsibilities adopts Ross's construing of morality and his response to the question, "What makes a right action right?" It affirms Ross's awareness of the role of intuition in ethics, as well as his key insights into the pluralistic bases of moral obligation. With Ross, this theory advances a duty-based theory of moral responsibilities in which individuals find themselves facing a slew of *prima facie* obligations, in addition to any duty to bring about the positive outcomes of their actions.

In presenting this theory ("that yields a clear, coherent, and comprehensive description of the moral system that thoughtful people actually use when deciding how to act or in making moral judgments," to co-opt Bernard Gert's comments about his own rule-based theory of morality), a conscious effort has been made throughout the theory's explication and justification to incorporate (successfully I trust) Ross's judiciousness and his realism, as well as the Oxford scholar's regard for the "plain" person's integrity and common sense. As done in earlier chapters, an effort has been made as well to let writers speak for themselves, so that distinctive voices will be heard as they express personal (sometimes quite original) insights into Christian understandings of the mystery of life in the human condition.

Morality and Ethics: Clearing the Ground

Purists who write college philosophy textbooks define the term *ethics* to mean something different from what is implied by the term *morality*. Such authors use the first term to refer to what one finds in college moral philosophy textbooks, i.e., the systematic efforts to rationally establish, justify (critique and demolish) normative theories, rules, and principles of conduct, while they reserve the latter term for the interests of sociologists and research psychologists who are studying moral development. However, in this age of pluralism, current usage shows that authors now use (as I do) both words interchangeably, as generic terms for construing and examining either the science of morality or the moral life.

Some current ethical theories focus on consequences; others on character or self-fulfillment. Few Anglo-American writers support the Stoic's natural law approach to morality, or exhibit Dewey's optimism about objective goods or values. Fewer still show positive interest in existentialism or personalism; while fewer still show any loyalty to Kant's understanding of "intuition," or his distinction between "acts of wisdom" and "moral acts," or his belief that "prudence" belongs to the province of aesthetics (beauty), whereas morality pertains to the study of ethics (moral excellence). Furthermore, while "deontological" theories are separated from "teleological" ones, just as "altruistic" theories are distinguished from theories that are "egocentric," modern writers have broadened (as I will) Kant's usage of the term *deontology*.

As well, this ethic supports the Aristotelian position that "ethics" and "morality" should not be confined to theoretical contexts, since the aim of ethics is practical, and a moral theory should enhance clarity, order, and precision in our thinking about behavior viewed in the light of our own "post-conventional" norms (Kohlberg), or the social conventions and moral rules that form a religious or secular community's stable consensus about "right" and "wrong" (Beauchamp and Childress). Moreover, the term *moral theology* or *religious ethics* will be used to describe the systematic results of religious thought about morality in the light of a particular theological tradition, e.g. Jewish, Muslim, or Christian.

The ethic being developed here is sensitive to Ross's conclusions that Western morality is concerned with the task of defining "right" and "good," and with understanding moral awareness. As a result, this chapter will begin with an analysis of these subjects. Because the ethic affirms Ross's historical observation that Western morality has been shaped by two irreconcilable streams (the Hebrew with its emphasis on duty, obedience, and revealed laws; and the Greek with its stress on goals and ends, the satisfaction of desires, happiness, and pleasure), this ethic is based upon the belief (held by Ross) that the two streams cannot be easily related, that "right" cannot be reduced to "good," and that all "goods" are not simply different expressions of one basic "good," e.g. pleasure. Further, as will be shown, this theory of responsibilities defends a mixed-rule deontological and pluralistic understanding of "right" and "wrong" that is grounded in intuited knowledge about the fundamentals of morality.

Finally, a well-articulated moral theory will provide a solid framework that allows agents to make reasoned judgments about behavior and character. Any ethic claiming to be adequate will be clear and sufficiently complete; it will contain enough information to assist students and critics to understand its conception of the moral life; and it will accord with common moral experience, standard terminology, and usual expectations, because, should it cause confusion or distort established ethical canons, it will find its way blocked—as Joseph Fletcher's theory found when first presented in the 1960s.[3] It is my hope that the following description and defense of this Christian ethic of responsibilities will respect these formal requirements, as well as others that have been proposed by E. O. Wilson and Avery Dulles.

Roman Catholic Moral Theology Today: Toward A
New Construing

The moral theory being developed in these chapters stands firmly within the Western tradition of ethics. With Aristotle, this ethic holds that the discipline of ethics touches upon subjects close to politics and economics, and involves the discussion of the human good, happiness, virtue, moral virtue, and the ideal life.[4] It maintains that every art, inquiry, action and pursuit aims at some "good," but because there are many actions, arts, and sciences, their ends are also many ("the end of the medical art is health, the end of shipbuilding is a vessel"). Subsequently, just as Aristotle concludes that the subject of ethics is the "good for man"; and the good for man is happiness (*Ethics*, 1095a14–b8)—which is "activity of the soul in accordance with the virtue" (the "best and most complete virtue"), this moral theory sees that since "one swallow does not make a summer, nor does one day," we must immediately add "in a complete life" (ibid., 1097b22–1098a20).

In Aristotle's opinions, as all know, moral goodness is a middle state intermediate between two vices—one of excess, the other of deficiency; to be virtuous is no easy task, and ethics, although it does provide useful knowledge, is a general science not nearly as precise as mathematics—which means that nobody should expect conclusions from ethicists to be similar (in their accuracy and precision) to those one expects from mathematicians.[5]

The Australian philosopher, Peter Singer (in spite of his focus on contemporary issues in health care, animal rights, and the environment) construes ethics in ways similar to both Aristotle's realistic approach and to this moral theory.[6] Ethics is about living according to standards that are "somehow *universal*" and go beyond our likes and dislikes; ethics involves looking at our or another's behavior from the standpoint of an "ideal observer," Singer states (ibid., 11). Ethics, for the professor of philosophy at Princeton University, is a patently rational endeavor; indeed, it is rational for us to act ethically (ibid., 207), because ethics involves judgments about interests and happiness, calculations dealing with optimizing the interests of those affected by our actions, and using standards (reasonable, reliable) to assess the morality of taking human life, slaughtering animals for human consumption, making decisions about reducing poverty, or taking care of disease.

Although Singer holds that "Human nature is so diverse that one may doubt if any generalization about the kind of character that leads to happiness could hold for all human beings" (ibid., 214), nevertheless, with Aristotle (and this theory) he is firmly convinced that life has meaning, and the study of ethics plays a definite role in providing meaningful insights into life. In this, as in other ways, ethics (as Aristotle, Aquinas, Kant, and Mill taught) is essentially a practical, not a theoretical, discipline; it deals with life and death—not simply speculation.

The moral theory being presented in this book stands with Aristotle and Singer in other ways. It is realist; it is humble. This ethic sees the formal study of morality and the activity of making moral decisions as essentially a search for order, or (to adapt Hobbes's insight into human behavior) a quest for happiness through the reduction of pain or the acquisition of inner (emotional, mental) as well as temporal satisfaction, peace, and prosperity. While *moral philosophy* seeks answers using the human heart and head within a framework of concepts and rules that can be justified by reason (observation, induction, deduction), this theory holds that *religious ethics* uses the human heart and head within a framework that can be justified not simply by reason, but also on the basis of faith. It sees the relationship between faith-inspired theology and natural reason in the same way as Aquinas did (following Anselm) when he wrote, "Sacred doctrine (theology) also uses human reason, not indeed to prove faith ... but to manifest some other truths which are delivered in this doctrine. For since grace does not eliminate nature, but perfects it, it must needs be that natural reason subserve faith ... And hence it is that sacred doctrine uses also the authorities of philosophers, where they have been able to know truth through natural reason."[7]

With the majority of feminist ethicists, this ethic accepts the validity of twentieth century insights into the limits of human knowledge expressed by C. S. Lewis in *God in the Dock: Essays on Theology and Ethics* (1970), and analyzed in Derrida's better-known critique of one of the central tenets of Levi-Strauss's *Mythologiques:* namely, that any attempt to interpret the underlying structure of cultural myths or the religious images basic to a person's faith assumes the ability to stand outside the interpretative structures—i.e., the ability to free oneself from one's own intellectual, cultural, religious, and political understandings in order to discover the forces (objective) that lie beneath nature, culture, and consciousness. However, a person, Derrida argues, cannot transcend his or her own religious or cultural paradigms in order to study and provide a scientific analysis of the nature of cultural paradigms. Consequently, in much the same way as Einstein saw in developing the implications of his theory of relativity, there is no "absolute" center from which such an analysis can be undertaken.[8] There is no objective or neutral vantage point.

This realization does not undermine the usefulness of building frameworks, or render void a worldview's observations about reality. Nor does it mean that frameworks are above criticism. It simply means that as long as humans inhabit Plato's cave—and have no access to any realm of ideas (unchanging, eternal)—there is no place to stand within the universe of thought that is the "center."[9]

There is a second major assumption at the core of this theory, one that was also championed by C. S. Lewis in his *The Discarded Image* (1964), and by more recent critics of history who have stressed two conclusions important for ethics. First, that all reconstructions of the past bear signs of the historian's religious preferences, cultural and ideological (Marxist, capitalist) biases. Second, that such reconstructions—even the most complete and careful—are inevitably unable to recover "how it actually was." In Lewis's judgment, for instance, the medieval worldview that he knew well and deeply admired—extraordinary in its "splendour, sobriety, and coherence"—had a serious flaw: it was not true. The reason? "No model is a catalogue of ultimate realities, and none is a mere fantasy. Each is a serious attempt to get all the phenomena known at a given period, and each succeeds in getting in a great many. But also, no less surely, each reflects the prevalent psychology of an age almost as much as it reflects the state of that age's knowledge....Nature gives most of her evidence in answer to the questions we ask her."[10]

There is a third important assumption within this ethic: all moral thought, whether an adolescent's efforts to construct a worldview or an expert witness's testimony in a complex biomedical ethics hearing, involves language—its facticity, ambiguity, and discontinuity. The ethicist, like the poet, is involved in biography and autobiography, in explanation and demonstration, in occasionally using comedy and parody, persuasion and intimidation. As we find in Simon Blackburn's *Being Good* (2003), some ethicists will write a witty book and use a popular touch to enlighten their readers.[11] Others will follow the authors of the Old Testament's narratives on some occasions, and employ analogy in order to strengthen his or her meaning in much the same way that Virginia Woolf uses imagery in her novels.[12] However, even in the hands of the expert, ethics is frequently exploratory and evolutionary as it reaches down into the recesses of cultural metaphors, explores human anxieties, and assesses religious inspirations through the always delicate instrument of language (civil, special) to express, evoke, and communicate.

This assumption means that, while sensitive to the rules of logic and grammar, the religious ethicist (again like the poet and novelist) will sometimes, as G. M. Hopkins did, write with the deep-seated conviction that there are more important values at stake than permitting a reader to grasp his or her meaning "at first glance." It also means that like Chaucer, Shakespeare, T. S. Eliot, or Jacques Derrida, an ethicist will sometimes prize ambiguity more than clarification; he or she will put imagination above practical reason, as the nineteenth century poet and illustrator William Blake did.[13] From time to time, seeing themselves as descendants of Origen and Abelard, the author of *The Cloud of Unknowing,* or the medieval dialogue *Mirouere des Simples Ames,* some ethicists will rank originality more important than tradition. Style, voice, vocabulary, context, and point-of-view—visionary insights and social convictions—will suffuse their presentations just as one finds when studying Picasso's drawings or Denise Levertov's poems.

Any theologian who seeks to present a contemporary moral theory (as I am doing here) must take the language of ethics seriously, as James Gustafson has done. An ethicist cannot ignore the fact that Jesus' moral teaching is a complex tapestry involving social values, cultural perceptions, and the interaction between text and reader.[14] He or she needs to know that the Bible frequently uses contiguous terms arranged in sequence without any definition of the links between one term and the next, and that the Bible's authors employed this literary device in order to better describe the wayward paths of human freedom: "the quirks and contradictions of men and women seen as moral agents and complex centers of motive and feeling," as Alter tells us (ibid., 46). In presenting their own theories, and in making use of biblical narratives, Christian, Jewish, and Muslim writers must take into account that the Hebrews who wrote the Bible's narrative of Eve's creation (Genesis 2), for instance, used literary devices different from those within Homer's mythological episodes. They should remember as well that the large cycle of stories about David, one of the stunning achievements of ancient literature in Alter's opinion, involves the intertwining of fiction and history, the skills of gifted writers (or series of gifted writers), remarkable intuitions into the psychology of the narrative's characters, and freedom, inventiveness, and creativity—sophisticated resources of poetry and prose—equal to what one finds centuries later in Shakespeare's history plays (ibid., 3–22).

There is an another assumption at the heart of this ethic that is larger (perhaps) than those already mentioned: while Christianity can be usefully described as an autonomous, continuous, self-organizing thought-world, with its own border guards and demarcations to set it apart and protect its integrity, it is (at the same time) an institution (faith community) that keeps a series of revelatory "moments" alive across the centuries through the proclamation of a prophetic message which is restated and redescribed—only with great difficulty—under the varying pressures of time and circumstance, but which, by its very nature, is unchanged and unchangeable.[15]

Such a view means ironically that Christianity is open to "change" as the nineteenth and twentieth Catholics (Alfred Loisy, Friederich von Hugel, and George Tyrrell) who were called "modernists" argued. But at the same time, it is not open to change as their critics (Orestes Brownson, Pius X) maintained. The centrality of the Sermon on the Mount and Lord's Prayer for Christian ethics, and Christianity's defined position on the Trinity ("three persons in one God") are "unchangeable". However, the Church's use of Greek philosophical terminology ("person") in its creed is always open to change, because of pressures upon the Church to restate its core belief at some future time in positive response to legitimate catechetical needs within a particular culture.

According to this theory's construing of Christian ethics, a *Lutheran* moral theory, for instance, will be structured on the basis of the rules of language (English, German), and the principles of logic. Where its judgments involve science, it will incorporate correct biology, physics, and history (and the accepted methodologies of these disciplines). The demands of scientific honesty and competence will apply no less to the Christian ethicist than they do to the psychologist or historian.[16] Since it is a *Lutheran* ethic, the theory will embody Luther's theological and moral teaching as interpreted by contemporary Lutheran scholars and Reformed communities. Contrary to the general optimism and confidence in reason current in U.S. society today, such an ethic (one supposes) will emphasize human sinfulness, reason's limited powers, God's sovereignty, and the Bible's supreme authority in moral matters.

Such an ethic (as we see in James Gustafson's theocentric ethics) will apply these central beliefs, as well as Luther's understanding of faith and righteousness, Luther's reading of the Bible, and Jesus' moral teaching, as understood by Gustafson himself and other contemporary Lutheran scholars, to issues such as abortion, euthanasia, and capital punishment.

The validity of a theory's claims to be Lutheran, as well as the correctness of its practical conclusions, will be judged on the basis of the soundness of an ethicist's scientific and theological knowledge, the strength of his or her interpretation, and the ability of arguments used to meet criteria set down by respected philosophers (consilience, coherence, consistency) and Lutheran theologians (fidelity to Evangelical principles, Lutheran synods). However, no matter how hard the effort, no matter how competent the scholarship, each Lutheran theologian's ethic will embody his or her biases and preferences; each will be a personal reconstruction of facts, an individual reordering of doctrinal tenets and ethical principles; it will inevitably embody the ethicist's language system, point-of-view, time, place, culture, and his or her self-view, worldview, life-history, and social experience. Consequently, it will always be *a* Lutheran ethic—never *the* Lutheran ethic. Like Christianity, the theory will be a personal effort to express for one's own time and place the life-implications of what one has come to know from others, past and present, about a unique revelatory "moment" —God's saving work in Christ.

Obviously, Christian, Jewish, and Muslim ethics make their own use of philosophy and science according to their traditions. It is a mistake, however, to argue (as some philosophers do) that religious ethics does not contain logic's rules or reason's insights—or that the term "religious ethics" describes all ethical knowledge that lies beyond or outside reason. Reason and faith, the human intellect, and human imagination, philosophy, and theology overlap in their interests and goals, in their desires and subject matter. Each ethical theory formulated within the great monotheistic religions will be "religious," however, no matter what "science" it uses, because of its reliance on *religious beliefs* (in an all-knowing God, revelation, in Jesus as God's Son, Muhammad as the last of the prophets), as well as *religious moral teaching* ("Love your neighbor as you love yourself," "Forgive others as I have forgiven you") in the building of its formal structure and in arriving at its practical conclusions. It will give respect to *religious authorities* (Bible, Koran; pope, liturgy). At the same time, because of its framework, preferences, and use of language, the ethic—even the most impressive and convincing—will be inherently imperfect ("untrue"), and subjective (caught up in its own webs).

Roman Catholic Moral Theology Today: Toward a New Unifying Metaphor

This moral theory takes the position that both the informal and formal disciplines that we call philosophical and religious ethics, as well as the actually lived experiences (thoughts, deeds, words, actions) —indeed all human manifestations and expressions of "morality-in-history"—comprise a distinctive *genre of literature*, and are best described and assessed in terms of the traditions of literature, art, and music, rather than in terms of today's physical sciences (with their strict methodologies and rules for verification). This metaphor for ethics, based upon recent work in literary studies, reunites ethics with aesthetics, and separates it from biology and psychology.

This position admits that ethics, like history, has its objective aspects (in events, actions) and its universal features (shared common desires, goals, projects). But because *ethics as a genre of literature* necessarily embodies authorial aspects (style, voice, syntax, point-of-view) that are personal, as well as linguistic features, narrative modes, and metaphors that are cultural (Anglo-American, Hindu-Buddhist), it inevitably possesses subjective and creative features inherent in all human efforts to express and reconstruct experience—whether one's awareness of injustice, the image of falleness in the novels of one's century, or the nostalgic emphases at the heart of contemporary feminist moral theories.

This model of ethics provides an understanding of the discipline that satisfactorily explains the pluralism, originality, change, and diversity that the historical record illustrates. From the theological point-of-view, this view incorporates Vatican II's convictions about the Spirit's cosmic role and the universality of Christ's saving work, both of which are captured in Gerard Manley Hopkins's reminder that "Christ plays in ten thousand places/ Lovely in limbs, and lovely in eyes not his/To the Father through the features of men's faces." Finally, associating ethics with literature allows us to see the seeds of objectivism and utilitarianism in the primate's first uncertain stirrings of aesthetic and moral awareness; it finds in the same wellspring both the sources of the great streams of music, art and literature, and the great rivers of Christian, Jewish, and Muslim ethics.[17]

A Summary Defense of This Depiction of Ethics: Learning from Past and Present

Twentieth century moralists with classic mentalities tend to associate ethics with physics and biology. They consider moral philosophy to be a rational science involved in achieving objective values and universal principles. They are convinced that, whether the focus of a college student's informal musings or of a consultant's expert opinions, the subject matter of objective ethical analysis or subjective moral decision-making is something "solid" and "hard." As late as 1985, the neo-Scholastic ethicist William E. May, for example, stated that God's "unchanging truths and laws can be known by human intelligence in so far as these truths are rooted in the being of the human person and in the constitutive elements of human nature," and that these laws included not only general precepts, but more particular and specific ones that are "absolutely binding and transcend historical and cultural situations."[18]

For such thinkers, the central models that best describe the ethicist are those of the laboratory scientist or the research academic. Their approaches, in spite of particular differences, all prize order and control. Their theories seek structure and pattern; their epistemologies can be fairly described as naive realism, since ethical values are viewed more as facts than as opinions, and there is no solid conviction that sociological, cultural, and psychological circumstances make any real differences to their conclusions. In its geography of the human body, the classical mindset views the intellect as the highest, most noble power; the passions as lower, inferior. Further, while there is a history of ethics, the record, according to this point of view, should resemble the history of mathematics—a record of achievements and breakthroughs, of small changes in stable structures and repeating patterns that underlie reality, and are best expressed in precise formulae $(E=Mc^2)$ and universally recognizable symbols (1,2). Ethicists—in this framework—resemble the disciples of Pythagoras.

Since the goal of ethics, according to some theorists, is to define concepts such as "justice" and (for others) to resolve human dilemmas ("Is it ethical to execute serial murderers?" "Is it right to withhold nutrition and hydration from a seriously impaired newborn?"), the neo-Scholastic approach to the discipline is understandable. Human nature does not change (in this view); such aspects as gender, culture, and religion do not influence the mind's ability to think or the tongue's capacity to speak. Should ten people be given the task of determining the answers to a moral question, and they think correctly and judge accurately, there will be one answer only—not ten—regardless of where they live, their gender, or their native languages. The rules of morality, like the rules of mathematics, are objective and universal.

While sympathetic to these opinions (I was educated in them), a case can be made that such thinkers fail to realize five truths that are basic to modern and postmodern thinking about ethics.[19] First, there is the insight central to Freud's psychology and the founding of psychoanalysis: namely, that the mind is active and imaginative in the organization of its own experience.[20] Second, that the agents of ethics are "persons" with all the unique aspects that modern moral philosophers like Heidegger and Ricoeur, Karl Rahner, Louis Janssens, and Norbert Rigali recognize.[21] This means that while ethics is capable of formulating generic moral rules (what is right for Christian men, for instance), it is not able to describe norms for persons, because each person is unique and unrepeatable, a distinct essence. Three, that culture, gender, and one's place in a group all play filtering roles in one's assessments of "right" and "wrong." This means that the human mind is not like a PC—simply a clone—but a separate and different processing and communicating system.[22]

The fourth argument contends that Wittgenstein grasped something important in 1947 when he observed in his notebooks, "It strikes me that a religious belief could only be something like a passionate commitment to a system of reference," and that the correct way to educate in religion, therefore, is through portrayals and descriptions.[23] The fifth is that as soon as a person wishes to speak about morality, whether as theory or as practice, the form of these activities involves the selection and organization of words, terms, images, and language-systems—with all the limitations, hazards, and difficulties that this immediately sets in motion.

True, each of these arguments might not be insurmountable on its own. However, their combined force poses a major hurdle for ethicists educated in the classical tradition. Because of their weight, contemporary ethicists (such as myself) see less objectivity and universality in morality; they admit the creative role of the imagination, intuition, and the passions in ethical analysis, as well as in actual decision-making; they recognize the discontinuities in texts and the ambiguities in language. Unlike ethicists with classic mindsets, those who are open to modern and postmodern opinions are careful to avoid Oedipus's flaw (to have understood the Delphic oracle too easily); and they do not assume that meaning is transparent to human reason, or communication is available to willing correspondents.

For modern and postmodern writers, the central models that best describe the ethicist's work are those of the person falling in love, the swimmer, and the artist. They posit new images of the intellect—and of its products, whether spoken or written.[24] For those who hold such opinions, both literature and science are the work of people with passion as well as objectivity; reality is not only as stable as a rock, but also constantly in motion like the sea; the ethicist is both a thinker like Auguste Rodin's and an experienced swimmer—a person whose actions generate both pauses and waves. In the eyes of these writers, the goal of ethics is like a far-off shore—ahead, distant, sometimes achieved (but not by every person), and always only after serious effort and careful work.

In the view being proposed here, although every Christian, Jewish, and Muslim ethicist seeks to answer the question, "How should we live?," the ethical theories and specific positions developed by black American Baptists have been and will continue to be different from the ethics developed by Irish-American Catholics. While they will share the same goal (to describe the Christian moral life, to resolve current ethical dilemmas) and they will use the same Bible, employ careful reasoning processes, Black American Christians will develop their social ethics in the light of their own distinctive understandings and convictions about God's creating-saving work in Christ, their own literary sources, metaphors, and personal experiences. Irish-American Catholics, on the other hand, will formulate their clanship ethics in the light of their distinctive grasp of the implications of the Bible's doctrines, their knowledge of papal and conciliar statements, and their own personal, community, and faith experiences. Both groups of Christians will be caught up in creative activity that, like prayer, involves expressing and communicating religious affectivities and cognitive insights and the influence of charismatic leaders, as well as the frustrations of human interactions.[25]

The inevitable presence in this activity of passionate persons (zealous, angry, frustrated), religious frameworks (Christian, Muslim), and metaphorical language (imagistic, rhythmic) means that ethics (religious ethics, in particular) as it is orally expressed or set down in writing has more in common with the humanities than with the sciences; that the communication of ethical beliefs and the resolution of moral dilemmas (as Martin Heidegger came to appreciate) stands closer to good poetry than to solid physics—to schools of spirituality than to systems of sociology. And ethics has these features, because it possesses characteristics (affectivity, subjectivity) more central to the humanities (literature, art) than the sciences; it involves reason *and* the heart, logic *and* intuition, knowledge *and* belief, persons *and* communities—because it is an *art-science*.[26]

The theory being presented here admires Adam Zachary Newton's *Narrative Ethics* because of the book's numerous helpful insights into ethics: for instance, that narrative itself *is* ethics, that the act of telling stories initiates responsibilities toward the other and others, and that this activity is the key to subjectivity because of the results of encounter and recognition resulting from hearing, telling, reading, and witnessing dramas. Newton builds upon Nietzsche and Heidegger, Livinas and Ricoeur to provide a theory that emphasizes postmodernism's "difference" in place of modernism's "similarity." His theory realistically explains how humans learn moral knowledge and grow as ethical agents. At the same time, it respects personal individuality; it understands that narratives dealing with moral situations (the death of one's child, the loss of one's boat, the betrayal of one's brothers) are not only singular, unrepeatable experiences, but also events that fall (if not always safely) within the interpretative scope of humans living in later centuries and in different cultures, and thereby possess the ability to educate, develop, and form consciences and cultures.

One of the implications of this construing of ethics is the following: a person's response to ethical values is similar to his or her response to a public speaker, novelist, teacher, or law enforcement officer—it will be guided by one's personal "grasp" of standards. As Peter Edwards says, "The inculcation of grammatical rules, of a role's responsibilities and duties, or of the norms of practical conduct more generally, are a means that further the spontaneous production of accepted linguistic and other forms of practical behavior, but they neither create new values nor capture all existing ones."[27] Or, as every parent and teacher quickly learns, just as the best and brightest will take one's own "laws" and creatively reinterpret them or apply them in new and unexpected ways in keeping with that child's own understanding and circumstances, his or her insights into rules or altruism, so "the investigation of ethical value must retain a keen sense of the significance not only of the unpredictable, of life's vicissitudes, but of the uncomfortably and disarmingly admirable, of what we really value in the world, of how this sometimes comes about in ways that involve the suffering of innocent people" (ibid., 56).

As the Church seeks to renew its ethics, those working to assist the Church should incorporate into their theories the implications of the following truths:

- The discipline of Christian ethics always involves a person's or group's distinctively human (creative, contingent) efforts to communicate (as Vincent McCabe said), deals with culturally-bound insights and contextually-framed affective responses to the *humanum*—as well as to that which lies beyond, yet always within the *humanum*: divinity (Norbert Rigali).
- Christian ethics, whether it is seen as an individual theory or as a wide river of thought, must possess some of the features found in its classics, as well as in the mystic's dance; it shares a number of the features central to Mozart's music and Picasso's art.
- However, just as there is no "objective" basis to music (in the classic sense of the term "objective") nor any universally correct style of painting, in a similar way, it is important to remember that there is no "objective" ground to Christian ethics, nor any Platonic form of good.
- While there is empirical evidence that provides a rational basis for the Christian teaching that "adultery is wrong," this tenet, as well as the guiding principles of Christian ethics, are essentially grounded on shared beliefs, the authority of the Bible, and the respect shown to certain authors and leaders. The arguments of Christian ethics are essentially arguments from authority. And consequently, Christian ethics is basically a positivist discipline. The Catholic Church's position on the treatment of captured soldiers during a war, for example, is grounded on the Church's past and present insights into human rights, duties, and respect. It is based upon the Church's understanding and interpretation of Scripture, its reading of the Church's moral traditions (what Augustine wrote, what Aquinas taught); it will look for guidance from the social encyclicals of popes, the decrees of councils. What the Church decides involves the use of research skills and logic—but the Church's conclusions are not "scientific" or "rational." Morality, as feminist ethicists have correctly reminded us, is about memories.
- Further, the Church's morality is shaped by the "power of *dangerous* memories," as Sharon Welch emphasizes. The Church's ethical teaching sits firmly on its memory of Abraham, Job, Christ, Mary, and Paul. To convince and persuade, the Church must speak

in the language of its hearers, as well as in the phrases and images of its authorities. The Church's authentic and lasting insights into moral truth will resemble its grasp of beauty—and neither lies simply in the eye of the beholder.

• Where there is disagreement, no firm consensus, the Church will have a right to expect that its positions possess an *a priori* right to respect, and that what the Church teaches will not be rejected out of hand by its critics, because Christian theology affirms that "the Church is the pillar and ground of truth."

• However, the Church's leaders should accept the wisdom contained in the aphorism *"In certis unitas. In dubiis libertas. In omnibus, caritas."* And they should appreciate Peter Edwards's words about the normative role of values—that they will always be creatively incorporated into the minds and hearts of individuals, being adapted and synthesized into life—just as creative musicians, artists, poets, and writers have always done.

• This view of ethics does not mean either the relativization of morality or its collapse into subjectivity. Each moral theory will be critiqued on the basis of *formal criteria* such as coherence and consistency, its fidelity to its roots, and its harmony with normal moral experience. An original or radical ethic (e.g. Gustafson's, Sartre's) will also have to defend itself on the basis of criteria prized by philosophy or theology.

• It will have to pass tests concerning its pastoral usefulness, whether or not it will cause scandal, or undermine society.[28] Like Joyce's *Ulysses*, an ethic's claims to be "Western" or "Catholic" will be measured by established rules; its individual expressions of Christianity or Judaism will be judged in terms of professional standards and expert opinions, a community's creed, or a group's material rules. *"Lex orandi, lex credendi"* will apply to moral as well as to dogmatic theologies.

• On the basis of such criteria, it will be possible for Christians today to recognize immoral individuals as well as immoral behavior, just as it was possible for Christians in past times to recognize the possibility of heretics and heresy.

• Further, although a person will not promote triumphalist views about any particular movement or tradition, no Christian will have to deny his or her loyalties or betray religious preferences. James Gustafson's creative fidelity to and imaginative revisioning of the Reform tradition's ethics will set the standard for future scholars.

In spite of its modern features, on the basis of its regard for formal criteria and its respect for material rules, the moral theory being presented here stands firmly within the Catholic tradition—as we will further demonstrate throughout the following chapters.

Notes:

[1] Herbert McCabe, *What is Ethics All About?* (Washington: Corpus Books, 1969), 92.

[2] For essays on Ross's life, writings, and contributions to philosophy, Tom Regan, W. D. Ross, in *Encyclopedia of Ethics*, Lawrence C. Becker, editor, Vol. II (New York: Garland, 1992), 1111–1112; Jonathan Dancy, "An Ethic of Prima Facie Duties, "in *A Companion to Ethics*, edited by Peter Singer (Oxford: Blackwell, 1991, 1993), 219–229, and Jonathan Dancy, "Intuitionism," Ibid., 411–419; *Cambridge Dictionary of Philosophy*, Robert Audi, General Editor (Cambridge: Cambridge University Press, 1995), 697–698; *Oxford Companion to Philosophy* edited by Ted Honderich (Oxford: Oxford University Press), 779–800; *Biographical Dictionary of Twentieth century Philosophy,* edited by Stuart Brown, Diane Collinson and Robert Wilkinson (London: Routledge, 1997, 2002), 674–675; Copleston Frederick, "Realism in Britain and America," in his *A History of Philosophy*, Vol. VIII: Modern Philosophy (New York: Doubleday, 1967, 1994, 380–401

[3] For further on Fletcher's ethics, my study, "Joseph Fletcher's Situation Ethics: Twenty-Five Years After the Storm," *Irish Theological Quarterly*, 56, 3 (Summer, 1990), 170–190 .

[4] On these topics, Aristotle, *Nicomachean Ethics* (London: Blackwell, 1989). Also, Stephen R. L. Clark's impressive analysis of Aristotle's thought that emphasizes his skills as a philosopher of biology, in particular of medicine, "The Doctrine of the Mean," and "*Eudaimonia*," in *Aristotle's Man*: *Speculations upon Aristotelian Anthropology* (Oxford: Clarendon Press, 1975), 84–97, 145–163.

[5] For an invaluable synthesis of Aristotle's ethical thought, Sir David Ross, *Aristotle* (London: Methuen, 1971, first published in 1923), 187–234.

[6] For Singer's statements on the shape of ethics, *Practical Ethics* (Cambridge: Cambridge University Press, 1979), 1–13.

[7] Thomas Aquinas, *Summa Theologiae*, I, II, Q. 1, Art. 9, reply to 2nd objection, as quoted by Raphael T. Waters in "The Relationship of Moral Philosophy to Moral Theology," *Listening* 18, 3 (Fall, 1983), 235–255, at 243–244. This is a useful study. However, it is tied too closely to neo-Scholastic assumptions about reason, "natural law," and Jesus' moral teaching.

[8] Ernesto Cardenal, priest, revolutionary, and one of the towering figures in modern poetry, captures Einstein's point in the following lines from the major achievement of his poetic work, "Cosmic Canticle," where he says:

We cannot speak of where.
There is no cosmic limit and therefore
There's no cosmic center.
We're in a world without center or border.
(Cantiga 22)

[9] On this exchange, Vincent B. Leitch, *Deconstructive Criticism: An Advanced Introduction* (New York: Columbia University Press, 1983).

[10] C. S. Lewis, *The Discarded Image* (Cambridge: Cambridge University Press, 1964), 222–223. As Dietrich von Hildebrand notes in his *The Trojan Horse in the City of God*, op. cit., 27, a case can be made that Lewis is not quite correct in what he says here, because just as a cup that is 90% full should not be called "empty," likewise one seems to be saying too much when one disagrees with Hildebrand's position that "an incomplete truth is not an error."

[11] Simon Blackburn, *Being Good* (London: Oxford University Press, 2003).

[12] For a fine analysis of these features—and others—that render biblical texts not more fanciful or imaginative but more precise and more reliable, Robert Alter, *The Art of Biblical Narrative* (New York: Basic Books, 1981).

[13] For a fine new study that depicts Blake as visionary rather than mad, a genius whose imagination puts him in a special class of thinker and artist, G. E. Bentley, Jr. *The Stranger from Paradise: A Biography of William Blake* (New Haven: Yale University Press, 2003).

[14] On this subject, Vernon K. Robbins, *The Tapestry of Early Christian Discourse: Rhetoric, Society, and Ideology* (London: Routledge, 1996).

[15] Some readers will realize that these remarks adapt and join together statements made about Islam by Clifford Geertz in "Which Way to Mecca?" *New York Review of Books* (June 12, 2003), 27–30, at 28.

[16] On this point, Raphael T. Waters, "The Relationship of Moral Philosophy to Moral Theology," *Listening* 18, 3 (Fall, 1983), 241.

[17] For the seeds of this construing of morality, Henri Bergson, *The Two Sources of Morality and Religion*, translated by R. Ashley Audra and Cloudesley Brereton (Garden City: Doubleday & Company, 1956), especially on the role of religion on the formation of morality; Vincent McCabe, *What is Ethics?* While some readers will find my description of ethics unsettling, in a sense, it simply extends what has been seen in the past, namely, the co-existence of Franciscan theology alongside Thomistic theology, the Roman rite and the Oriental rite, gothic churches nearby baroque cathedrals—in other words the constant appearance within the Church of different forms of theology, spirituality, liturgy, and church architecture.

[18] William E. May, "The Vatican Declaration on Sexual Ethics and the Moral Methodology of Vatican Council II," *Linacre Quarterly*, 52, 2 (May 1985), 116–129., at 121.

[19] The term "postmodern" stands for an extremely broad movement or attitude that has been described as "contingent, ungrounded, diverse, unstable, and indeterminate." As used here, the term is used not to identify this ethic with any particular theorist (Marxist, feminist, multiculturalist, nihilist), but with a general "spirit" that looks beyond the "Enlightenment" and the "Modern Era" in its sense of self, human rights, and especially in its understanding of the relationship between intellect, language, and reality—which might be best summed up in Richard Rorty's conviction that the mind is not a mirror of reality—a central principle of science in the "Age of Reason." For a valuable analysis of postmodernism's projects and problems, Terry Eagleton, *The Illusions of Postmodernism* (Cambridge: Blackwell Publishers, 1996).

[20] This opinion has become widely accepted in 20th century psychological circles. It is crucial to the thought of Michael Polanyi and Sidney Callahan (as we will see). Carol Gilligan's *In a Different Voice: Psychological Theory and Women's Development* (Cambridge: Harvard

University Press, 1982) also incorporates recent philosophical thinking about the role of age, gender, and culture in moral development and moral decision-making.

[21] Karl Rahner's formal existentialist ethics rises in part on the realization that while what a person ought to do on a particular occasion cannot lie outside the implications of objective and universal norms, at the same time a person's perception of such norms cannot be merely a simple deduction from a general ethical principle. "It would be absurd for a God-regulated theological morality to think that God's binding will could only be directed to the human action in so far as the latter is simply a realization of the universal norm and of a universal nature," Rahner wrote in 1963. In the German Jesuit's opinion, God's creative will is directly and unambiguously directed toward the concrete and the individual as such—as it really is—in its material uniqueness. And "God is interested in history not only in so far as it is the carrying out of norms, but in so far as it is a history which consists in the harmony of unique events and which precisely in this way has meaning for eternity." *Theological Investigations*, II (Baltimore: Helicon, 1963), 227.

[22] This realization explains why generations of Catholics, while able to pass college level exams in ethics, did not really think like their instructors, and why women's moral opinions and worldviews were actually quite different from their male classmates—although not expressed.

[23] The importance of this shift in thought will be developed when we deal with moral development and the role of laws and stories in the development of values, models, tenets, character, and decision-making skills.

[24] For a scholarly study of human behavior, as described in the informal world of "intentional states" and in "the world of the physical sciences," Kathleen Lennon, *Explaining Human Action* (La Salle: Open Court, 1990).

[25] What is stated here can be more clearly seen when one examines not simply Irish-American Catholics or African-American Baptists, but the fast-growing and diverse Asian-American communities (Chinese, Japanese, Korean, Vietnamese, Laotian, Cambodian, Thai, Mong), in which one finds distinctive views of literature ("writing is fighting"), ethics (the individual is the law, revenge is vital), and Christianity (seen by some as *the* primary source of racial hatred, genocide, self-contempt, and self-annihilation). On this subject, Frank Chin, "Come All Ye Asian American Writers of the Real and the Fake," *The Big Aiiieeeee! An Anthology of Chinese American and Japanese American Literature*, Jeffrey Paul Chan, et al. editors (New York: Meridian, 1991), 1–93; Frank Chin, "This is Not an Autobiography," *Genre* 18 (1985), 109–130.

[26] In recent centuries Roman Catholic moral theology has disdained creativity. However, Augustine's *Confessions* and Aquinas' *Summa Theologiae* are filled with their author's original insights and their highly personal language sets and literary styles. As seen in the Church's architecture, its ancient missals and sacramentaries, its high crosses and rose windows, style, color, craftsmanship, and creativity were once central to the Church's efforts to express and communicate its faith.

[27] Peter Edwards, "The Future of Ethics," in *The Future of Philosophy: Towards the 21st Century*, edited by Oliver Leaman, op. cit., 41–61, at 56.

[28] Historically, the avoidance of scandal has been one of the Catholic Church's major concerns when assessing change, whether in its canonical practices concerning marriage or in its policies about priests. As recent events in America and Canada have shown, this concern was sometimes excessive and undermined other important moral principles, for instance, justice.

Chapter VIII

A Christian Ethic of Responsibilities: Informing Beliefs, Key Images, Central Narratives

> The truth is rarely pure and never simple. Modern life would be very tedious if it were either, and modern literature a complete impossibility.
>
> Oscar Wilde
> *The Importance of Being Earnest*

> That science has found reality in its physical aspect to be incomparably more majestic and awesome than we had supposed suggests—it does not prove—that if we could see the full picture we would find its qualitative depths to be as much beyond what we normally suppose as science has shown its quantitative ones to be.
>
> Huston Smith
> *Beyond the Postmodern Mind*

> The symbolic model presupposes that human individual and group behavior is organized around the symbolic meanings and expectations that are attached to objects that are socially valued.
>
> Bruce Malina
> *The New Testament World*

Christianity is a pictorial religion.[1] Furthermore, Christianity respects mythopoeic knowledge.[2] Unlike Judaism and Islam that have generally not encouraged icons or statues, Christianity has been expressed from its beginnings in pictographs and symbols, stone carvings, mosaic, and stained glass. Furthermore, Augustine's thought is colored by a dynamic vision of the cosmos as a "structured hierarchy"; Augustine's morality is shaped by his belief that all humans are essentially "wayfaring souls."[3] Gerard Manley Hopkins's worldview, for all its modern and postmodern insights into created reality and the language of poetry, is dominated by awe-inspiring biblical images of God.[4]

While modern science presents itself as value free and objective, analysis shows that all human thought, whether in poetry or physics, is influenced to some degree by images, and these images—whether of natural realities or supernatural agents—are central to building answers, philosophical or religious, to the questions that Paul Gauguin answered through his famous painting, "Who am I? Where did I come from? Where am I going?" The role of narratives, images, and metaphors in the development and expression of moral understanding leads to such questions as: "What are the distinctive images in Christian ethics? In what ways are Christian, Jewish, and Muslim ethics really different from each other? What are the stories and metaphors that shape Christian morality, whether in terms of individual self-awareness and self-understanding, or the academic discipline known as Roman Catholic moral theology?"

Although these are somewhat narrow questions, they are important both to ethics and to the moral theory being presented here. Any ethic attempting to be part of the "renewal" in Catholic ethics mandated by Vatican II must address these questions.

First, however, some clarifications: A *philosophical* ethic grounds its foundations and justifies its conclusions on a structured analysis of some form of "empirical" evidence: e.g. the results of research into biology, cultures, experience, language, and social benefits. This means that E. O. Wilson's sociobiology is a philosophical ethic. A *religious* ethic (Jewish, Christian, Muslim, Hindu-Buddhist) on the other hand is one that is shaped (at least to some conscious degree) by: (a) beliefs or norms that do not have empirical evidence to support their validity: for instance, the belief in eternal life and happiness for the "just" following life on earth; or (b) by beliefs that, while coloring the theory's vision of life, society, or the times, do have some empirical evidence to support them: for example, the belief that adultery is immoral.[5]

Next, in keeping with the emphases of twentieth century theologians—e.g. Karl Barth, Paul Tillich, Yves Congar, Tielhard de Chardin, Joseph Sittler, Richard McCormick, Stanley Hauerwas, Germain Grisez—*theology* is much more than a "linguistic-intellectual activity," as James Gustafson says (I, 159). It is, primarily, a distinctive way of "construing the world" (I, 158). However, on the basis of their study of Scripture and their reading of theologians such as Athanasius, Basil, Augustine, Aquinas, Loyola, Luther, and Calvin, these theologians see that, in terms of method and procedure, both an individual's and a tradition's theology (Orthodox, Lutheran, Roman Catholic, Baptist) involves the *selective* arrangement of particular tenets (creedal beliefs, doctrinal formulae) into coherent strands (traditions) that determine the ordering of other (doctrinal) beliefs—an observation that has greater merit when we examine how Celtic monks like Patrick and Kevin emblazoned their "construing of the world" on Ireland's high crosses, or how Norwegian Lutheran composers skillfully arranged their guiding tenets and expressed them musically in their great traditions of community hymn singing.

This conclusion means that Athanasius's overarching belief in the Logos's divinity, for instance, moderates what Ambrose has to say in later years about Christ's weaknesses and fears; that Augustine's deep sense of sin forever colors Luther's understanding of justification and human freedom; while Aquinas's vision of divine law and his creative use of Aristotle shape the Council of Trent's sixteenth century teaching about conscience and its authority. The role of creeds and doctrines in coloring and shaping personal and communal insights and public statements on moral issues means that Christian ethics is not so much biblical, but doctrinal—the lived faith of believers.

Finally, in an insight that has definite implications for religious ethics, these theologians see that "The dominance of certain theological tenets shapes the prescriptive ethics [of a community] and deeply informs the [its] analysis of the human predicament and the circumstances of human action" (words again from James Gustafson's *Ethics from a Theocentric Perspective*, I, 161). In other words, Paul's insights into Christ's divinity colors what he has to say about discipleship; Calvin's sense of God's sovereignty colors his analysis of human freedom; and Bonheoffer's emphasis on Christ being a "man for others" shapes what he has to say about the cost of discipleship. Christian ethics—Catholic, Lutheran, Anglican—is shaped by a selective body of doctrines—emphases that embody beliefs central to particular faith-communities.

The moral theory being presented here derives its shape and form, its central moral principles from the *Christian story*. More specifically, it derives these from the Christian story as told and expressed over the centuries within the *Catholic Church*. More specifically still, this ethic gains its meaning from the Christian story as told within the *Roman Catholic Church* rather than the Anglican or the Orthodox, both of which have their roots in the Catholic Church. Furthermore, in some of its features, this ethic gains its meaning from the Christian story as its has been committed to memory, recalled and re-expressed over the centuries by *U.S. Catholics*—those communities of immigrant Irish, Italian, Polish, German, French, Spanish, and Czech heritage who came to North America directly from Europe or via Mexico at different times following the day that Columbus landed in the New World. This latter point merits a brief comment.

Just as Quakers, Mormons, and Congregationalists made their homes in America and found their identities in their own Protestant stories and metaphors taken primarily from their readings of the Bible's narratives, the Roman Catholics whose stories shaped some aspects of this ethic settled in New York, Boston, Chicago, Dubuque, and Omaha with worldviews, senses of selves, family traditions, and value systems that were Catholic, while at the same time historically, culturally, ethically—and spiritually distinctive because of the homelands, historical experiences, culture, piety—identity-shaping stories and metaphors from which these immigrants came.[6]

The particular features of the ethic being presented here, its organization and structure, its method of making concrete moral decisions, result from the dominant places that (a) certain theologically-informing *Christian* beliefs hold within its framework, and (b) the roles played by specifically *Catholic theological images* within that framework and subsequently within the memories, imaginations, and consciences of the moral agents who will accept this ethic and use it to make professional and personal moral decisions.

Among the assumptions that are central to this ethical theory is the belief that authentic Christian doctrines should not only shape the individual Christian's vision of reality and his or her conscience, but also that these doctrines should be foundational to the moral theory itself, to its premises and building blocks, its ordering and arrangement of illuminating and normative tenets. To build a "Christian" moral theory on inherently "Marxist" insights, especially on perceptions antithetical to Christianity's established theology or social teaching seems (to me) to be theoretically flawed.

The following are this ethic's principal theological orientations, tenets, and characteristics:

a) This moral theory is *God-focused*

The Word was God (John 1:1). Jesus was the Word of the invisible God, and the "nearest to the Father's heart (John 1:18). As Jesus said to Philip, "He who sees me, Philip, sees the Father" (John 14:9). Further, Jesus did not come to preach himself, but God; and in this (as Matthew sees it) Jesus was a prophet in the tradition of Moses and Elijah (Matthew 17:3). For these reasons, this moral theory is like Jesus'—a *theocentric ethic*. Christ, as we will see below, is the center of this moral theory, but God is its focus. This means that (a) doing God's will and (b) acting in ways that God acts (commands, empowers) form the core of the Christian life—as they did in Jesus' own life (John 16:28; 17: 1–26).

This theory embodies an image of God different from Sharon Welch's, with its concerns about God's power—its strong emphasis on God's immanence to the expense of God's transcendence.[7] It is different as well from the image of God revealed in the political commentaries of the powerful TV evangelist Pat Robertson, who uses the biblical theme of God's gift of the land to the Israelites to support the annihilation of all Palestinian land rights, as well as to condemn Palestinian efforts to end the Israeli military occupation of Gaza.[8] Third, this ethic does not embody James Gustafson's Reform (and rather idiosyncratic) image of God, nor is the ethic grounded in Gustafson's central theme that Christian morality should be shaped by a concern about what God is calling Christians to be and do at this point in human history.

The central motif in this theory's way of construing the world is the distinctive result of a series of always-imperfect insights into God's being, purposes, and dynamic actions: *the Catholic "idea" of a transcendent God who is kind, merciful, and diffusive by nature.* To explain: the doctrine of God taught by John Chrysostom and Gregory of Nyssa, by Origen and Basil, is filled with the realization that all knowledge of God is inadequate, and that all language about God's majesty, for instance, cannot express God's greatness, because God is greater than the mind, the tongue, and every word. In this tradition of theology, the human mind glimpses "aspects" of God, but human reason and language cannot grasp ("master") God.

Hans Urs van Balthasar explains: "In having to resign itself to not knowing *what* God is, the failing spirit divines *that* he is; and this "Is" can therefore not be added to that of the creatures, but shows itself as the altogether Other and Greater than all in the failing of all images and notions."[9] For those who support this approach (their membership includes both Alexandrian and Cappadocian theologians who shaped the Church's creeds), "The Father sends the Son, and the visibility of the Son must point to the invisibility of the Father.... (ibid., 99).[10]

At the same time, the moral theory being presented here sees God's mercy and generosity as central to the Christian life because they are central features within God's self-revelation to Moses, "YHWH, YHWH, a God merciful and gracious, slow to anger, and abounding in steadfast love and faithfulness" (Exodus 33:12–19). This ethic views the God of Israel as the same God who made himself known in Jesus, as forgiving and faithful—in spite of sin and the punishment that it deserves, and as a God who is rich in mercy. With the *Catechism of the Catholic Church*, this theory rises upon the belief that "In all his works, God displays not only his kindness, goodness, grace and steadfast love, but also his trustworthiness, constancy, faithfulness, and truth." This approach professes that this God is Father, Son, and Spirit—Creator, Lord, and Judge.

This ethics flows from the same center as Gustavo Gutierrez's liberation ethics and Richard McCormick's renewed natural law moral theory. It fully accepts that "An ethic that claims to be theological will root itself in God ... Its primary referents will be God's relation to us, and ours to God. The primary analogate—to use scholastic language—of the term 'morality' will be this relationship" (*Corrective Vision*, op. cit, 25). However, the God who forms the originating center of this ethic and colors its moral insights is not exactly the same as John Howard Yoder's, who has chosen to build his moral theory on his own separate and original understandings of the Reformed tradition's theology of God as synthesized in the past by Calvin and Luther, and more recently by Barth and Brunner, who selectively chose certain Reform tenets and arranged them to speak effectively to their communities about crucial theological and moral issues.[11]

As mentioned in examining Gustafson's ethic, his theocentric moral theory sets aside some traditional affirmations about God: God's full and total foreknowledge; that God will come at the end of time to judge both living and dead; that God possesses intellect and will; and God as person. The theory being presented here maintains current Catholic theological positions on these aspects of theology. This theory encourages emphases that John Wijngaards makes in *God Within Us*, a book rich in its knowledge of Chinese philosophy, medieval mysticism, and Arab and European scholars (Aquinas,

Newman, Levi-Strauss, Otto, Maritain, E. L. Mascall, Barth, Levinas, Pannenberg).[12]

At the same time, this ethical theory stands firmly within the Roman Catholic theological tradition that sees God's essential attributes in Moses' words about YHWH's mercy and steadfast love—and rather than employing Jesus' *agape* (as Joseph Fletcher did), it will use these attributes as the basis for its primary moral principles. This theory focuses on the God whom Luke and John depict in their retelling of Jesus' parables and Paul describes in his missionary letters—a God who is not bent on sending humans to hell, as Bertrand Russell saw.[13] This is also the *Triune God* found in the creedal formulae of the Church's theologians Athanasius and Chrysostom, the Councils of Nicaea and Chalcedon; the God who inspired Martin of Tours, Ephraem of Syria, Leo, Augustine, Patrick, and Boniface, the "Apostle of Germany."

In a real sense, this moral theology of responsibilities embraces the image and attributes of the God found in Aquinas's *Summa Theologiae*, where God's actions *ad extra* are described in terms of the inherent and spontaneous ability of "goodness" to expand, radiate, and diffuse itself, so that the essential feature of God is generosity.[14]

Finally, this moral theory construes women and men, human life, and the human future within the all-encompassing vision of a God whom Gerard Manley Hopkins depicts in his now-famous, awe-inspired double images "World's strand, sway of the sea: … giver of breath and bread."[15] Act as God has acted in history, with generosity and mercy, is the basic principle of this moral theory.

b) This moral theory is *Christ-centered*

"It is characteristic of Christianity that choice is made not of principles but of a person, of the living God, of Christ," Paul Tournier writes toward the close of a chapter on morality in *The Meaning of Persons* (1957).[16] Because of the truth embodied in this remark, the center of the ethic being presented here is Jesus Christ, "the image of the invisible God, the firstborn of all creation; for in Him all things were created in heaven and on earth … all things were created through Him and for Him. He is before all things, and in Him all things hold together" (Col. 1:15–17). Christ, as Paul, John, and the Christian creeds state, was sent by the Father that we might have life (John 3:1–3). Christ is the Alpha and the Omega (Apoc. 22:13), Christ is the fulfillment of the law (Rom. 10:4). Christ is salvation and law (Gal. 6:

2; I Cor. 9:21). He is "our wisdom, our righteousness, and sanctifica-
tion and redemption" (I Cor. 1:30). Christ is also the "firstborn among
many believers" (Rom. 8:29). He is, as Karl Rahner said (and Thomas
Merton accepted), the kenotic Christ present today throughout the
diaspora, in the "post-Christian crater of the spirit," in the resilient
hopes of the weak, the abused, and damaged of the earth.[17]

Two obvious conclusions from these New Testament statements
are: (a) Jesus is the full and complete embodiment of right human
action and human virtue; (b) being a Christian means living in Christ,
the personal following of Christ, abiding in Christ's love (John 15:10),
walking as Christ walked (I John 2:16), to have Christ's mind (Phil.
2:5), to "put on Christ" (Rom. 13:14)—not simply to passively adhere
to a complex set of religious doctrines or to blindly observe a weighty
moral code.[18] In the minds of Yves Congar, Richard McCormick,
Joseph Sittler, Enda McDonagh, Paul Ramsey, Bernard Haring,
Teilhard de Chardin, and Norbert Rigali, a *Christian* ethical theory that
seeks to be taken seriously by theologians must be developed in such
a way that it has a definite relationship to Christ, whether it be
to Christ's moral teaching (as in Joseph Fletcher's situation ethics),
Christ's prophetic lifestyle (as developed in Norbert Rigali's
Christocentric ethics with its strong existentialist emphases), or
Christ's saving-creative role in eternity and history (as seen in Oliver
O'Donovan's resurrectional moral theory).

Such an ethic should bring out the dialogical and responsive character of God's saving initiative and Jesus' response—a characteristic
of the theories developed by Charles Curran, Enda McDonagh, and
Germain Grisez.

*This ethical theory holds that God's saving work in Christ and
Christ's response to God's saving work in Him comprise the basis of
Christian ethics.* As seen above, this means that God's mercy, fatherly
care, forgiveness, and generosity are central to Christian morality; it
means that while we cannot reproduce Jesus' historical existence, we
can imitate or relive in our own distinctive ways Jesus' life in our own
lives, because Christ works in and through us by his power, and as
Bonheoffer saw, the starting point of Christian ethics is the power of
God's grace in Christ. For Christians living today who wish to live as
Jesus did, the key question that women and men must ask themselves
is not "How can I be good?", but "What is the will of God?"[19]

Further, rather than depicting the Christian life in terms of Jesus'
passion as Thomas A. Kempis did in his *Imitation of Christ*, this

theory emphasizes that just as Christ's life led to the paschal mystery, the Christian's imitating and following Christ should be seen in the light of that same mystery—it is a *eucharistic* passage with Christ, in Christ, and through Christ to eternal life in the Father. Both the Lord's Prayer and Jesus' major sermons (Matthew's "On the Mount", and Luke's "On the Plain") are central to this Christ-centered, eucharistic ethic, because, as *The Catechism of the Catholic Church* says: "God, infinitely perfect and blessed in himself, in a plan of sheer goodness freely created man to make him share in his own blessed life. For this reason, at every time and in every place, God draws close to man. He calls him to seek him, to know him, to love him with all his strength. He calls together all men, scattered and divided by sin, into the unity of his family, the Church. To accomplish this, when the fullness of time had come, God sent his Son as Redeemer and Savior. In his Son and through him, God invites men to become, in the Holy Spirit, his adopted children and thus heirs of his blessed life" (I, 1).

c) This moral theory is *Spirit-filled*

Because the approach being developed stands within the Catholic moral tradition, it sees (as George Lobo, Oliver O'Donovan, Yves Congar, and Karl Rahner do) that a person's moral development and his or her moral decision-making will be assisted at every point by the power of God's Spirit.[20] This theory affirms that authentic Christian living is not so much the exercise of natural virtue (as Pelagius taught), but conscious cooperation with the actions of the Spirit in a world-order that has been restored by God's saving work in Christ. It accepts, further, that the Spirit makes the reality of redemption present in *authoritative* ways—through special gifts (charisms), ritual sacraments (baptism, eucharist), and creation ("the world is charged with the grandeur of God")—raising up women and men to be spiritual leaders and moral guides because they have been given the Spirit's gifts of wisdom, courage, love, generosity, and forgiveness.[21]

This theory holds that the Spirit makes redemption present in an authoritative way through the Church's liturgy, its preaching and hymn singing, its missionary work, and apostolic initiatives.[22] With Aquinas, following Paul, this ethic holds that "the new law of Christ consists mainly in the grace of the Holy Spirit which is inscribed in the hearts of the faithful—and given by faith in Christ."[23]

Furthermore, in this theory the Spirit is seen to evoke our personal responses as moral agents (as Paul said in Phil. 2:13), and does so in such a way that our responses and the actions that flow from them are free.[24] Further, using themes central to Teilhard de Chardin, this theory holds that because the redemptive work of the Spirit involves both the restoration of the natural and human orders, as well as our access to reality (as O'Donovan says), all genuine moral effort is, in fact, working with Christ—to "amorize the cosmos," i.e., to bring love into it, since "love alone is capable of uniting living beings in such a way as to complete and fulfill them, for it [love] alone takes them and joins them by what is deepest in themselves."[25]

Monika Hellwig describes the Spirit's role in history in these words: "the work of the Spirit which is the power of grace, is to liberate human creativity, not to crush it or substitute for it."[26] Moreover, such love in the lives of Christians who are striving to follow Christ and to respond to the Spirit will be more than an assertion of themselves—it will be a conscious effort to recognize others, as Stanley Hauerwas writes.[27] It will be a love (at its infrequent best) that does not impose upon another an agent's preconceived image of who he or she is, nor a love that makes him or her simply aspects of an agent's own plans. This human love—Christ-like and Spirit-filled—will strive (but usually fail) to avoid loving others whom we have created in our own likeness through fantasy.

Finally, in recognizing the place of the Spirit in human action, this theory sees that human efforts aimed at restoring creation and building God's kingdom cannot be achieved (as Karl Raher realized) in "gnostic mystic interiority alone," but in mutual brotherly love—in relationships with others, in expressing our solidarity with those working for social justice, clean environments, improved health care, the elimination of the scourge of TB, polio and AIDS. This ethical approach gives contemporary meaning and relevance to John's words, "If anyone says 'I love God' and hates his brother, he is a liar; for he who does not love his brother whom he sees, cannot love God whom he has not seen (I John 4:20). It appreciates that "God is experienced in and through our love toward our fellowmen [sic] and the world, realizing fully that we ourselves are not the ultimate source of this human love and the secular involvement," as Edward Schillebeeckx's wrote in 1969.[28]

d) This moral theory is *biblical*

Sufficient has been said on this subject in earlier chapters. What the *Catechism of the Catholic Church* says about Scripture, its place in the Church's life, and its authority in the Church's thought, should be incorporated into this moral theory, in particular such statements as: "in sacred Scripture, the Church constantly finds her nourishment and her strength, for she welcomes it not as a human word, 'but as what it really is, the word of God.' In the sacred books, the Father who is in heaven comes lovingly to meet his children, and talks with them" (104).[29]

e) This moral theory is *ecclesial*

Current Catholic theology sees the Church as "the people of God established by Christ in his body through the power of the Holy Spirit in order to realize the kingdom of God," as Kevin McNamara wrote in 1965.[30] It considers the "people of God" as a *holy people*—whose vocation is to separate itself from "the world" (evil, sin, impiety) and to cling to God (a calling with obvious and far-reaching moral implications). From the time of John and Paul, Christians have consistently affirmed that "God wants to save men through community. He wants one organism, one medium of His saving presence in the world. This is the Church, the Spirit-filled community, the Body of Christ," as Vatican II says in *Lumen Gentium* (52). While God calls all persons to salvation, and calls individuals (as history shows) into culturally, linguistically, religiously, and geographically diverse communities, nevertheless, God (we believe) calls people—in God's own mysterious ways—to the Church, God's instrument of union and unity (ibid., 1), which does not exist for itself, but for the sake of humankind—to be humanity's family, beacon of light, and leaven of communion for all.[31]

Just as James Gustafson's ethic falls consciously within the Reformed tradition, this moral theory no less consciously lies within the Catholic tradition. Furthermore, the approach being presented here sees any ethic, even the most original and independent, as necessarily being sensitive to the morality and teaching structure of the faith-community to which it adheres. Like Kansas City jazz or Russian literature, the ethic (to merit the title Reformed or Catholic) should respect certain theological images and doctrinal tenets central to its community; it should give due respect to established moral positions on fundamental matters within its tradition. To be worthy of the name that it is taking, an ethic should adjust (where possible) to its faith-community's stands on such matters as authorities, the rules for responsible criticism, and dissent from the community's moral teaching. Such an ethic will have the prophetic responsibility of calling back its "home" community to moral insights that have been forgotten (e.g. to show greater concern for the poor).

This means that those who follow this moral theory will form ethical opinions and make moral decisions within the context of Catholic theology's current ecclesiology, with its insights into the teaching authority of the Church, council, pope, bishop, and the respect that these should be shown by individuals within the Catholic Church. The Catholic position on the authority of conscience will be important in forming one's opinion on this subject. Works such as the *Catechism of the Catholic Church* will have their place in Catholic life and thought.

At the same time, Catholics should remember that God calls women and women to respond to the Spirit as Paul, Augustine, Francis of Assisi, Joan of Arc, and Dorothy Day did. God calls Christians to build the future. At all times, any ethic seeking to be Christian should assist Christian individuals and communities to see that they must "at all costs avoid giving the impression that moral answers to particular problems are quite evident in advance of any research into the economic, psychological, medical, or social facts of the matter," as Gerard J. Hughes warns.[32] The ethic should be communicative (as Sharon Welch's); it should build *solidarity* (like Gutierrez's)—and advance God's kingdom of justice, love, and peace.

f) This moral theory is *personal*

The person is not the central focus of this moral theory. However, as George V. Lobo rightly says, "Christian morality is not an abstract, lifeless system of imperatives, a maze of laws and principles. What is distinctive about Christian ethics is the basic structure of God's self-gift to man and man's response to that gift in Jesus Christ. It is the way of life that is derived from the covenant relationship into which God has entered with man [*sic*] through the Christ-event."[33] Christian morality, as argued above, is therefore God-focused.

At the same time, Louis Janssens, Bernard Haring, Richard McCormick, Monika Hellwig, and others are right to emphasize such aspects of the human person as autonomy and self-realization, creativity and responsibility, to stress dignity and freedom in an age of unparalleled organization and socialization, as George V. Lobo points out (op. cit., 96). They are correct to emphasize that Catholic theology sees the person as an "image of God," and the Christian life as a personal response to the call of a personal God—that implies a call to community (personal relationships with the Church), as Lobo further explains (ibid., 102–105).[34]

g) This moral theory is *liberational*

The goal of any authentic Christian ethics should not be pleasure or rational self-interest, nor should such an ethic be focused on achieving "personal" goods or maintaining the *status quo*. Since, as Enda McDonagh rightly points out, the Christian ethic is "the living expression in human activity of God's self-gift to man in Jesus Christ," it follows that such a moral theory is "an ethic of the kingdom or kingship (sovereignty) of God."[35] The purpose of this ethic is to establish God's kingship in human hearts, and "to make this kingdom a reality on earth as it was in heaven" (ibid., 39).

At the same time, this is an ethics of "love and freedom, truth and conversion" (ibid., 40). Further, any authentic Christian ethic should be an ethic of freedom and liberation—one that emphasizes the liberating or saving aspect of God's activity in revelation" (ibid., 40). Jesus, Francis of Assisi, Joan of Arc, Martin Luther King, Jr. Dorothy Day, and Cesar Chavez will be this ethic's models.

Consequently, as Enda McDonagh argues, this means "community building becomes the criterion or norm of morality"—and one of the primary principles of this moral theory becomes clear: whatever human activity promotes this community is a correct response to God and morally good activity; "Whatever activity hinders or disrupts the community is a failure in response, morally bad activity" (ibid., 53).

Given the support which the theory being presented here gives to W. D. Ross's insights into morality and moral decision-making, the statements above mean that morally right and morally wrong decisions will be assessed largely in terms of how an agent responds to his or her discerned *prima facie* responsibilities about community-building actions. One's *prima facie* responsibilities toward self-improvement, for instance, will be balanced by one's responsibilities toward repairing the damage one has done to another's reputation or financial security. Whether a person has acted in a way that is morally good will be judged in terms of that person's correct weighing of her *prima facie* responsibilities toward avoiding pain and suffering in a dying neighbor, and one's responsibilities toward one's profession, one's family's good name, and one's own future and financial livelihood.[36]

Returning to Mount Athos: How Theology
Works in This Theory

"Modern society is not geared to produce, receive, or respect 'the educated mind,' and it is hard to imagine anyone in his senses claiming the title as an honor," Jacques Barzun said in 1950. The same might be said about the "theological mind." However, this state of affairs, as well as the fact that millions cannot sit still in a room, should be a cause for lament, not joy—for concern instead of indifference. Christians committed to the "natural law" approach and those who use the Bible in a literal way in business or bioethics will not support the methodology being proposed here: namely, that scriptural narratives and images (final judgment, God as judge), as well as central theological doctrines (Trinity, Incarnation) have legitimate places as forces shaping personal consciences and moral imaginations, to be sources of ethical motivation and inspiration.

This theory also supports the use of Scripture, Jesus' moral teaching in particular, as "second order" (specific norms) that provide both framework and direction in making individual moral decisions. It is not opposed to a person's using one of the commandments in the Decalogue or one of Jesus' aphorisms about forgiveness ("But I say to you, if your brother does something wrong, reprove him, and if he is sorry, forgive him. And if he wrongs you seven times a day and seven times comes back to you and says, 'I am sorry,' you must forgive him" (Luke 17:4) in somewhat the same way that authors recommend the use of philosophical standards ("quality of life", "care," or "best interests") to make decisions in bioethics.

Further, as James Gustafson argued, this ethic sees that there is more justification for Christians using specifically scriptural standards in making moral decisions than for using purely "rational" norms. This ethic prefers that Christian ethicists should apply Jesus' example and words about mercy, for instance, in making decisions about the appropriate care for a woman in a persistent vegetative state like Terri Schiavo, rather than seeing them argue about whether or not the treatment that she is receiving constitutes "ordinary" or "extraordinary means." The theory sees greater justification for using specifically "Christian" arguments rather than the argument that care in these cases does not constitute an intelligent use of medical resources, or that the treatment's burdens outweigh its benefits.[37]

However, this moral theory sees Christian creeds and central Christian doctrines as the primary sources of Christian morality and spirituality. It advocates a return to developing ethics and making moral decisions on the basis of these foundations instead of reason or natural laws. It encourages greater affinity with Orthodox moral methods rather than the "modern" methodology encouraged by Enlightenment philosophers.[38]

This shift will mean that Catholic positions on justice issues, for example, will flow from creedal statements and prayer forms that specifically reflect the Church's longstanding lived traditions about care for "the widow, the poor, and the orphan." Rather than canon laws that embody punitive and punishing prohibitions that destroy "sinners," Catholic moral theology will proclaim the message of redemption and liberation, of unconditional forgiveness found in the Church's baptismal liturgy, its prayers for the dead, and its sacramentaries and books of blessings.

Lex orandi lex credendi will once again be central to moral (not simply Catholic) dogmatic theology. The Church's faith, its long-held yet ever developing beliefs about life and death, wealth and poverty, honesty and truth, as well as the Christian community's insights into human values and weightiest duties—whether it is "just" to give a huge tax cut to the nation's wealthiest, or wage pre-emptive war against a dubious enemy—will be the ground and basis of Catholic ethical statements by bishops, female or male lay leaders who are presidents of Catholic colleges and universities, or CEOs of medical centers sponsored by the Sisters of Mercy or the Dominican Sisters.

This moral theory construes Christian morality as a thoroughly Christian way of being and acting—as embodying the virtues that Jesus taught, the actions central to Jesus himself, his disciples, and the legions of Christian saints who have embraced God's revelation in Christ at different times and places, in times of crisis and calm, in cultures as different as medieval Italy and modern day Australia. In other words, this approach sees the real possibility of Christian communities and individuals articulating an authentic Christian ethic adapted to culture, gender, and age, in much the same ways as communities and individuals develop authentic Christian spiritualities or aesthetics—distinctive expressions of religious beliefs, worldviews, and understandings of life and death, self and others.

This ethic rejects Richard McCormick's hybrid moral methodology, in which "faith-informed reason" has the ability to reach the ethical principles embodied in God's self-revelation in Christ as proclaimed in the lived prayer and spirit of the authentic heroes (saints) of the historic Christian community. It rejects the opinion that

a person's "potential for human relationships," for example, is a satis-
factory norm for resolving decisions about the care of seriously ill
newborns. It does not support McCormick's position that Christian
morality makes good sense apart from the Christian story, whether
lived or written. As well, this theory rejects both Roman Catholic and
Evangelical "fundamentalism." Contemporary Christian life in today's
complex economic, political, social, and cultural problems cannot be
solved by knee-jerk recourse to Bible texts, nor to the encyclicals of
Pius XII, John XXIII, or Pope John Paul II.

Positively, this means that American Christians will hold opinions
and behave in ways different in both literary content and behavioral
features from their neighbors who are secular Jews, European
Marxists, or Trobian Islanders. In the way they formulate and express
their moral positions, as well as in the way they justify their decisions,
Catholics will be authentically Catholic, just as Jews, Muslims, and
Hindu-Buddhists will be genuinely themselves—in their own times,
places, cultures, and linguistic and thought patterns.

Of course, all people who seek justice will possess some common
aspirations and moral norms; their general principles and practical
norms will not be radically different. However, those who profess
Christian beliefs will be guided by narratives and images, leaders
and models that are religiously and ethically distinctive—and their
justifications for their specific decisions will be drawn from sources
peculiar to the Catholic traditions—the lives of saints, the poetry of
mystics, and the high crosses of Ireland, Scotland, and France.

Spearheading This Renewal: Authentic Christian Voices

Besides the well-known Catholics (Karl Rahner, Bernard Haring,
Yves Congar, Eduardo Boff, Gustavo Gutierrez, Hans Urs von
Balthasar, Charles Curran, Enda McDonagh, and Edward
Schillebeeckx's) and Protestants (James Gustafson, Joseph Fletcher,
Paul Ramsey, Paul Ricoeur, Sharon Welch, Stanley Hauerwas) all of
whom have been leaders in the worldwide, post-WWII efforts to renew
Christian ethics, a number of other (if less well-known) contemporary
authors have spearheaded this "renewed" way of doing Christian ethics.
And their work that builds upon earlier leaders of the renewal, and
embodies original insights as well, should be mentioned here.

Stephen H. Webb provides an illuminating example of the use of
doctrine to make moral decisions in *The Gifting God: A Trinitarian*

Ethics of Excess (1996).[39] From what Christians have come to con-clude about God's gift-giving activity and its appropriateness as a Christian virtue, Webb defends human acts of altruism and generosity. On the basis of his reading of Scripture and theology, Webb employs the classic principle *Bonum est diffusivum sui* (Goodness is diffusive of itself) to justify gift-giving, and the inter-related convictions, first, that *divine excess begets reciprocity* (ibid., 90), and second, that "God is also persistently involved in our giving, sustaining our participation in the unfolding of God's great generosity" (ibid., 91). Consequently, gifts are able to be reconstrued as neither pains nor rewards. Gift-giving does not necessarily involve self-punishment or loss, Webb affirms. "Gifting is a process that combines elements of risky and disruptive excess with anticipated and grateful mutuality in a circle ... that never ends where it begins, but keeps spiraling outward in increasingly inclusive loops of expansion and consolidation, movement and rest" (ibid., 158).

The Oxford theologian Oliver O'Donovan has developed a moral theory in which Christ's resurrection and the impact of that liberating and restoring event on the world-order become the basis for under-standing human freedom, history, and morality in terms of thanks-giving and response to God's grace. In the revised 2nd edition of *Resurrection and Moral Order: An Outline for Evangelical Ethics* (1994),[40] O'Donovan depicts morality as participation in the created order (ibid., 76) and Christian morality as the "glad response to the deed of God which has restored, proved, and fulfilled that order" (ibid., 76).

Finally, Celia Deane-Drummond provides a third example of this approach in her *Creation Through Wisdom: Theology and the New Biology* (2000),[41] where she argues that the theological motif of Old Testament "wisdom," that becomes more manifest in the New Testament and Patristic theologies, needs to be recovered by Christians as a response to current developments in biology (ibid., 234–248). Deane-Drummond suggests the use of Aquinas's use of wisdom as a practical basis for ethics, and shows how strands of both the Eastern and Western wisdom traditions might be used as a framework for an authentic Christian theology of creation (ibid., 73–111).

Each of these authors assists in throwing light upon the way that today's Christians might be inspired, motivated, and guided in making decisions as spouses, health care providers, corporate managers, or military officers. In distinctive ways that reflect their personal selves, cultures, religious and philosophical experiences and traditions, Webb, O'Donovan, and Deane-Drummond imply that Paul's exhortation to his readers that they might have in them the mindset that was in Christ Jesus (Philippians 2:5) will be the standard by which today's Christians will assess motives; that Jesus' concern for the "widow, poor, and orphan"—embodied in Christians like Justin, Martyr, Martin of Tours, Ambrose of Milan, Catherine of Siena, Nano Nagle, John Hughes (New York's Archbishop "Dagger" John Hughes, who founded Fordham University and built the first St. Patrick's Cathedral), Dorothy Day, and Mother Teresa—women and men in whose spirits and behavior we see lived expressions of God's mercy and compassion: the correct norms for assessing the morality of human behavior toward others—whether neighbors or enemies.[42]

While such theological theories do not provide a set of common "rules of thumb," or practical principles as we find in traditional Catholic medical ethics—and the approaches might confuse and divide both the religious and scientific communities (one of the major criticisms against using specifically religious theories in bioethics discussions, according to Richard McCormick)—the time has come for Christian theologians to follow in the footsteps of James Gustafson and Gustavo Gutierrez, and all others who recognize that renewing Catholic moral theology means developing a "religious" ethic—one grounded in Christian theology and focused on grace, righteousness, and life (both here an in the future) in the Spirit.

Conclusion: A Trinitarian Ethic of Personal Responsibilities

Catholic theology depicts God's actions ad extra in terms of boundless expressions of love; it sees the appropriate human reaction as eucharistic response. Consequently, Thomistic moral theology has frequently expressed the ethical life not in terms of one's obligations to obey the commands found in the Decalogue (the approach we find in *The Catechism of the Catholic Church*), but in terms of responsibilities—to God, self, neighbor, church, and society.[43]

The Christian ethic being presented here stands in this tradition; it maintains that moral maturity means creative awareness of one's personal responsibilities, rather than scrupulous observance of general rules or moral commands; it implies wrestling with one's weighty duties rather than making careful calculations of the consequences of one's actions. In keeping with the thrust of Sir William David Ross's writings, in particular his emphasis on "mental maturity" as a requirement for making correct moral decisions (*Right*, 31), this theory encourages not only being aware of the central tenets of one's theological tradition, the long-held stand of one's religious community on baptism, justification, the authority of conscience, the priesthood of the laity, the seriousness of deliberate sin, the importance of mercy, compassion, caring, but also: (1) an emphasis on creativity and responsible autonomy in decision-making, and (2) reasoned respect for social relationships. It treats moral agents with dignity; it takes rights and duties seriously.

In this theory, moral maturity means taking up all the loved details of one's ethical and religious inheritance, the painful lessons of one's mistakes, as well as the happy memories of one's ethical successes, and weaving them into behavior (one's own story) in which one's own and one's community's historical past and personal present are inter-mingled, as they are in the Jewish celebration of Passover or the Christian celebration of Easter (especially in the new Roman rite for the Easter Vigil) in which one sees one's life and fate, one's birth and eternal future, situated in one's own and one's generation's sense and grasp of time—as imperfect as that grasp and understanding will always be.[44]

To recap: Besides accepting the positive place of mythopoeic thinking alongside metaphysical and functional modes of thought, this moral theory recognizes the *pictorial* nature of Christianity. While scholars have spread Christ through theological tomes, pictures and pictographs have been the far more common means of instruction—because those who created them were pastors who knew that much of Christianity's power lay in its ability to move hearts as well as minds; that Christianity's painted portraits and colored walls depicting the sin of Adam and Eve, or Jesus' death on the cross, spoke not simply to the unlearned but to the scholar, reminding both that each was created in God's image, saved through God's work in Christ, and destined to be blessed forever.

Further, this ethic supports liberation theology's emphasis on the importance of *praxis* in the building of an authentic Christian under-standing of reality, the moral life, and ethical character. Using this approach and illuminated by the Christian "story," children will not be encouraged to make moral decisions in terms of "What's in this for me?" Nor will they be taught to look at issues in terms of "What course of action will produce the greatest amount of personal success or pleasure?" Rather, they will be tutored to learn the lessons that

Christianity sees embodied in its foundational narratives, parables, and life-histories—to ask themselves, *"What is my responsibility?"* They will be encouraged to see Christ's story as their own, his fidelity to God's will and his willing acceptance of his responsibilities as the core of the Christian moral life.

In order to do this, children and adults (as we will see in greater detail when discussing moral development) will be educated through examining Christian narratives and stories: (1) to recognize the moral qualities that reside in human actions and personal characters, to notice by head and heart "goodness" (mercy, generosity, simplicity) and "nobility" (forgiveness, bravery) in much the same way as they recognize "beauty" in music, painting, dance, nature, and sport; (2) to appreciate that there are both general and special responsibilities arising from their own and others' past or present actions (that result in harm or benefit), as well as from acts which put them under immediate obligations (e.g. vows, oaths, contracts, promises, verbal agreements). They will be guided to see that they have definite respon-sibilities toward themselves (self-improvement, health, avoiding danger), neighbors (to build fences, healthy communities, schools), God (worship, liturgy), society (to be responsible, informed citizens), and church (to be involved, active); and (3) to know that mature moral decision-making means well-reasoned, informed discernment (listen-ing to one's heart, using one's head) about their actual responsibilities in specific circumstances, given their relationships, roles, commitments, and the consequences of acting or not acting, doing A, B, or C.

By learning in supportive settings to make decisions in this way, children and adolescents will not only be developing moral maturity (skills, knowledge) as well as moral character (habits, virtues), but they will also be building stable relationships and healthy communities—they will be engaged in personal and social liberation, as they will be overcoming the twin demons of fear and guilt, and they will be creating healthy networks. While this approach recognizes the place at times for "tough love," it discourages harsh discipline that older gen-erations still associate with their years at Catholic schools sponsored by the Christian Brothers or the Presentation Sisters.

This ethic recognizes the significance that affirmation plays in healthy psychological life, and the destructive power of deprivation.[45] It is concerned as well that parents and teachers do not crush a child's "creativity" or "spontaneous confidence in life"—one of the great dangers of the modern age in the opinion of Gabriel Marcel—who believed that, "It is this, and this alone, which enables man [*sic*] to establish his roots in the universe and to develop to his full stature."[46]

However, children will not be told to make decisions in terms of theology's cosmic relationships (as Gustafson's theory implies), but simply in terms of their established relationships—and those relationships within their horizons. (There are sufficient difficulties here, and no moral theory should demand the impossible).[47] Education, especially that sponsored by Christian communities at times like First Communion and Confirmation, will emphasize sensitivity as well as cognitive development, emotional as well as intellectual maturity—it will emphasize "wisdom" as Celia Deane-Drummond suggests, and developing the moral imagination.[48] Such education will teach that caring, knowledge, generosity, and character are crucial to both the process and the implementation of moral decisions.

In order for a Christian to possess an adult, mature morality and a developed, personal character, the Christian story, its metaphors and symbols, must be creatively communicated so that they result in *passionate zeal*—the distinctive feature of Judean religion—and *creative thought*.[49] The authentic telling of God's work in Christ—purified from its un-Christian elements—must be the foundation of the Christian's life-style and being-in-the-world. Christian ethics cannot be separated from Christian theology and spirituality. Christian morality cannot be separated from God's saving-work-in-Christ, and the multiform account of the Christian story-intime.

Notes:

[1] It is important to note here Clifford Geertz's remark that "narrative is the form of rationality especially appropriate for ethics." In his *The Interpretation of Cultures* (New York: Basic Books, 1973), 89.

[2] David Tracy writes, "It is true that the historical memory of a people is the principal carrier of the history of effects of the classic texts, persons, events, symbols, rituals of that people. It is also true that a loss of those memories, in either an individual or a communal sense, can be fatal to participation in a culture. For without them we cannot act." In *Plurality and Ambiguity*, op. cit., 36. Because of Amos Wilder's realization of the positive place of myth and the importance of mythopoeic language within Christianity, myth-making and memory, the place of poetry and imagination have been central themes throughout the life of the journal *Christianity and Literature*. For comments on these subjects, Martin E. Marty, "Christianity and Literature: Covertly Public, Overtly Private," *Christianity and Literature*, 47, 3 (Spring 1998), 261–283; Eleanor J. McNees, *Eucharistic Poetry: The Search for Presence in the*

Writings of John Donne, Gerard Manley Hopkins, Dylan Hopkins, and Geoffrey Hill (Lewisburg: Bucknell University Press, 1992).

[3] On this subject, Robert J. O'Connell, *Soundings in St. Augustine's Imagination* (New York: Fordham University Press, 1994).

[4] Michael E. Allsopp, "G. M. Hopkins, Narrative, and the Heart of Morality," *Irish Theological Quarterly* 60, 4 (1994), 287–307.

[5] Some examples: Abraham's morally correct obedience to God (his acceptance of the fact that he would be the father of a great nation although Sarah was past the time of having children) reflects the first view of religious ethics, whereas Paul's writings indicate that he made some moral decisions (about marriage, wealth, service) not only on the basis of common sense and Jewish custom—but also because of his "religious" belief that "the time is short," and therefore, that "those with wives should live as though they had none".

[6] For an interesting study concerning the way that the 18th century English authors Pope, Richardson, and Fielding, as well as English Protestant educated society in general, interpreted the story of Job in conflicting ways to explain and deal with life's disappointments, failures, and sufferings through plays, essays, sermons, cartoons, and novels, Jonathan Lamb, *The Rhetoric of Suffering: Reading the Book of Job in the Eighteenth Century* (Oxford: Clarendon Press, 1995). The religious, cultural, ethical, and political opinions that marked Irish-American Catholics and set them apart from Italian-American Catholics can be seen when Eugene O'Neill's plays or John O'Hara's novels (*Appointment in Samarra*, in particular) are compared with Mario Puzio's novels. These differences are even more marked when one compares Irish-American Catholic experience as recorded by O'Neill and O'Hara with the African-American experience as found in James Weldon Johnson, Toni Morrison, and Ralph Ellison.

[7] Following her presentation during the annual meeting of the Society for the Study of Christian Ethics held in Oxford in fall 1998, Welch made it clear that she no longer held a traditional concept of God, and that her "image" of God had changed significantly since the time she wrote *A Feminist Ethic of Risk*.

[8] Because a mature image of God must be inevitably complex, and using God's actions as a model for one's own behavior will lead to behavior that is morally questionable among contemporary Christians, this ethic uses the Catholic theology of God, and the Church's current moral teaching as guides for today's Catholics as they seek to develop ethical frameworks, visions of life, and value systems.

[9] Hans Urs von Balthasar, *The God Question & Modern Man*, edited by John Macquarrie (New York: Seabury Press, 2nd Printing, 1967).

[10] Ethical monotheism is not the distinctive feature of biblical religion, since all higher religions proclaim the high moral standards of their deity. Rather, transcendent monotheism—the conviction that God is beyond nature, and nature's creator—is the unique aspect of Judaism and its daughter faiths, or as Stephen A. Geller says, "The logical relationship of a zealous transcendent God lies at the heart of biblical religion and runs through all its aspects." Stephen A. Geller, *Sacred Enigmas: Literary Religion in the Hebrew Bible* (New York: Routledge,1996),168–194.

[11] On this subject, John Howard Yoder, *The Politics of Jesus* (Grand Rapids: Eerdmans, 1972).

[12] John Wijngaards, *God Within Us* (London: Collins, 1988).

[13] Bertrand Russell, *Why I Am Not a Christian* (New York: Simon & Shuster, 1957). On this subject, James Gaffney, "Is God a Retributivist?," in his *Matters of Faith and Morals* (Kansas City: Sheed and Ward, 1987), 16–28.

[14] For a recent illustration of the way that this understanding of God can be used to ground a case in support of generosity in modern life, Stephen H. Webb, *The Gifting God: A Trinitarian Ethics of Excess* (New York: Oxford University Press, 1996), 123–158, 182–189. As Webb admits, his model of God is based largely on that found in Catherine Mowry LaCugna's *God for Us: The Trinity and Christian Life* (San Francisco: HarperCollins, 1991).

[15] For a valuable study that attempts to speak to contemporary adults, John Wijngaards, *God Within Us*, op. cit., 57–72, 104–114, 155–163.

[16] Paul Tournier, *The Meaning of Persons* (New York: Harper & Row, 1973), 221. This work was originally published in French in 1957.

[17] For an invaluable study on the development of Merton's Christology and the role of Rahner's theology on Merton's thinking, George Kilcourse, *Ace of Freedoms: Thomas Merton's Christ* (Notre Dame: University of Notre Dame Press, 1993).

[18] On this subject, George V. Lobo, "Christocentric Morality," in *Guide to Christian Living*, op. cit., 107–124; Joseph Fuchs, "The Law of Christ," in *Moral Theology Renewed*, edited by Enda McDonagh, op. cit., 70–84; Enda McDonagh, "The Natural Law and the Law of Christ," in *Invitation and Response*, op. cit., 22–37; Richard A. McCormick, "Tradition in Transition," in *Riding Time Like a River: The Catholic Moral Tradition Since Vatican II*, edited by William J. O'Brien, op. cit., 17–33; Paul M. Quay, "The Theological Position and Role of Ethics," *Listening* 18, 3 (Fall, 1983), 260–274. Vincent MacNamara, *Faith & Ethics*, op. cit., 14–36, 69–94. N.H.G. Robinson, *The Groundwork of Christian Ethics*, op. cit., 94–99, "*Imitatio Christi*," 100–120. Gerard J. Hughes, "The Authority of Christian Tradition," in *Authority in Morals*, op. cit., 1–25; Vincent MacNamara, "Moral Life, Christian," *The New Dictionary of Catholic Social Thought*, op. cit., 635–650.

[19] Dietrich Bonhoeffer, *Ethics* (New York: Macmillan, 1955), 18, 55.

[20] George V. Lobo, *Guide to Christian Living: A New Compendium of Moral Theology*, op. cit., 142–167; Oliver O'Donovan, *Resurrection and The Moral Order: An Outline for Evangelical Ethics*, op. cit., 101–120.

[21] For an important study that provides the medieval and reformation contexts for contemporary discussions about God's Spirit, Stanley M. Burgess, *The Holy Spirit: Medieval Roman Catholic and Reformation Traditions* (New York: Hendrickson, 1997).

[22] As mentioned earlier, the position is taken here that such activities are inducive of salvation, moral growth, and right thinking—it does not hold that such activities are "truthful." Such activities are "prophetic" not "scientific"—and their goal is "conversion" not "information." Although written in 1965 and somewhat limited in its focus, I recommend the essay by Kevin MacNamara, "Life in Christ: Life in the Church," in *Moral Theology Renewed*, edited by Enda McDonagh, op. cit., 85–102. Also, Dermot Ryan's "The Mass in the Christian Life," ibid., 103–129, because this essay is rich in its appreciation of Scripture, although it does contain some (needless) insensitivities, e.g. about the "avoidance of strife with one's fellow worshippers" (128).

[23] Aquinas' *Summa Theologiae*, I, II, 106, i. Also 106, ii.

[24] "It is this freedom that makes Christian ethics meaningful, and indeed demands it," O'Donovan writes. "For freedom is the character of one who participates in the order of creation by knowledge and action. That man is free implies that he can know and act; thus moral enquiry is a meaningful undertaking for him" (ibid., 107).

[25] Lobo, op., cit., 152. Teilhard's words are from *The Phenomenon of Man* (London: Collins, 1959), 265.

[26] Monika K. Hellwig, *Understanding Catholicism*, 2nd Edition (New York: Paulist Press, 2002), 3.

[27] For Hauerwas' own words, *Vision and Virtue* (Notre Dame: Fides, 1974), 33–52.

[28] Edward Schillebeeckx's, *God and Man* (New York: Sheed and Ward, 1969), 164–165.

[29] For a valuable summary and critique of recent work on this subject, Bernard Brady, "The Bible and Ethical Theory," in his *The Moral Bond of Community: Justice and Discourse in Christian Morality* (Washington, D.C.: Georgetown University Press, 1998), 71–89, 161–163. There is much to reflect upon throughout this chapter, as well as in Brady's positions that "moral discourse addresses the conditions for the possibility of human flourishing" (77), "Jesus was not a philosopher" (88), and in his acceptance of Philip Selznick's conclusion that justice "does not invoke the noblest human virtues—love, sympathy, courage, self-sacrifice; it is not a promise of moral perfection" (89).

[30] Kevin McNamara, "Life in Christ: Life in the Church," in *Moral Theology Renewed*, edited by Enda McDonagh, op. cit., 85–102.

[31] For further on this subject, Enda McDonagh, "The Christian Ethic: A Community Ethic," in *Invitation and Response: Essays in Christian Moral Theology*, op. cit., 38–58. Also, Richard A. McCormick, "Moral Theology from 1940–1989," in *Corrective Vision: Explorations in Moral Theology*, op. cit., 1–22, esp. "Vatican II and Ecclesiology" (5–6); McCormick's "Moral Theology in the Year 2000," ibid., 23–39, esp. 28–30, 34–35; "The Search for Truth in a Catholic Context," ibid., 69–82; "Theologians and the Magisterium," ibid., 82–99; Joseph Selling, "Authority and Moral Teaching in a Catholic Christian Context," in *Christian Ethics: An Introduction*, op. cit., 57–71; Francis A. Sullivan, *Magisterium: Teaching Authority in the Catholic Church* (New York: Paulist Press: 1983); Gerard J. Hughes, "Authority in the Christian Community," in *Authority in Morals*, op. cit., 91–121, 135–136, and 122–131. And the valuable collection of essays in *The Magisterium and Morality, Readings in Moral Theology #3*, edited by Charles E. Curran and Richard A. McCormick (New York: Paulist Press, 1982).

[32] Gerard J. Hughes, *Authority in Morals*, op. cit., 125.

[33] Goerge V. Lobo, op. cit., 90.

[34] For further on this subject, Louis Janssens, "Personalist Morals," *Louvain Studies* 3 (1970), 5–16; Bernard Haring, *Morality is for Persons* (New York: Farrar, Straus & Giroux, 1971); Joseph Selling, "The Human Person," in *Christian Ethics: An Introduction*, op. cit., 95–109.

[35] Enda McDonagh, "The Christian Ethic: A Community Ethic," *Invitation and Response: Essays in Christian Moral Theology*, op. cit., 38–58.

[36] As readers will have realized, the above builds upon Enda McDonagh, "Moral Theology: The Need for Renewal," in *Moral Theology Renewed*, op. cit., 13–30;

George V. Lobo, *Guide to Christian Living*, op. cit., 18–22; Richard A. McCormick, "Moral Theology in the Year 2000," "Theology and Bioethics, in *Corrective Vision*, op. cit., 23–39, 133–148.

[37] The use of such "rational" principles, central to Richard McCormick's ethics, implies—as we have seen—that Christian morality is identical with rational morality, that the moral standards that Christians should use in making decisions in bioethics, for instance, are no different from those that "good" philosophers would use, an assumption that McCormick simply assumes and nowhere justifies.

[38] The Orthodox ethicist, Stanley Harakas, who authored the volume on *Health & Medicine in the Orthodox Tradition* in the widely used Crossroads Series, and a frequent contributor to recent debates in bioethics, provides a moral methodology that all Catholics should study carefully. Grounded in the great creeds and the theology central to the key prayer statements of the Church, this approach leads to practical moral conclusions that are more authentically Christian than those derived from William May's construing of "natural laws," and at the same time, they are much more sensitive to persons, cultures, and specific circumstances.

[39] Stephen H. Webb, *The Gifting God: A Trinitarian Ethics of Excess* (New York: Oxford University Press, 1996). This book provides a needed rehabilitation of altruism and sacrifice that have been pushed aside by the influence of Ayn Rand's objectivism (the most powerful ethic within the U.S. business community), and a strong undercurrent of Darwinism that continues to sweep through Western economics, emphasizing the "naturalness" of the superiority of the strong over the weak, and the harm done to the "natural order" when one assists the poor through compassion or beneficence.

[40] Oliver O'Donovan, *Resurrection and Moral Order: An Outline for Evangelical Ethics* (Grand Rapids: William B. Eerdmans, 1986, 1994). This major work in Christian ethics argues (first) that moral action must be "true" to the world, and (second) that this "truth" is constituted by adjusting one's own knowledge about the world to one's faith in what God has done for the world and for humankind—through his saving and empowering work in Christ. Thus, what O'Donovan calls the "Easter" principle must be combined with the "realist" principle. Separating his approach from both Matthew Fox's "creation ethics" and theologians who propose a "kingdom ethics," O'Donovan develops an ethic in which the order established by Jesus' resurrection flows into Christian baptism—with its regenerative impact and gifts of the Spirit, plus the "eucharist" in its sacramental and inspirational forms, both of which support the call to humans to new life, new vision, and new being and living—to become new persons (priests, prophets, kings) in community, members of the "people of God" that have both authority to instruct and authority to command.

[41] Celia E. Deane-Drummond, *Creation Through Wisdom: Theology and the New Biology* (Edinburgh: T&T Clark, 2000). Dedicated to Sergii Bulgakov (1871–1944), this book builds upon the author's earlier published essays on "Sophia," biology, and genetics, to argue that as the new millennium begins, science need not be as secular as it appears to nonscientists (an insight support by Paul Tournier in the 1940s), and that a meaningful point of contact between science and theology can occur in "the theological meaning of wisdom" (xiv). By elaborating the Bible's themes about Wisdom (as Eternal Feminine, Holy Spirit), and illustrating their places in the theologies of Bulgakov and Teilhard de Chardon, the author proposes the use of wisdom as

a basis for Christian ethics—in much the same way that Nel Noddings has proposed "care" in biomedical ethics, and Joseph Fletcher presented "love." "A creation theology understood in these terms [that creation emerges in Love, but it is through Wisdom] has a bearing on theology's relationship with science," Deane-Drummond writes. "For now wisdom becomes the key underlying process, rather than simply information" (xv). And with Aquinas, she sees the final end of creation in "wisdom expressed through beauty."

[42] Using such standards in the way that the U.S. bioethicist Nel Noddings uses care to assess motives and actions, will mean, for instance, that the desire for vengeance following a murder of one's daughter will be seen as understandable but not Christian, while the widespread attitude among contemporary American Christians that they have no serious moral duty to share their wealth with the less fortunate, especially those who are outside their "family" (natural, religious) will also be viewed as unethical.

[43] For an example of this, Paul J. Gleason, *An Introduction to Philosophy* (St. Louis: Harder Book Company, 144, 10th printing, 1955), 383–395.

[44] There is wisdom in Monika Hellwig's reminder that "the message of God's self-revelation in Jesus has come to us through a number of channels, none of which is free from human error and the ambiguities of history." *Understanding Catholicism*, op. cit., 3.

[45] For an important study on these subjects, Jack Dominian, "The Cycle of Human Affirmation," in *Affirming the Human Personality: Psychological Essays in Christian Living*, op. cit., 152–169.

[46] Gabriel Marcel, *Homo Viator: Introduction to a Metaphysic of Hope*, translated by Emma Craufurd (New York: Harper & Brothers, 1962), 119.

[47] Critics of utilitarianism claim that it is too demanding (a) in its emphasis on always maximizing the benefits of actions, and (b) in not allowing any purely selfish behavior. *A fortiori*, Gustafson's ethic seems to be even more demanding.

[48] This has been a subject of greater interest in moral education programs. One useful new work is Edward Stevens, *Developing Moral Imagination: Case Studies in Practical Morality* (Kansas City: Sheed & Ward, 1997).

Chapter IX

A Christian Ethic of Responsibilities: The Ground of Morality, Right Actions, Ethical Principles

The greatest commandment in the law is to love God with one's whole heart and one's neighbor as oneself (cf. Mt. 22:37–40). Christ made this commandment of love of neighbor His own and enriched it with a new meaning.

Vatican II
Decree on the Laity

That which is right is right not because it is an act, one thing, which will produce another thing, an increase in the general welfare, but because it is itself the producing of an increase in the general welfare.

W. D. Ross
The Right and The Good

The will is absolutely good if it cannot be evil—that is, if the maxim, when made into a universal law, can never be in conflict with itself.

Immanuel Kant
Groundwork of the Metaphysic of Morals

To see is an act of judgment; to see clearly is an obligation of moral dimension. To choose not to see is an act of self-obliteration.

Marion Montgomery
Virtue and Modern Shadows of Turning

Ours is an age that reads too much, perhaps, to be wise, and thinks too much to be beautiful, as Oscar Wilde once said. However, in order for the ethic being proposed to be more complete, it is important to ask, "What is the subject matter of moral knowledge? What is it precisely that makes people feel moral obligations, or that they are doing the 'right thing'?"

The "Moral" and What Makes a "Right Action" Right?

Some ethicists argue, following A. J. Ayer, that moral judgments have no "real" subject matter, certainly no matter like the judgments made by physicists or biochemists, because moral judgments are essentially expressions of feelings, likes, or dislikes. The majority of Anglo-American philosophers, as well as the majority of Christian theologians, however, maintain that moral decisions do have some specifiable content. Ayn Rand, for instance, confidently defines morality in terms of "rational self-interest." Grisez and Finnis locate "right" and "wrong" in an action's respect or lack of respect for "basic human goods"; while Max Scheler posited a hierarchy of "values" grounded in ascending forms of love.[1]

Classic utilitarianism affirms not one but two interconnected foundations of moral obligation: one associated with producing pleasure, the other with maximizing pleasure. Because pleasure is the utilitarian's *summum bonum*, and moral acts are essentially pleasure-producing behavior-events, it follows that humans have a moral duty, first, to perform such acts; and, second, since it is rationally-persuasive to perform P5 rather than P1, P2, P3, P4 (where P1 stands for the least amount of pleasure an action produces, and P5 for the most), humans have a related duty to effectuate those acts which produce more pleasure than the other actions open to them as agents. In this theory, all "goods" are reducible to pleasure, and moral obligation is tied to securing and optimizing pleasure for oneself and/or others.[2]

The moral theory of responsibilities being proposed here affirms that moral decisions have definite and specific content. It rejects, however, Bentham's hedonistic as well as the more recent utilitarian responses on this subject. Pleasure does have its legitimate place in Christian living; it is a powerful motivator, but pleasure cannot be the Christian's *summum bonum*, nor can the moral life as construed by Christians be a "pig" morality—even a high-class "aesthetic" morality.

Furthermore, the Christian life cannot be adequately understood in terms of maximizing the socially beneficent outcomes of one's actions. The reason? There are six serious flaws in the utilitarian's theory of optimizing and maximizing socially useful benefits. First, the utilitarian's emphasis on maximization might be rationally cogent, but it is historically groundless. Where is the evidence that Socrates, Jesus, Muhammad, Martin Luther, or Mother Teresa sought to maximize the pleasurable (or socially useful) results of their actions? Second, the utilitarian is always forward-looking; his or her concern is exclusively about the outcomes of actions. Morality, however, requires that sometimes we look backward to what has taken place in the past: e.g., to a promise or vow made at a wedding ten years ago, or to the commitments associated with a mortgage on a house made fifteen years before. These past actions possess moral force regardless of the good consequences of some here-and-now action, and they cannot be dismissed or set aside simply because of "good" that might be produced in the future by our actions.

Third, utilitarianism is an ethics of calculation, not commitment; it is always weighing and balancing outcomes. The utilitarian has only one real responsibility—and that is not to persons, but to the maximization of optimum pleasures or socially useful goods. Fourth, the utilitarian's emphasis on maximizing pleasure does not make all "right" actions right. As Ross argues, "When a plain man fulfils a promise because he thinks he ought to do so, it seems clear that he does so with no thought of its total consequences, still less with any opinion that these are likely to be the best possible.... What makes him think it right to act in a certain way is the fact that he has promised to do so—that, and, usually, nothing more" (*Right,* 17).[3] In other words, there is something about the very nature of promise keeping or fidelity that is "right," and this cannot be outweighed simply by the act's pleasure-producing consequences.

There is a fifth reason to reject utilitarianism. The theory ignores (or at least does not do full justice to) the highly personal character of duty. As Ross says, "If the only duty is to produce the maximum good, the question who is to have the good—whether it is myself, or my benefactor, or a person to whom I have made a promise to confer that good on him, or a mere fellow man to whom I stand in no such special relation—should make no difference to my having a duty to produce that good. But we are all in fact sure that it makes a vast difference (ibid., 26).

Clearly, utilitarians oversimplify the moral relationships in which we stand toward others. They are soft on human rights, and hard on minorities, since their theory is, by definition, a majoritarian theory in which the happiness of the many will always have more weight than the rights and pleasures of the few.

Finally, the utilitarian ethic neither needs nor demands any specifically theological supports, since, like natural law morality, it is inherently an autonomous and naturalistic approach. As such, it renders revelation unnecessary; it severely undermines Christ's unique place in the history of morality—a weakness that it shares with all natural law moral theories, whether neo-Scholastic (William E. May's) or renewed (Richard A. McCormick's).[4]

All analyses of "right" and "good" are hazardous and leave room for debate. Nevertheless, there is rational support for the following positions: there is no need to collapse "rightness" and "goodness" into one principle or feature (*Foundations*, 82).[5] Certain moral dispositions and actions appear to be "good" in ways which depend entirely on their "intrinsic nature," i.e., they are conscientious or benevolent (ibid., 283). With Ross, the moral theory being presented here holds that an action's tendency to be "wrong" or "right" is a "*parti-resultant attribute*": i.e., one which belongs to an act in virtue of some component of its nature (*Right*, 28).

Further, morally good actions are "good" in a sense which is largely indefinable, but which may be paraphrased (as they are by Ross) by saying that they are "fine or admirable activities of the human spirit, and by adding that they are good in such a way that any one who has them or does them is to that extent being good himself. Pleasure is never good in this, which I should call the most proper sense of 'good'" (*Foundations*, 283).[6] It follows, therefore, that the primary basis of our awareness of moral duty lies first and foremost in a self-evident necessity (for Ross, a *prima facie* duty) to produce, to the best of our ability, these "fine or admirable activities."[7]

And how do we establish what are these "fine or admirable activities"? By looking hard (using reason, emotion, intuition) in an informed, educated way at our own and others past, present, and future actions in order to see which are "worthy" objects of satisfaction (ibid., 283). Now, as Ross indicates, some of these actions are "fine and admirable" because they lead to such "goods" as happiness,

self-improvement, or repayment of financial obligations, or they avoid
such "evils" as personal harm, injury, or loss of trust. Other actions are
simply "good" in themselves: e.g., promises, oaths; they are not
"good" because of what they cause, e.g. justice.[8]

"Goodness" therefore, in Ross's mind (and I share the belief),
though it is essentially intuited, is a property "inherent" in an action or
character; it is not, as it were, "stuck on objects or actions like postage
stamps, quite indifferently to any other features of those objects or
actions, nor are other properties quite irrelevant to goodness," as
Geoffrey Warnock notes.[9] And, as has been said above, we have a
prima facie duty to produce these "good" actions "to the best of our
ability, irrespective of whether it is ourselves or others that are going
to have or do them" (ibid., 283).

The Right, The Good, and Moral Responsibilities: Their Pluralistic Bases

I support the conclusion that the ground of morality is multiple,
not single, as Ross argues in his remarks about the ground of rightness
and moral obligation (*Foundations*, 57ff.), and also in his comments on
his provisional list of "authentic conditional duties" (*Right*, 26ff.). The
human awareness of "good" and "bad", "right" and "wrong" is associated with actions, relationships, duties, and outcomes. For instance, we
recognize that we have a duty to perform certain actions, and not to
perform others; that we have moral duties associated with the "mere
fact that there are other beings in the world whose condition we can
make better in respect of virtue, or of intelligence, or of pleasure" (ibid.,
24). We also know that we have other duties arising from obligations
both not to harm others and to resist an inclination to harm them (ibid.,
24).[10]

Furthermore, as Ross says, our actual experience of *prima facie*
duties arises "in highly complex ways" (ibid., 28). Their recognition is
grounded in our sense of self and respect for others, in our appreciation of others' kindnesses and sacrifices, and in our acknowledgment
of what we owe to those who have gone before us (parents,
colleagues), as well as those still to be born. "Or again, the sense of
general obligation to bring about (so far as we can) a just appontion-
ment of happiness to merit is often greatly reinforced by the fact that
many of the existing injustices are due to a social and economic system which we have not indeed created, but taken part in and assented

to: the duty of justice is then reinforced by a duty of reparation" (ibid., 28).

This means that moral "talk" is conversation about responsibilities, not principally about socially desirable goods or community values; it is discussion about *prima facie* duties, not consequences (benefits or burdens, potential for human relationships). It is conversation (with ourselves, others) about our *responsibilities* to ourselves, neighbors, state, and church—because of who we are and the roles that we have selected or been given—when we are faced with specific decisions about what we ought to do here and now because we are a soldier in combat, a ICU physician called to attend to a patient who might have AIDS, an exhausted teenage mother on welfare who has to take her two children to day care before being at work by 7:30 A.M.[11]

What is a "right" action? For an evangelical ethicist like John Jefferson Davis, a morally right action is one that is in keeping with and respects the Bible's infallible and divinely inspired ethical teaching. In the opinion of conservative Roman Catholics who have excessive respect for papal or episcopal magisteria, Catholics act morally when they faithfully and strictly adhere to papal or episcopal moral instruction, regardless of the arguments given, their own moral opinions, or those of other authoritative teachers, e.g., Bible, theologians. Loyalty and respect for papal teaching, regardless of its lack of inherent force, makes one's actions "right."

Further, as seen in Chapter 3, for Richard McCormick, "right actions" are those that respect both the *ordo bonorum*, and "right reason," whereas, "wrong actions" are those that disrupt both the *ordo bonorum,* and violate "right reason." Allowing somebody to die by removing nutrition and hydration would normally be immoral, because it would show a disregard for the *ordo bonorum* (human life, personhood). However, where a person is in a long-term persistent vegetative state and the prognosis is bleak (the person would most likely never again know his or her world or reestablish any human relationships), discontinuing nutrition and hydration would not be immoral because, on the one hand, it would "free" the patient from suffering and allow the medical community to make better use of expensive resources, on the other hand, it would allow him or her to enjoy paradise, and it would relieve the family and society from serious burdens. In other words, these "proportionate reasons" would permit disrupting the *ordo bonorum* in these particular circumstances—and would make an otherwise "wrong" action "right."

The theory being articulated here finds its answer to the question "What is a right action?" from a careful examination of human experience, the moral decision-making process, and the lives of women and men respected for their ethical stature. First, it holds that a right action when properly performed should not be the result of a simple (brain-jerk) reaction. Every life-changing decision (to divorce a spouse, kill a soldier in military combat, to allow one's own child to die) should involve mind and heart, prayer and research, private reflection, and public discussion.

Such actions should result from a complex process of sifting and sorting, separation and rejection. As those who have made major ethical decisions know, right actions are frequently fluid—what a person thought was right today can change tomorrow because of new knowledge, a new perspective, or one's emotional health. To be right (to have the feel and thought of being right) such actions must be compatible with one's self and one's value system—as well as the lives and belief-systems of significant others (peers, family, community).

On the basis of careful analysis of the historical record, right actions (in the Christian moral tradition) seem to have little to do with such things as pleasure (Bentham), happiness (Mill), personal integrity (Sartre), wholeness (Kennedy), self-interest (Rand), caring (Noddings), respecting "basic human goods" (Finnis, Grisez), or natural laws (William E. May). Being faithful to the pope might be in keeping with the virtue of "respect," but it does not guarantee that one's decision is morally correct.

In the approach being proposed, a morally right action (*personal*) is one that flows (as McCormick observed) from one's awareness of "goodness." However, rather than positing a hierarchy or *ordo bonorum*, and justifying exceptions to this order on the basis of proportionate reasons, this ethic proposes that "good" actions are those associated with one's intuitions of "goodness," while right actions are linked with one's considered decisions about an actual or absolute duty to perform a specific act in particular circumstances (ibid., 28). And a wrong act is one that, while it possesses "goodness," flows from what one knows is not in accord with one's weightiest duty, e.g. to spend money on one's own leisure (beer, cigarettes) as a way of responding to a duty to self (relax, reduce stress) when one knows that one has a weightier responsibility to spend the money on one's children's food, housing, or health care.[12]

Universally, a right act is one that respects not simply one's own awareness of goodness and an actual or absolute duty, but also corresponds and respects one's moral community's convictions about goodness and weightiest duties. It is an action that like "universal" beauty bears the force not of one's own considered opinion about goodness, but the added authority of one's moral (Christian, Jewish, Muslim) community's collective judgments.[13]

One example: a Catholic adult who is gay and who honestly holds that his actions are good and his weightiest duty is a duty to his sexual self-hood will have a *personally* correct moral belief; but since neither of this person's considered opinions will have the support of this person's wider faith-community (Church) his convictions will simply be *personally* correct decisions. Now, were the Catholic Church to consider this person's "considered opinions" to be morally correct, then they would not only be subjectively right, but also universally correct.[14]

Here the truth contained in a community's moral convictions ("Gay behavior is not OK for Christians"), as well as in the individual's existential judgments ("Gay behavior is OK for me") are both grounded not simply in subjective "feelings," but in a community's historic and widely-held (if always fallible) "considered opinions"—a position that explains not only the inevitability of a "pluralism" of moral convictions among Christians, Jews, and Muslims, but also the soundness of John Henry Newman's teaching about the *sensus fidelium* as the secure test of the truth of the Church's doctrines in the areas of faith and morals. The "people of God's" awareness of what is good and its collective decisions form its ethical teachings.

A cautionary comment here: the fact the Church judges an action to be wrong does not mean, of course, that this assessment is final. As we have seen in recent years on the issue of the Catholic Church's position on the morality of capital punishment, some changes in Christian morality will be possible in the future due to new insights into the *humanum,* or as a result of cultural changes that attain the Church's approval (divorce, ordination of women to priesthood).[15]

While it is hard to see that some of the Church's judgments will change—e.g., about the cold-blooded murder of an innocent child, or about a thoroughly dishonest historical character (Hitler)—it is not impossible that just as some past judgments (e.g., about slavery, divorce, birth control) have changed, some changes will take place in the future. Obviously, the greater the evidence that an action lacks goodness, the longer the record of opposition, and the more conservative the Church's leadership, the less likely change will be—but the recent history of Christian ethics shows that moral theology is an inexact "science" in which the unexpected is possible.[16]

All students of biomedical ethics know Ross's list of good actions, as well as his categories of *prima facie* duties. However, it must be noted that he nowhere does he claim that these lists are either complete or ultimate. Rather, his enumeration of *prima facie* duties, for example, is simply "a prima facie classification of the duties which reflection on our moral convictions seems actually to reveal" (*Right*, 26). Therefore, Ross's well-known list permits additions. For instance, it admits of goodness and resulting duties based on relationships and attributes not mentioned by Ross: e.g., acts associated with God, faith-community, pets, parks, the wilderness, and future generations.

These are significant relationships for many contemporary humans, as well as for Christians; and they create their own general and particular *prima facie* duties—which means that one has a responsibility to fulfill them unless one is, in the circumstances, subject to other competing obligations of greater weight. For example, a duty to worship is considered to be less important on a particular occasion than a duty to one's health; a responsibility to participate in a son's tenth birthday is seen to be weightier than a duty to attend a monthly meeting of a committee on which one serves—a person's actual duty being, as seen above, that which he or she judges to be the most urgent or weightiest in particular circumstances.[17]

This Ethic's Principles: Mercy, Solidarity, Generosity, Forgiveness, Simplicity

Toward the end of his *Confessions*, Augustine says that it is hard to discuss "time." Every person knows what time is—until he or she starts to speak about it. In the same way, writing about "norms" and principles leads to silence. First, care must be used when using the terms norms or principles in Christian ethics. The reason? Norms and principles which are usually equated with *kanon* and *arche* in Greek, have meanings in Aristotle's *Nicomachean Ethics*,[22] that are different from what one finds in Aquinas's *Summa Theologiae*,[23] or in Joseph Fletcher's *Situation Ethics*, Sharon Welch's *A Feminist Ethic of Risk*,[24] or the internationally respected textbook *Principles of Biomedical Ethics*, written by Tom Beauchamp and James Childress.[25]

Some aspects of the terms principle and norm as used in this moral theory are different from Aristotle's usage. They are not used in the way that Aristotle does, when in speaking about "equity," for example, as something that is a corrective to "legal justice" where it is defective owing to its universality, he says, "When a thing is indefinite, the rule (*kanon*) is also indefinite, like the leaden rule used in making the Lesbian molding; the rule adapts itself to the shape of the stone and is not rigid, and so too the decree is adapted to the facts" (Book V, 10, 1137b29).[26]

In other contexts, Aristotle gives *kanon* a personalized meaning; it stands for a "living standard" in the sense that some people's own changeable self is the *kanon* for judging their friendship toward others. I do not use the term "principle" as Aristotle does when he uses *arche* to mean "beginning" or "foundation" (frequently translated into English as "first principle"). However, for Aristotle, the very first *arche* of human conduct is "choice" (*proairesis*), but since a "person" exercises choice, Aristotle can say with confidence "A man is the first principle (*arche*) of his actions." Thus, among Scholastic philosophers and theologians writing in the twelfth and thirteenth centuries, *arche* comes to mean—quite naturally—"*liberum arbitrium*" (free choice).

Further, in Aristotle's moral theory, virtuous actions are called *kalai,* and they become "virtuous" actions (as Kant saw) when they are done for the sake of the *kalon*. And it is *intuitive reason* that grasps "first principles" (arche). This means that, differing from Joseph Fletcher's analysis of norms and principles, for Aristotle, adultery and murder— even theft—are always wrong, regardless of the circumstances, because the *kalon* consists in always avoiding them, while acts of bravery and temperance are always morally good because of their *kalon*.

Besides differing from Aristotle's usage, this theory will not use the terms "principle," "norm," and "standard" (this last term is central to the Hasting Center Report's essays in bioethics) in exactly the way as they are used in *Principles of Biomedical Ethics*. When Beauchamp and Childress use the terms, they do so in ways that have their own specific senses. In their eyes, principles in other frameworks might be developed as "rights," "virtues," or "values" (ibid., 37); and the four principles (autonomy, nonmaleficence, beneficence, justice) that are central to their ethical theory (it has been called *principlism*) are derived from "coherence" and "considered judgments in the common morality and medical tradition" (ibid., 37)—they have not been reached by an "argued defense" (ibid., 37). Beauchamp and Childress state that they will "operate with only a loose distinction between rules and principles" (ibid., 37).

Why? "Both are normative generalizations that guide actions, but, as we analyze them, *rules* are more specific in content and more restricted in scope than principles. Principles do not function as precise action guides that inform us in each circumstance how to act in the way more detailed rules do. *Principles* are general rules that leave considerable room for judgment in specific cases and that provide substantive guidance for the development of more detailed rules and policies" (ibid., 37–38). The goal of the authors throughout their work is to "specify and balance" principles (ibid., 37).

Now, as all must know, Protestant and Catholic moral theologies use the terms "norms" and principles in a variety of distinctive ways too. First, Catholic texts are full of principles such as the "principle of double effect," the "principle of totality," the "principle of ordinary and extraordinary means," the "principle of proportionality," the "principle of subsidiarity," and the "principle of preferential option for the poor." Aquinas's "natural law" theory, when used correctly, renders (according to Thomists) a set of "primary" and "secondary" moral principles that is identical (in its scope) with the Decalogue and Jesus' moral commands.[27]

When I studied Christian ethics, we quickly learned that the "fundamental principle" of the Church's pastoral ministry was embodied in the aphorism, *Salus animarum suprema lex* (The salvation of souls is the supreme law). However, what exactly one means by terms like "law" or "principle" in these contexts is as difficult to determine as when reading Aristotle's *Ethics* or *Principles of Biomedical Ethics*.

This ethic uses these terms in ways that reflect the current thought of mainstream sociologists, Scripture scholars, and contemporary Anglo-American ethicists—the acceptance of their postmodern insights into morality, metaphors, and stories in particular. To illustrate: whether these "norms" and principles are absolute or relative, objective or subjective, and whether they are "exceptionless" or they "admit of exceptions," has been the subject of serious discussion during the last forty years. Back in the 1960s, Joseph Fletcher argued that "principles or maxims or general rules are *illuminators*. But they are not *directors*."[28] In his mind, "circumstances alter rules and principles" (ibid., 29) For Fletcher, there was "only one norm or principle (call it what you will) that is binding or unexceptionable, always good and right regardless of the circumstances. That is 'love'—the *agape* of the summary commandment to love God and the neighbor. Everything else without exception, all laws and rules and principles and ideals and norms, are only *contingent,* only valid *if they happen* to serve love in any situation" (ibid., 30).

Arguing in his own way against the immutability of natural law's norms in 1971, Josef Fuchs says: (a) that Aquinas held that human nature is changeable, and (b) that biology and history confirm that mutability belongs to man's immutable essence, and that even those *a priori* and inalienable elements in human nature subsist in it in variable modes.[29] One conclusion—following Durban's Archbishop Hurley and contrary to Aristotle's position—"killing, stealing, lying, etc. are intrinsically evil, yet they might be warranted in view of important opposing obligations" (ibid., 118) Another is that "error in the moral sphere" cannot be excluded *a limine* from the Christian communities in which moral norms were established (ibid., 128).

The moral theory being presented here holds that while principles and norms both provide moral guidance and direction, embody authority (truth), and sanction (law), they are different in their scope, as well as in their applicability. Although it was established within a community that is always subject to error, the fundamental Christian principle "Love your neighbor as you love yourself" admits of no exceptions—within the Christian community. Further, just as Jesus, his person and character, his willingness to do God's will, and his compassion for others (as the embodiment of God's revelation) is the foundation of Christian morality, Jesus' primary moral principle is foundational for Christian ethics in the sense that other more specific and more concrete norms ("Give to this person in need") are derived from it.

Unlike Fletcher's ethic, however, this theory uses a set of principles (broad, general) derived from Jesus' life and teaching, his parables and sermons (Matthew's Sermon on the Mount, Luke's Sermon on the Plain) in much the same way as those found in *Principles of Biomedical Ethics,* and just as Tom Beauchamp and James Childress do, it specifies and balances these principles in order to resolve real-life issues such as euthanasia, capital punishment, or killing in warfare.

Given an adolescent's powers of judgment, the complexity of some moral issues, plus other variables such as peer pressures, point-of-view, moral education, and spiritual development, this theory holds that explicit norms—"Do this!"—where "this" is lying to a high school teacher"—are inherently fallible, contextual, individual, and personal, although this does not mean that such decisions are wrong, flawed, immoral or lacking in ethical truth or goodness. With Ross, this ethic affirms the basic decency of people and their awareness of morality. Further, this theory finds wisdom in Carol Gilligan's analysis of women's moral behavior and development, in Sidney Callahan's descriptions of the roles of norms and principles in moral decision-making, and in the words that Erick Erikson used in once reminding Gandhi, "'Truth', you once said, 'excludes the use of violence because man is not capable of knowing the absolute truth and therefore is not competent to punish.'"[30]

Biblical scholarship has come to the conclusion that the morality described in the Bible has undergone development over time, and that the Bible's moral traditions have been "distilled by a community of piety and faithfulness from their own perceptions and understandings of the divine governance through the course of their history" (to quote James Gustafson).[31] This moral theory holds similar views concerning the origins and growth of Christian moral traditions, not just during the age of the patriarchs. During the Middle Ages, Aristotle's four central moral virtues (prudence, justice, fortitude, and temperance) rose to eminence to become the "cardinal virtues," displacing in the process key virtues that the ancient Irish prized (beauty, generosity, bravery).[32]

The Greek virtues displaced some Hebrew virtues, as well: those that Paul encouraged in his letter to the Galatians 5: 22 ("love, joy, peace, patience, kindness, goodness, trustfulness, gentleness, and self control"), and in his letter to the Colossians 3: 12–15 ("You are God's chosen race, his saints; he loves you, and you should be clothed in sincere compassion, in kindness and humility, gentleness and patience. Bear with one another; forgive each other as soon as a quarrel begins. The Lord has forgiven you; now you must do the same. Over all these clothes, to keep them together and complete them, put on love. And may the peace of Christ reign in your hearts, because it is for this that you were called together as parts of one body. Always be thankful").

During these same years, as the Franks and other tribes rose to power within Christendom, rather than adopting Paul's virtues, they extolled and spread military virtues, strengths of mind and body vital for success in warfare, conquest, and political administration. In the process, these fighting peoples laid the foundation for the rise of knightly chivalry and courtly love, ethical traditions that further pushed aside the central place of the New Testament's quieter domestic virtues.

Since the Renaissance, Western thought has seen the elevation of mind over being, according to respected U.S. critic and poet Marion

Montgomery's survey of history. Consequently, the Western person has experienced a new awakening marked by an "infectious optimism, advanced under the banner of progress, a code term signaling the deconstruction of being through which the recovery of a new Eden at some far-off divine point in the future is promised through that higher reason which I have termed satanic."[33]

Now, while Joseph Fletcher's moral theory is able to reduce the Church's ethical principles simply to one moral principle, and *Principles of Biomedical Ethics* resolves moral dilemmas by relating and balancing four principles, the moral theory being developed here, after looking back over the Bible and the Church's theological and moral traditions (its view of God, Christ, humans, life on earth, church, salvation, sin) since the days of Paul, Matthew, and John (just as Bernard Hoose has done in *Received Wisdom: Reviewing the Role of Tradition in Christian Ethics*, and James Reston has also undertaken in *The Last Apocalypse: Europe at the Year 1000 A.D.*), offers five moral principles: **mercy, solidarity, generosity, forgiveness,** and **simplicity**.

This ethic sets forward these principles, since each is derived from what the Church has come to know of God, God's saving work in Jesus, and God's governance in the course of history. Each of these principles is *theocentric* in its origins, and foundational in its relationship to God's Word and to the Christian vision of reality and life. Each principle embodies the Catholic understanding of God's saving-work-in-Christ, the moral message contained in Jesus' life and teaching, and what the Church has come to know about the role of God's Spirit in the world. Using these principles in a way similar to the way that Nel Noddings recommended that "care" be used in making moral decisions or assessing past actions, will (I believe) result in personal behavior and social policies that are unambiguously Christian, whether one is dealing with questions about physician-assisted suicide, the torture of terrorists, or a community's budget allocations for homeless children.

No case for these principles will be made here. The validity of each, its cornerstone place in the Christian life, might be argued, however, from an examination of (a) what the Bible and Christianity have said about God; (b) Jesus' doctrinal and moral teaching in word and action; (c) the lives of undeniably Christ-like women and men, such as Martin of Tours, Ambrose, Patrick, Francis of Assisi, Catherine of Siena, John of the Cross, Thomas More, John Henry Newman,

Mary MacKillop, Dorothy Day, Martin Luther King, Jr., and Archbishop Romero.[34]

Further, in the theory being presented here, there is no need to have separate moral principles for business ethics, bioethics, or military ethics. For a Christian ethic to be true to its name, it must be grounded in the life-implications of God's saving work in Christ. True, there will be some adjustments at the second or third levels because of concerns such as roles and relationships, but there will be no wholesale abandonment of central moral principles.

Conclusions: Positions More Cogent, Consilient, and Contemporary than Rivals

The method of resolving conflicts among and between actions being proposed here has more to commend it than either Joseph Fletcher's or Richard McCormick's ethical theories. Fletcher's theory makes the process too simple and violates the complexity of human moral experience; McCormick's ethic of "proportionate reasons" provides some clarity about moral responsibilities, but his analysis does not lead to insight about the "rightness" of a specific moral decision, nor does it possess inherently "Christian" characteristics. Further, McCormick's analysis does not take one safely to the realm of authentic morality, or to Kant's kingdom of duties. McCormick's renewed natural law approach does not adequately accord with human experience; it does not provide either coherence or consilience.[35]

Making a right moral decision (in the theory being proposed) involves a judgment about goodness and one's known moral responsibilities. The method of decision-making respects creativity and safeguards personal autonomy, as well as human dignity. It does not subject the person's freedom to the tyranny of the "ontic" or the phenomenological, as Janssens's decision-making method does. It is more realistic and accords better with common experience than the decision-making method proposed by John Finnis and Germain Grisez, who argue that a decision is inherently immoral when made directly against a basic human good, and that the decision to execute a criminal can only be licit when the principle of double effect is employed—something that defies human experience (in consulting with judges), as well as human psychology.[36]

This pluralistic theory of morality involving attributes that generate "compounds" or "bundles" of teleological and deontological *prima facie* obligations, resolves the problems inherent in utilitarianism. It is consistent, coherent, and accords with normal moral experience; it is a reasoned and intellectually satisfying response to the human experience of moral duty. As well, contrary to the remarks of his critics, Ross's comments on how to make reasoned decisions about the most urgent of two or three *prima facie* duties provide morally sensitive agents with adequate guidance for resolving everyday moral problems, as well solving those less frequent dilemmas faced by nurses, physicians, police, and investigative journalists. Finally, the norms and principles central to this ethic are undeniably Christian.

This ethic views moral decision-making (as we will see in the next chapter) as Sidney Callahan does: as a complex and creative process involving reason, intuition, and emotion. It affirms, on the basis of history and experience, that humans possess a direct grasp of the fundamentals of morality; and that this knowledge (coupled with the results of civil and religious education) takes the form of an awareness of "good" or "bad" qualities associated with an action. In this ethic, the moral life is associated more closely with relationships than consequences; *prima facie* responsibilities more than keeping rules.

The three-thousand-year-old rivers of Western and Eastern ethics, which began in Baghdad, Jerusalem, and Anyang, are viewed as colorful and complex experiments in the humanities, and closer to literature and music than to current research into evolutionary biology or abnormal psychology.

This theory develops a mixed rule deontology in which agents make specific moral decisions on the basis of considered opinions about existent responsibilities toward themselves and others, and what they here and now sensitively consider to be their weightiest duties.

Two final points. First, in this theory, when we think ourselves justified in breaking, indeed morally obliged to break some commitment (a promise, appointment) in order to relieve some distress or to secure some benefit, we do not cease to recognize the *prima facie* duty to honor our prior commitment, a fact which causes us: (a) to feel compunction, or the need to repent for our behavior; and (b) to know that we must make up (as best we can) for breaking the promise or missing the appointment.

Second, in this ethics, the obligation of fidelity or honesty is not so strong as never to be outweighed by an action's consequences; and one's actual duty is highly variable and dependent on the situation at hand. In other words, this approach to morality embodies a realistic and reasonable approach to decision-making, and flexibility consistent with the complexity and constraints inherent in the busy lives of today's parents, nurses, and politicians. It upholds Jesus' words about the law—that it was made for men, and that women and men were not made for the law.

Notes:

[1] On Scheler's moral theory that has had a major influence on European philosophy and religious thought (if not on Anglo-American circles), Max Scheler, formalism in ethics and non-formal ethics of values: a new attempt toward the foundation of an ethical personalism (Evanston, IL: Northwestern university press, 1973).

[2] On the development of utilitarianism during the second half of the 20th century, Peter Edwards, "The Future of Ethics," in *The Future of Philosophy: Towards the 21st Century*, edited by Oliver Leaman, op. cit., 46–47. Also, Mark Timmons's chapters on "Classical utilitarianism," and "Contemporary utilitarianism," in his *Moral Theory: An Introduction* (Lanham: Rowman & Littlefield, 2002), 103–129, 131–150 *respect.*

[3] W. D. Ross, *The Right and the Good* (Oxford: Clarendon Press, 1935). Afterward simply referred to as *Right.*

[4] For a number of other difficulties associated with utilitarianism, especially when compared with Kant's moral theory, Bernard Williams and J. J. C. Smart, *utilitarianism: For and Against* (Cambridge: Cambridge University Press, 1973). Also, John Rawls, *A Theory of Justice* (Cambridge, Harvard University Press, 1971); Richard Brandt, "Toward a Credible Form of utilitarianism," in his *Morality and the Language of Conduct* (Detroit: Wayne State University Press, 1963), 107–140.

[5] W.D. Ross, *The Foundations of Ethics* (Oxford: Clarendon Press), 1939. Afterward simply referred to as *Foundations.*

[6] Ross was deeply influenced by his teacher H. A. Prichard (1871–1947), who held that some types of actions are "right" by their very nature, and that a person can apprehend when something "ought" to be done by a simple "act of moral thinking," according to Theodore C. Denise, Sheldon P. Peterfreund, and Nicholas P. White, in *Great Traditions in Ethics*, 8th Edition (Belmont, CA: Wadsworth Publishing, 1996), 332, n. 1.

[7] utilitarians and other supporters of moral monism "are overly reductive: they attempt to boil all morally relevant considerations down to a single, fundamental feature possessed of moral relevance," writes Mark Timmons. Moral pluralists such as Ross, on the other hand, maintain "that there is a plurality of equally basic morally relevant features and thus plurality of moral principles or rules" op.cit., 190.

[8] For an important discussion of intuition, Bernard Williams, "What Does Intuitionism Imply?" in his *Making Sense of Humanity* (Cambridge: Cambridge University Press, 1995).

[9] Geoffrey Warnock, the object of morality (New York: Methuen, 1971).

[10] While Ross does not develop this basis of "duties," it seems clear that some of our "responsibilities" result as well from chosen or elected "offices" or "states of life"—the fact, for instance, that we have decided to be in law enforcement, the armed forces,

a firefighter, a nurse, or a physician, and, consequently, have assumed certain "responsibilities" (to risk our lives, to treat the infectious) as a direct result of being in such lines of work.

[11] The practice of developing concrete moral "responsibilities" from a person's natural or chosen "roles" is part of a tradition that predates Cicero's *De officiis*. It can be found in Greek and Indian philosophies, in Luther's understanding of vocation, and the writings of the Oxford philosopher F. H. Bradley, author of "My Station and Its Duties." Early Christian writers developed this approach when they expanded upon the image of society or church as an organic body in which people have their roles or places. The most influential example of such a work is St. Ambrose's *De officiis ministrorum*—that joins pre-Christian and Christian ethics in a structured analysis of the philosophical basis of morality—both ordinary (expected of everyone) and honorable (beyond the normal call of duty), a work that has been called the "sole Christian example of a comprehensive ethical treatise before the time of the *Summa*." For further on this subject, James Gaffney, "The First Christian Ethics Text," in *Matters of Faith and Morals* (Kansas City: Sheed & Ward, 1987), 214–230; Jan L. Womer, *Morality and Ethics in Early Christianity, Sources of Early Christian Thought* (Philadelphia: Fortress Press, 1987), 27, 87–107—for introduction and extracts from Ambrose's work.

[12] Using the criteria set down in this ethical theory, the judge in Albert Camus' *The Fall* is a classic example of an immoral man, while individuals such as Socrates, Jesus, Dietrich Bonheoffer, and Teilhard de Chardin are good examples of moral men—because they were responsive to what they saw (judged, felt) to be their weightiest duties.

[13] For a helpful, if too summary outline of Ross's moral theory, Mark Timmons, *Moral Theory: An Introduction*, 189–209, at 196 for the author's own restatement of Ross's understanding of "right conduct."

[14] In Protestant communities, the fact that an individual's opinion is compatible with or clearly supported by Scripture will render it "objectively" right.

[15] The recent changes in Roman Catholic morality—eating meat on Friday, not fasting on the Fridays within Lent—bear out the validity of the case being presented here. Nowhere is it being held that all of the Church's moral teaching is subject to change, but simply that some changes in the Church's ethical teaching are possible—and for the reasons stated.

[16] I think of the Anglican community's changes on the matter of the ordination of women to the ranks of bishops, its developments on birth control, abortion, gay and lesbian marriage.

[17] John Finnis's position that every act of birth control, for example, necessarily involves a decision directly against a basic human value—and therefore is always immoral—seems both arbitrary and fictional. Surely, McCormick is right in positing (along with Catholic philosophers like Max Scheler) an *ordo bonorum*, or (as I prefer) with W. D. Ross, a world of *prima facie* duties. And construing moral decisions in terms of well-reasoned resolutions of the conflicts surrounding these goods or duties.

[22] Aristotle, *The Nicomachean Ethics*, with Introduction and Translation by W. D. Ross (Oxford: Oxford University Press, 1925, 1990).

[23] On this subject, Brian Thomas Mullady, "The Meaning of the Term 'Moral' in St. Thomas Aquinas," *Studi Tomistici* 27 (1986).

[24] Sharon D. Welch, *A Feminist Ethics of Risk*, op. cit. 124–129.

[25] Tom L. Beauchamp, James F. Childress, *Principles of Biomedical Ethics* (New York: Oxford University Press, 1979, 1994).

[26] On this subject, Sir David Ross, "Ethics," in *Aristotle*, op. cit., 187–234; Also, Joseph Owens, "Aristotle's Contribution on the Nature of Ethical Norms," *Listening* 18, 3 (Fall 1983), 225–234.

[27] On this subject, Enda McDonagh, "The Natural Law and the Law of Christ," in *Invitation and Response*, op. cit, 22–37, 201; Joseph Fuchs, "The Law of Christ," in *Moral Theology Renewed*, edited by Enda McDonagh (Dublin: Gill and Son, 1965), 70–84; George V. Lobo, "The Natural Moral Law," in *Guide to Christian Living*, op. cit., 169–198.

[28] Joseph Fletcher, *Situation Ethics* (Philadelphia: Westminster, 1966), 31.

[29] Joseph Fuchs, "The Absoluteness of Moral Terms," in *Moral Norms and Catholic Tradition*, in *Readings in Moral Theology #1*, edited by Charles E. Curran and Richard A. McCormick (New York: Paulist Press, 1979), 94–137, at 107.

[30] As quoted by Carol Gilligan, *In A Different Voice: Psychological Theory and Women's Development* (Cambridge: Harvard University Press, 1982), 103–104.

[31] James Gustafson, *Ethics from a Theocentric Perspective* I, op. cit., 339.

[32] On this subject, Thomas Cahill, *How The Irish Saved Civilization* (New York: Doubleday, 1993).

[33] Marion Montgomery, *Virtue and Modern Shadows of Turning: Preliminary Agitations* (Lanham: University Press of America, 1990), 33–34.

[34] A case will not be made in support of these "principles," just as no case was made for the four principles that are central to *Principles of Biomedical Ethics*—primarily because no case is really necessary.

[35] As mentioned earlier, McCormick's standard for allowing severely handicapped newborns to die—their "potential for human relationships," for instance—has no foundations in the New Testament, and flies in the face of Jesus' words about those who should be shown care and mercy.

[36] On this principle, James F. Keenan, "Double Effect, Principle of," in *New Dictionary of Catholic Social Thought*, op. cit., 300–303.

Chapter X

A Christian Ethic of Responsibilities: Moral Development, Moral Decision-making

The authority of morals is the authority of truth, that is, of reality.

Iris Murdoch
The Sovereignty of Good

Conscience is not Jiminy Cricket or a guardian angel on one's shoulder or the voice of a little man inside a person .... In fact, conscience is not a static "it" at all, but rather a human activity, a developed predisposition for activity of a special kind.

Sidney Callahan
"Conscience"

Virtue itself, which is not among the primary objects of nature, but succeeds to them as the result of learning, though it holds the highest place among human good things, what is its occupation save to wage perpetual war with vices—not those that are outside us, but within; not other men's, but our own.

Augustine
The City of God

What is however undeniable is that the return to the fundamental character of God as the basis of Christian morality means an increasing readiness to seek decisions appropriate in that light and a refusal to accept precedents as binding.

J. L. Houlden
Ethics and The New Testament

66 T o exist as a person means to act. And action means choosing, deciding. What is the right choice? What ought I do? What ought we do? This is the question before which every human is objectively placed," Karl Barth once wrote. However, choosing and deciding are far from easy.

Psychologists such as Robin Hogarth point out that much is still unknown about how the human mind works and how it influences human behavior.[1] Given the importance of making sound life choices, any ethical theory seeking to gain acceptance today within the Catholic community must provide an up-to-date description of moral development, as well as an intellectually convincing answer to the question, "How do humans make moral decisions?" Any model of mature decision-making must embody current thinking about the ways that minds and hearts are colored by philosophical and theological beliefs and shaped by contemporary social values, as well as emerging ethical perspectives.

This chapter will examine the ways that descriptions of the moral decision-making process have changed in the thinking of Catholic philosophers and theologians working in the field since WWII. It will look at the role of cognitions, emotions and intuitions, and the parts played by metaphors and language in the analyses of authors who reflect both the neo-Scholastic and more recent philosophical traditions. Indirectly, it will examine current research into moral development as a basis for an authentic Catholic understanding of the goals and process of moral education.

Drawing upon the research of Bernard Lonergan, Daniel Maguire, Herbert McCabe, Paul Ricoeur, Sidney Callahan, and Sharon Welch, as well as the investigations into cognitive development and critical thinking undertaken by Lawrence Kohlberg, Jean Piaget, Richard Paul, Linda Elder, and Carol Gilligan, the chapter will propose a model of moral maturity and decision-making that incorporates the best features from the past with convincing insights from those who have made major contributions to recent research: in particular, those who have explored the complex process of ego and moral development, and who have argued convincingly in favor of holism in making moral decisions, as well as for restoring the role of the human will— with its passions, sentiments, intuitions—to its traditional position in contemporary philosophical and psychological discussions about human development and sound ethical decision-making.

Besides providing readers with insights into the opinions of the writers just mentioned, the study will again focus on the contributions to ethics made by the British philosopher, civil servant, and respected translator of Aristotle's *Nicomachean Ethics*, Sir. W. David Ross, whose appreciation of the role of intuition, as well as his understanding of morality and decision-making, while overlooked by the great majority of Catholic philosophers and psychologists, provide a number of significant insights into these subjects.

Neo-Scholastic Analyses of Moral Decision-making: Reason's Judgments

Catholic moral education has been marked by an emphasis on obedience, legalism, and conformity. It has given little place to the role of creativity in moral development or decision-making. Consequently, the standard image of a morally "mature" Catholic adult lacks such strengths as initiative, independence, and self-determination. As a generalization, the great majority of Catholic authors who wrote about moral decisionmaking prior to the 1950s–1960s, emphasized the role of reason and logic in making moral decisions; they gave little or no support to the positive role played by the emotions in this behavior. Having a "good" and "sound" conscience meant possessing one that was fully in line with the teachings of the "official" Church.

Today however, the majority of current Catholic writers places less emphasis on the role of reason and logic in their analyses of decision-making, and they defend the positive place of emotion and intuition, as well as autonomy and the right of the imagination to be creative. The first group of writers employed institutional and forensic language in their writing (they used the terms judgment, deduction, motives, reason); current authors take their decision-making terminology from counseling and psychology (they prefer to use terms like decision, choice, values, feeling)—they are less patriarchal. Finally, the former were supremely confident in the results of reason; they saw "correct" moral judgments as objective and universal; they saw the Catholic Church as the sole "pillar and ground of truth." Current writers are tentative about the mind's powers; they do not claim that moral norms are objective or universal; they are less absolutist when it comes to the Catholic Church's claims to be a unique moral teacher or a special repository of moral wisdom.[2]

Austin Fagothey's widely-used *Right and Reason* (2nd edition, 1959), praised by reviewers as one of the "greatest and most successful" ethics books ever published, is representative of the former writers.[3] Sidney Callahan's *In Good Conscience: Reason and Emotion in Moral Decision-Making* (1991) represents the latter group. Both of these works, moreover, reflect the Catholic Church's changing political culture, its developing theology, its socially colored understanding of psychology, and its growing regard for personal autonomy, creativity, and freedom within society and church.[4] Both books attest to the relative nature of moral and aesthetic judgments.

Fagothey's book states that "the faculty to be used in discriminating right from wrong can be no other than the human intellect or reason." Such a view is implicit in Aristotle, Fagothey claims (ibid., 132). It is clearly held by the Stoics, who "seem to have come close to finding the correct norm. They insisted on reason as our guide in morals; that the good life alone is a reasonable life and anything else is folly; that right reason shows the good life to be a life in conformity with nature, both universal nature and human nature" (ibid., 132). The Stoic's thought is found (Fagothey states) in Aquinas's discussion of eternal and natural law (*Summa Theologica* I, II, 19, 3–4). For Fagothey, therefore, right reason is the "proximate norm of morality" (ibid., 133). And how do we know when our reason is right? Fagothey's answer: because, "logic teaches us how to draw the correct conclusions from premises" (ibid., 133).

In the American Jesuit's eyes, Adam Smith and David Hume, Ralph Cudworth and Samuel Clarke were quite wrong: there is no need for either an intuitive or an affective power or faculty to judge right and wrong. Why? Because "moral judgments are not of an essentially different nature from other judgments, for they are either self-evident truths or reasoned conclusions from self-evident principles. To understand is the function of the intellect. Any faculty other than the intellect would not understand why certain actions are good or bad. To make it the norm would lower man's moral life to the instinctive and brutish. It is absurd to expect man to use his reason in the fields of science, business, law, and politics, but not in the realm of his own personal conduct and in the achievement of his last end" (ibid., 131).

Conscience, for Fagothey, has quite a limited role in decision-making and the moral life. First, it is simply the norm of subjective, not of objective morality (ibid., 131). Second, it is not a special faculty, but "only the name for the intellect judging the morality of a particular concrete act here and now" (ibid., 131). Further, the judgment of conscience is simply "the conclusion of a syllogism arrived at by a strictly rational process" (ibid., 131).[5] Finally, according to Fagothey's philosophy, sentiments, even the noblest such as sympathy, cannot be reliable guides to right and wrong, since they are constantly changing depending on our physical condition and emotional mood (ibid., 131). Likewise, we have no direct intuition of the moral goodness or badness of concrete acts here and now to be performed. The intellect judges right from wrong by a process of reasoning, not by an instinctive sentiment or an immediate intuition.[6] Writing before there was general acceptance of the reality of "differentiated" consciousness, Fagothey makes no allowances for gender, culture, age, or religion in his analysis of decision-making. In the Jesuit author's mind, the Catholic Church possesses unique claims in the field of morality, and stands as a shining light among a history of moral error and human corruption.[7]

Recent Developments in Roman Catholic Thought: Lonergan, Maguire, Callahan

While some Catholic writers still support Fagothey's analysis, more recent authors show more humility in their assessments of Catholic morality, and a greater awareness of what Mary Midgley has called "the unity of the moral enterprise."[8] Bernard Lonergan's *Insight* (1957), and his Halifax Lectures in 1958, Daniel Maguire's *The Moral Choice* (1978), Sidney Callahan's *In Good Conscience: Reason and Emotion in Moral Decision-Making* (1991), as well as Karl Rahner's essays on existential knowledge, all show major departures from Fagothey's simplistic and excessively rationalistic understanding of the workings of conscience and the process of moral decision-making. They are less legalistic; they place less stress upon obedience and conformity; they view the morally mature Catholic adult as less servile and more autonomous, possessing greater generosity, forgiveness, and bravery.

Lonergan's paradigm-shifting *Insight*, for instance, deals with analyses and exercises in which a person moves toward the functionally operative tendencies that ground knowledge; it describes self-appropriation, ways to better appreciate human understanding and to achieve useful insights into the whole phenomenon of human "insight."[9] The book forces readers to become more aware of their own judgments and personal moments of epiphany. While Lonergan's book says little about moral decisions, his analysis of common sense and "invulnerable insights" emphasizes the personal and existential aspects of desires and values, and the role of deliberation and decision, choice and will in the intellect's efforts to bring the goodness of being to light.

Lonergan holds that persons are the basis of ethics; he accepts Heidegger's arguments about authentic and inauthentic existence; he treasures rational self-consciousness and is openly critical of the tendency to equate intellect with intelligence. Of special note is Lonergan's sympathy (as seen in his "Halifax Lectures") toward the place of *a priori* intuitions in Kant's philosophy. "If one has casual insights, one is kidding oneself if one continues to believe that one is deducing one's geometry from the axioms. It does not really flow from the axioms," he writes ("Halifax Lectures," 16). With Bernard Haring, Lonergan's ideal Catholic stands closer to Christ than to Therese of Lisieux, whose autobiography was a widely-used manual for the spiritual direction of Catholic clergy during the 1960s–1970s.

Daniel Maguire's award-winning book, *The Moral Choice*, advances the discussion of moral reasoning beyond Lonergan's analysis. "The moral is unique, and so too is the approach to it," Maguire writes.[10] "Ethics cannot be rationalistically reduced merely to induction plus deduction. Of its essence it involves us in creative imagination, affective appreciations, faith, insights mediated through tragedy and comedy, and full recognition of the social roots of knowing" (ibid., 121). In Maguire's analysis, moral discernment flows from the questioning mind in its fullness, because the goal of ethics is "moral insight"—a quite distinct activity (known to the detective) of organizing intelligence that places the full set of clues in a unique explanatory perspective (ibid., 121). For Maguire, a person's conviction that capital punishment is "generally wrong" does not have its basis in an intuitive perception of the action's implications, but is grounded in arguments about alternatives, consequences, and "all other morally meaningful circumstances" (ibid., 120).

Feminist ethicists have focused on the inadequacy of analyses of moral decision-making such as Fagothey's with their compartmentalized pictures of the self, together with their models of reasoning that ignore the particularities of settings, trivialize personal experience, and fail to appreciate the unities connecting reason and emotion, mind and body, culture and nature.[11] They have been responsive to research into the brain, its evolution, and development, the writings of Shanon Brownlee, for instance, who states that the "prefrontal cortex is the seat of civilization" in the course of a useful essay on the neurophysiological aspects of brain development during a person's adolescent years.[12] Feminists are sensitive to the opinion that "the brain was not made for learning but for survival," as Mark Reardon states in a valuable summary of recent research into the way that the brain acquires and processes knowledge.[13] Open to the implications of postmodernism, Sharon Welch, Nel Noddings (best known for advancing an ethics of care), and Rita Manning acknowledge that there is a "subjective" element in human experience—without supporting "subjectivism"; that the process of image formation is "unconscious" by nature; and that "differences" are the trigger to mental activity and growth in self-conscious awareness—themes central to Gregory Batson's research into the human mind.[14]

The theory of responsibilities being developed here respects these neurobiological insights. It sees the self-conscious self's growth as a moral subject as (a) a complex journey from an egocentric (almost totally affective) fixation on objects such as one's mother, play objects, and sounds, to (b) the zealous observance of rigid rules (as a crawling infant, emerging teen) imposed by external authorities (parents, siblings, teachers) to (c) personal, if always unstable and threatened self-conscious expression and self-determination—i.e., emotional, psychic, and ethical autonomy. Since the process of moral maturation and personal identity extend well beyond adolescence and Christian ethical theories must be directed toward contemporary adults as they return to religious communities, raise children in religion, and seek to deepen their spirituality or theological skills, this ethic understands the psychologically healthy and morally useful place of inspiring heroes, as well as specific self-accepted rules in children's lives—and in the lives of adults.

This theory's understanding of adult learning has been shaped by Malcolm Knowles's research into the ways that mature women and men acquire and process knowledge, as well as the insights into personal identity and moral growth proposed by Carl Rogers, in particular his essays on "student-centered learning." This ethic encourages decisions about careers and professions being associated with culturally and ethically worthwhile sports, cultural, religious, and political "celebrities" who become known, admired, and respected through the medium of "stories"—whether in print or in picture.[15]

Given the Catholic vision of moral maturity and its Scripture-based stand on the dignity of the human person, this theory holds that

(a) obedience (in particular, conforming one's behavior to rules or laws associated with some moral or political authority rather than living by rules or principles that are self-accepted because reasonable and personally persuasive) has limited place only in the moral lives of adults; and that (b) a mature morality involves creativity (seen as "divergent thinking"), independence, and self-determination that are based upon personally held and individually committed principles that leave room for reasoned decisions in specific cases, while providing sufficient guidance for the development of existentially relevant (and more explicit) concrete norms.

Both of these positions are central to the thought of those at the forefront of research into critical thinking. Stephen D. Brookfield, Associate Director of the Center for Adult Education at Teachers College, Columbia University, holds that "Central to critical thinking is the capacity to imagine and explore alternatives to existing ways of thinking and living."[16] And through this activity "we become skeptical of claims to universal truth or to ultimate explanations. In short, we exhibit what might be called reflective skepticism" (9). For Brookfield, critical thinking is associated with what Habermas called "emancipatory learning," which is described as "that which frees people from personal, institutional, or environmental forces that prevent them from seeing new directions, from gaining control of their lives, their society, and their world" (12).

Surely, the goals of critical thinking are central to any Catholic education faithful to the scholastic tradition. They remind us, as Socrates did, that central to the aims of education is the development of questioning, truth-seeking adults—not passive, servile drones— men and women fearful of discovery or anxious about questioning traditional beliefs or values. As Jacques Barzun wisely noted, surely higher education exists not to provide graduates with diplomas ensuring higher salaries, but "to put the next generation in possession of the social, political, and cultural heritage of the world," and to develop the skills for a "thoughtful life."[17]

The U.S. Catholic psychologist Sidney Callahan has provided a body of essays on moral reasoning that represent the most up-to-date analyses of moral development, conscience and decision-making by a psychologist writing in the Catholic philosophical tradition; they move the discussion beyond Lonergan and Maguire.[18] Callahan's respect for emotion can be seen in such statements as, "A completely rationalist view dismisses the role of emotion with the assertion that 'arguments are one thing, sentiments another, and nothing fogs the mind so thoroughly as emotion"' ("The Role of Emotion in Ethical decision-making," ibid., 23).[19] She makes passionate calls for a broader definition of conscience and for an acceptance of the place of intuition and emotion in moral decision-making, seen in such words as "Emotion and thinking are, in sum, complementary, synergistic, parallel processes, constantly blending and interacting as a person functions" (ibid., 25).

Callahan believes that intuition, when not overlooked, has been devalued; and that emotions "have been the most neglected and devalued aspect of moral decision-making throughout most of the Western tradition" ("Conscience," ibid., 106).[20] Callahan calls for a more robust Catholic morality in keeping with the tenet central to the aesthetic and ethical traditions found in Aquinas (1225–1274), Dante (1265–1321), Fra Angelico (1387–1433), and Michelangelo (1475–1564): namely, that the human heart is as reliable, and no less noble, than the brain.

"I prefer to define conscience as a personal, self-conscious activity that integrates reason, intuition, emotion, and will in self-committed decisions about right and wrong, good and evil," Callahan writes. "Mature human beings while alive and awake are always actively making decisions; but the decision-making of conscience is devoted to moral standards of worth, or to responding to some ethical pull or demand" (ibid., 99). Unlike Fagothey, Callahan accepts Gordon Allport's view of conscience as a form of "generic self-guidance," and "a sovereign monitor" of behavior (ibid., 102). She sees it (speaking religiously) as "the voice of God within" (ibid., 100); she considers conscience's moral decisions as "unique, personal" (ibid., 99). Furthermore, the scope of these decisions is broad. "We are not confined to the domain of what some have called 'judicial conscience,' making retrospective moral decisions about past behaviors. We also engage in acts of 'legislative conscience,' deciding what we ought to do now and in the future" (ibid., 99–100). Conscience governs small matters as well as large ones—life and death decisions.[21]

When it comes to describing moral reasoning, Callahan has little in common with Fagothey. She sees the process as "holistic" and "complicated" (ibid., 103). Rather than seeing "cognitions" opposing "emotions", she depicts both as working together to produce a more complete and reliable decision. Furthermore, Callahan depicts ethical reasoning as much more complex than Aristotle did.[22] She writes: "I see an adequate process of self-invested moral decision-making to

be anything but an orderly, linear, rationalistic, or deductive process of
running through some decision tree or algorithm" (ibid., 103). In
Callahan's mind, moral decision-making involves "checking one's
principles in the light of one's sympathies" (a quote from Jonathan
Bennett).[23]

Mature moral development will mean a genuine respect for the
differing moral sentiments of others ("The Role of Emotion," Ibid.,
33). It means sensible and appropriate risk-taking and not being afraid
of making normal mistakes; it sees moral maturity in terms of becoming a larger and more complete "personal" whole rather than in terms
of ethical "dwarfism"—with its scrupulous attention to moral minutiae
and nonexistent "sins" that must be too-frequently confessed and
excessively expiated.

The activity of conscience will more likely be a "recursive, oscil-
lating, interactive, dynamic process involving all of one's human
capacities for reason, intuition, emotion, imagination, moving in many
different directions" ("Conscience," ibid., 103). For Callahan, reason,
intuition, and emotion are important resources that mutually influence
each other in the complex decision-making of conscience. Moral
deliberation involves mutual cross-checking and testing of all of one's
capacities and resources; it seeks congruence and fusion of reason,
emotion, and intuition because the whole self is involved (ibid., 103).

With Alasdair MacIntyre, Callahan sees the self developing and
finding its ethical identity (its values and principles) in and through
overlapping and interconnected "communities"—cultural, artistic,
social, political, and religious—in which charismatic leaders play significant roles.[24] Persons inhabit and frequent multiple environments
chosen and organized in terms of their significance—their excitement,
their restfulness, their convenience, and their safety—an observation
that will be developed later in this study.

Creativity has never been given a major emphasis in Roman
Catholic descriptions of decision-making. However, creativity in
adolescence and in later life plays a central part in Callahan's understanding of mature moral decision-making.[25] As she sees it, the art of
making decisions involves *reason* judging and tutoring emotions; *intuition* supplements, engenders new ideas and also monitors, checks, and
judges reasoning; *emotions* (gifts of the Spirit) tutor reason, intuition,
and other emotions. Within a creative person, these three capacities are
fostered and cherished; they are combined in experimental ways,
played with, used to conjure up original conceptions and imaginative

possibilities. "Our loves, aversions, sympathies, interests, and empathies trigger thoughts, intuitions, and reasoning processes," Callahan writes ("Conscience," ibid., 108).

Reason judges feeling; feelings and intuitions assess reasoning. Spontaneous or enacted emotions tutor emotions. It is the person seen as a unique center of energy and curiosity who knows and decides. And just as all five senses are involved in sensible knowledge, all cognitive and affective capacities are at work in making life choices and serious moral decisions. "All our capacities, dimensions, or sub-selves are plumbed and engaged in coming to a personal, wholehearted moral commitment" (ibid., 109).

There are two important conclusions to be drawn from Callahan's analyses: First, in this modern, indeed, postmodern view, moral decisions are not judgments of reason alone, because they are the products of reason, emotion, *and* intuition. Second, individual moral norms are not identical with reason's norms, because the heart has reasons that reason does not know.[26] In other words, there are some aspects of moral decision-making and some features of ethical norms that transcend reason's reflections on experience.[27] Here Callahan, Rahner, and the British philosopher and translator of Aristotle's *Ethics*, W. D. Ross are in agreement, for as Ross says, "When I reflect on my own attitude towards particular acts, I seem to find that it is not by deduction but by direct insight that I see them (particular moral acts) to be right or wrong."[28]

Moral Decision-making Today: The Whole Person Decides

Mark Twain once quipped, "I must have a prodigious quantity of mind: it takes me as much as a week sometimes to make it up." The models of moral growth and decision-making being proposed here support both Twain's candor and the recent developments in Catholic theology and moral psychology. The ethic embraces Lonergan's appreciation of "intuitions," Maguire's regard for the "creative imagination," and the broader, holistic understanding of "conscience" as described by Sidney Callahan. The model endorses, in particular, those aspects of morality and decision-making that accord with W. D. Ross's perceptive insights into the human person, morality, and the complex (nonlogical) character of moral knowledge that are contained in such statements as: "What I suggest is that both in mathematics and in ethics we have certain crystal clear intuitions from which we build up all that we can know about the nature of numbers and the nature of duty" (*Foundations,* 144). And "our judgments about our particular duties are not logical conclusions from self-evident premises."[29]

The contemporary description of moral maturity and the art of moral decision-making upholds what Ross said in the 1930s about the essentially rational quality of moral intuitions, as seen in *The Right and the Good,* where Ross states, "The main moral convictions of the plain man seem to me to be not opinions which it is for philosophy to prove or disprove, but knowledge from the start" (ibid, 29).

As indicated by millions of readers' responses to Plato's account of Socrates' death, or the worldwide reactions to this century's recent acts of genocide (Rwanda, Bosnia), humans, regardless of their cultures, ages, religions, formal educations or moral trainings, seem to possess genuine *knowledge* and valid *understanding* of fundamental morality—they are both affectively and intellectually aware of basic morality and general ethical responsibilities.

Further, while some people, it is true, are excessively respectful of religious authorities (Bible, pope), and see moral maturity in terms of passive obedience and being willing to accept moral principles simply on the basis of authority, with Ross the model of ethical maturity and moral decision-making being outlined here affirms the historically valid conclusion that "we can hardly fail to recognize in the best and most enlightened of men an absolutely original and direct insight into moral principles, and in many others the power of seeing for them-selves the truth of moral principles when these are pointed out to them" (*Foundations,* 172). It also sees major differences in the ways that men and women make moral decisions, distinctive characteristics that sepa-rate women's moral maturity from men's.[30]

The moral life of the teenage boy and adolescent girl is something that goes on continually, Iris Murdoch wisely reminds us.[31] It begins with the infant's first tactile awarenesses and continues throughout the years with change and uncertainty, contradiction and confusion, as individuals struggle to fuse identity and intimacy.[32] And becoming morally mature in the minds of contemporary Anglo-American philos-ophy and psychology means becoming progressively one's own person—a self-critical, involved, and sensitive moral agent who is not afraid to think for herself, to take sensible risks, and to accept the consequences of her actions.[33]

With Callahan, and distancing itself from Fagothey, this model views an individual's consciousness of basic morality as a dynamic and creative expression of a progressively developing self-conscious self; it sees "selving" as an essentially linguistic process by which a person goes out of "himself" and engages with others through language, then returns to his "self" changed—enlarged, shaken, converted, but with new or added meaning, understanding, and sensitivity.

This theory construes the road to maturity as a complex process by which an individual person responds to the dangerous and painful implications of the moral. It understands that this road, as Paul knew, implies constant risk and daily danger—that becoming an ethically healthy Christian man or woman comes about (when it does) not as the result of years spent as a passive student cowering at the feet of high school teachers more interested in "searing one's soul" (as one parent described it) with a fear of sin but with a spirit of curiosity or joy. Such "educators" who obviously never read Whitehead's words about the impossibility of moral education without the habitual vision of greatness, or knew Plato's advice about putting into the students' hands "the works of great poets" are no better than the blind guides of Jesus' parables—individuals (bitter, uninspiring) who in spite of their "vows" and "vocations" possess neither the personal desire nor the moral courage to walk in the footsteps of Christ, Patrick, Francis, Catherine, Joan of Arc, Martin Luther King, Jr., and Dorothy Day.

Conscience—one of the central activities of individual consciousness—is integral to the wider process of ego growth and personal decision-making, through which humans learn who they are and why they are, what is right for them and for others. Conscience, as Hebrew, Greek, Latin, and medieval Christian thinkers wrote, involves both cognitions and emotions—interest-excitement, enjoyment-joy, surprise-startle, distress-anguish, anger-rage, disgust-revulsion, contempt-scorn, fear-terror, shame-humiliation, guilt-remorse, love—as it warns and informs, steers human agents away from danger, and draws them toward what is safe. Conscience is a central human capacity, not simply an act of judgment; the term implies both heart and head—the person's moral awareness, both sensitive and sensible, and his decision-making center.[34]

This model of morality and moral decision-making sees Augustine's or Luther's morality as a fundamentally well-ordered and *personal* reflection on central questions and issues, e.g. killing in war, legitimacy of rebellion, marriage, and divorce. But this reflection is tempered and shaped by one's sensitivities (feelings, sentiments, intuitions); and that (for all its system, rationality, and loyalty to tradition) it sees these moral reflections (academic analyses, life-choices, and judgments) as highly poetic in character, figurative in their modes of perception, imagistic and metaphorical in their spoken or written expressions, as authors such as Michael Polanyi, Paul Ricoeur, Stanley Hauerwas, and William F. May, following Heidegger, have argued.

To explain. In *The Symbolism of Evil* (1969), and *Oneself as Another* (1992), and elsewhere in his books and essays, Ricoeur distances himself from Voltaire's statement that "Speech was given to man [*sic*] to conceal his thoughts." On the contrary, Ricoeur argues that humans are not so much "rational animals," as "word creatures," and that each human life is a quest for "selving" through conquering the pains and disunities inherent within human self-consciousness. "All *thought*," according to Ricoeur, "is an effort at unity." The "I" ("ego") must be fashioned and built; it must be constantly rescued from "self-alienation" (being lost in class-consciousness, malaise, anonymity) through the never-ending task of creating-maintaining-losing-recovering the meaning and sense of "self". And at the heart of this complex and always fluid process, moreover, lies *language*, because it is only through language (for Ricoeur) that humans achieve and express individualized self-understanding. And at the center of language lies *metaphor*—because it is through metaphor (images, similes) that reality is discovered, as concepts and insights are brought to light by teasing the mind into thinking something new and different, seeing and feeling something that did not exist before.

In Ricoeur's mind, poetic statements such as the opening lines of Hopkins's "The Windhover" ("I caught this morning morning's minion, king-/dom of daylight's dauphin, dapple-dawn-drawn Falcon, in his riding/Of the rolling level underneath him steady air ...") cause the reader's "self" to feel and think things new and different, because the poem's metaphors force the reader or hearer not only to see but also to experience resemblances previously unnoticed and unfelt—even by the poet who has been engaged in his or her own process of "selving" through the metaphors of his or her language. In the process of reading or hearing such texts, the human heart and mind (imagination, memory, conscience) engage in a creative, indeed life-generating and life-preserving activity, because "metaphors" possess what E. O. Wilson greatly values and has made central to his theory of the unity of knowledge: "consilience"—the ability to make the mind and heart "jump over," make connections, and cause sparks to fly, just as they do when certain physical surfaces (wool and glass) are rubbed together.

Whether these "stories" and "metaphors" are known through books or dolls, TV or movies, music or popular magazines—all of which have become central learning tools in advanced technological societies—the model of moral growth and decision-making being outlined here sees wisdom in Ricoeur's analyses—as well as in Carol Gilligan's insights into women's distinctive concepts of self and morality that depict being ethical as a movement from selfishness to responsibility—sees "goodness" as "self-sacrifice," and women's adult moral behavior in terms of nonviolence (not hurting others, what one is "comfortable" with, least possible injury to relationships).[35]

The whole person decides. Personal and community morality does not simply involve an individual's reason and its productions ("cognitions," to use Sidney Callahan's term). A person's lived morality and a community's ethics (the academic discipline) would be incomplete without the use of the affective powers (will, heart, emotions) that impel (as Aristotle, Augustine, and Aquinas argued) humans toward "beauty, truth, and goodness" with greater force than simply the intellect acting alone. One's personal sense of the moral and one's awareness of specific ethical responsibilities spring from one's reason *and* one's emotions, as Dan Maguire and Sidney Callahan argue. They are tied to our thoughts, feelings, and desires.

The Human Person: A Spiritual, Linguistic, Valuing, and Social Animal

Four features are essential to the Catholic understanding of the human person: she is spiritual, linguistic, valuing, and social. While grounded in Scripture and Thomistic philosophy and theology, these characteristics have been rediscovered, in a sense, by contemporary writers. For instance, on June 22, 1909, Gabriel Marcel wrote in his *Philosophical Notes*:

> This morning, quite by myself, it seems, I became aware of the eternal truth which alone can ground ethics .... The ego is only a negation, and we attain absolute thought only by becoming aware of the nothingness of our individuality: thus Hegel and Schopenhauer meet .... Our ego, our empirical

existence, our very consciousness, whether we want it to or
not, falls within this objective world; our individuality falls
within the totality of our representations, and it has no more
value or meaning than they do. Nothing is outside the eternal subjectivity; and while writing this, I have already lost
the intuition which carried me above myself a few minutes
ago ....The synthesis in us of a nature and of this absolute
consciousness, of this supraconsciousness, is, as Coleridge
understood it so well, the eternal mystery which religion
attempts to solve.[36]

For Marcel, "we participate in God only in the measure in which
we act freely" (ibid., 121), and faith "bears upon the relation between
thought and experience as a whole (in the past as well as in the future),
in its indivisible and yet complex unity" (ibid., 122). "The subjectivity
of religion and the abdication of the individual are essential to a
mature understanding of religion" (ibid., 37).[37]

While a relatively new term, and one dismissed by writers like
Allan Bloom as "barbarous" jargon, contemporary authors do not
hesitate to call the material objects of our morality our "values"—
those personal "beliefs" we cherish (and for which we are sometimes
willing to fight and suffer)—our personally held "appreciations" about
what is right, good, fair, and decent—and their opposites.

According to authors such as Sidney Callahan, Carol Gilligan, and
Dan Maguire, our "values" are the material objects as well as the shaping forms of personal morality. And while sociologists speculate
whether "values" are the result of genes or socialization, whether they
are instinctual or learned, there is general agreement that individuals
and societies arrive at their "values" by a complex process that
involves the following six forces: authority (religious, secular); reason
and logic; sense experience; will (sentiment, emotion); intuition
(largely unconscious perception); and science (experiment, structured
testing).[38] And at the center of authentic Catholic "values" are such
"goods" as life, liberty, peace, beauty, family, community, health, and
happiness.

"Man is the linguistic animal," Herbert McCabe argued in his
best-selling *What is Ethics All About* (1969).[39] Once one accepts the
validity of this insight and unites it with Karl Barth's words, then making moral decisions and expressing them are "acts" inseparable from
the central work of every human being. Consequently, it follows that
the creating of the psychic and ethical "self," as Paul Ricoeur sees it,

begins in simple intuitive acknowledgment, and then progresses with success and failure through the hazardous task of building authentic self-knowledge, values, and character, as well as a healthy self-image through social interactions, dialog with oneself, and communicating with others.

Each self is, to some degree, both a reiteration of the universal self so central to Jung's understanding of culture and reality, and also (and more so) a unique self-consciousness resulting from actively processing one's own singular yet universal affective and intellectual grasp of primordial human symbols and standards, as well as crafting one's distinctive personal history and moral experience into an ongoing self-expressiveness—or center of action and energy. Each *Christian self,* moreover, is—and should become (as Gerard Manley Hopkins saw so clearly)—a unique, culturally bound "reiteration" of Christ.

Finally, humans are social. The U.S. medical ethicist Carl Elliott has observed, "Ethics is one thread in the fabric of a society, and it is intertwined with others. Ethical concepts are tied to a society's customs, manners, traditions, and institutions—all of the concepts that structure and inform the ways in which a member of that society deals with the world."[40] However, just as no person is an island, no modern person exists simply in one society. Whether young or old, contemporary persons participate directly or vicariously in multiple societies, groups, and communities—in several families, faith organizations, political, and cultural groups. Except in countries such as North Korea and Iran, nobody lives in a society that is as homogenous or monolithic as Elliott's words imply. Whether we belong to developed or developing societies, all of us are pluralists, members of open and porous societies—something that the feminist religious ethicist Sharon Welch has emphasized.[41]

Aquinas taught, *"Nihil in mente nisi quod prius in sensibus"* ("There is nothing in the human mind that was not first in the human senses"). Henry James believed, "What we perceive comes as much from inside our heads as from the world outside." Each great thinker enshrines powerful traditions of psychology. The ethic being proposed here holds that individual self-consciousness and personal moral values are self-created systems, not simply passively ingested social threads. One's conscience embodies one's own personally validated insights into the appropriate role of women in society, for instance, and one's opinions about the proper care for the elderly who are dying. These are individually fashioned from emotions and cognitions derived from one's contacts with and reflections upon customs, traditions, and ways of being within multiple communities, as well as one's "associations" (reading, talking, TV) with different moral teachers and leaders, for instance, one's "contacts" with Gandhi, Margaret Sanger, Martin Luther King, Dorothy Day, or Archbishop Romero.

It is a mistake to depict morality or civilization as "natural" products or processes; they are not things that simply happen, but the consequences of the efforts (conscious and unconscious) of countless individuals, famous and obscure, who sacrifice some amount of personal ambition and gratification, forgo certain possibilities and pleasures, assume certain tasks, and, perhaps above all, accept their responsibilities—as siblings, parents, citizens, and civic leaders.[42]

As a result of these distinctive qualities and potentialities, to be a mature moral person (self-determining, ethically informed, and sensitive) means that one is curious and willing to be associated with others, an individual who is "risk taking," and aware of "dangerous memories," as Welch has argued (ibid., 123–124). Further, since, as Jonathan Swift once observed, "Man is not a reasonable animal but only capable of reason," persons are not simply members of families, but in order to become authentically moral, persons must be *active* members of "multiple communities with divergent principles, norms, mores." Why? Because only by actively participating in such communities (Welch reasons) will persons develop the awareness and skill to criticize structural or individual injustice within any society, or be aware of the ethical blind spots and other moral limitations that exist within a community.[43]

In view of these facts about humans and morality, the material object of conscience (to use Scholastic terminology) is both *universal objective* and *personal existential* knowledge—as Karl Rahner argued—and this knowledge is a complex fusion of objective and subjective morality, socially derived norms, and personal principles that are grasped by cognitions, emotions, and intuitions. Such knowledge is God's will for *persons* and *this* individual—viewed not simply as a singular agent, but as an eternally valuable "self," as well as a member of the "people of God," who stands in several worlds. In this analysis, and contrary to Fagothey's position, conscience does not simply deal with subjective morality, nor is it a simple deduction from a general moral principle.[44]

Before returning briefly to the place of religious beliefs in Christian character, decision-making, and conscience formation, it should be noted that the model being presented here (like Ross's) does not claim that humans have direct intuitions (i.e. God-given "infallible" answers) about the rightness or wrongness of specific actions. An "intuition" about the morality of letting one's patient die by stopping nutrition and hydration, for example, is not the same as a rationally justified "answer"—nor does having such an intuition exempt a physician from the serious study of biomedical ethics or prayerful decision-making.[45]

Further, this theory does not affirm that either "essential" or "concrete" (second or third order) moral rules or convictions are "non-rational." On the contrary, this model maintains (as Aristotle and Aquinas did) that: (a) human beings directly "know" general moral principles; (b) their "main moral convictions" i.e., their deeply-held ethical beliefs are "of the nature of knowledge" (*Right*, ibid., 27); and (c) these convictions are grounded in a rational, not an irrational, grasp of morality.[46]

As articulated in Ross's writings, as well as in Callahan's essays, moral intuition (the core both of his and this moral model) is not simply an irrational hunch or a neurotic feeling, but a complex emotionally felt and rationally perceived "conviction" about "rightness" or "wrongness"—discerned not in the "naturalness" of one's contemplated behavior nor in its "rational self interest," but in terms of an action's "goodness" and "rightness". Intuition is central to the self's growth, the self's crying, "What I do is me: for that I came" (as Gerard Manley Hopkins realized). Certainly, critics of intuitionism claim that the approach is "boring," and that it is "completely unhelpful" in answering such questions as, "What is the ground, or the grounds, on which rests the consciousness of moral distinctions? How do we, how should we, how far can we sensibly hope to resolve or diminish moral disagreements by discussion and argument?"

Deconstructionists and postmodernists point out the discontinuities and limitations in communicating moral understanding, and, with the majority of feminists, are cautious about the search for abstract, universalizable principles or rules. However, these hostile judgments about a person's moral decisions are unfair in connection with Ross's and Callahan's sophisticated and nuanced understandings of the role of intuitive knowledge in moral decision-making.

I do not deny that Ross rejects the opinions of those who hold that "reasons" and "emotions" in themselves are the ground of an individual's sense of "rightness" and "moral obligation" (*Foundations*, ibid., 57ff.). However, in keeping with the holism central to contemporary

Christian ethics, I support Ross's contention that "intuition"—along with feelings and reasons—are the keys to a person's knowledge of basic morality, and of his or her awareness of personal duties and moral responsibilities (ibid., 82). Likewise with Ross and Callahan, this model of decision-making does not deny the cognitive and affective aspects of "intuition", rather it emphasizes the importance of both.

As well, in keeping with the twentieth century's emphasis on realism, this description of decision-making adheres to Ross's "modest" understanding of intuition—the words he uses, for instance, in describing how we come to know "rightness" and "wrongness": namely, "The fitness or unfitness of an imagined act catches our attention" (ibid., 84). Or in speaking about his list of *prima facie* duties, "It is a *prima facie* classification of the duties which reflection on our moral convictions seems actually to reveal, and if these convictions are, as I would claim they are, of the nature of knowledge, and if I have not misstated them, the list will be a list of authentic conditional duties, correct as far as it goes, though not necessarily complete" (*Right*, ibid., 19).

Dialogues About Responsibilities: Focus of Moral Growth and Decision-making

The moral model for educated males is Shakespeare's Hamlet; the moral of morality for educated women is Shakespeare's Portia—writes Carol Gilligan.[47] Being bright does not guarantee that a person will make sound decisions. All of us know individuals with IQs over 170 who have no social skills or common sense. The fact that a person employs a highly structured decision-making process (as one finds in business training manuals and self-help books), does not guarantee that the chosen path will be right.[48]

However, nobody can deny that in the case of those who have taken any quality time to examine a life choice or complex personal or theoretical moral issue, the existential awareness (feeling, sense) of moral obligation and the intuitive recognition (knowledge, belief) that one has specific duties will involve the *intellect and will*—which are both actively at work throughout the decision-making process—that involves both creative reflection on moral convictions and the applied task of intelligently weighing responsibilities, choosing between them, and making decisions about an actual (specific, weightiest) duty.[49]

While neo-Scholastic philosophers such as Austin Fagothey are able to describe decision-making in terms of Descartes' clear distinctions, a respect for reality demands that we describe any process involving sense experience, emotion, intuition, logic, and science as both intellectual and volitional at all levels. Obviously, the *emotions* are involved in this process, because one's awareness of the twin duties of reparation and gratitude, for instance, and the task of making a decision about one's actual responsibility when torn between two *prima facie* responsibilities (to recoin Ross's terminology) cannot take place without the involvement of one's feelings.

Just as the whole person decides, the whole person is informed, inspired, and consequently shaped in the development of character and values, as well as in making specific moral decisions by a range of forces—some from religion, some from science, others from culture—with its female and male icons. For ethically mature and morally sensitive Christians, their values and ethics will be God-focused, Christ-centered and Spirit-filled, as mentioned earlier. Rather than James Gustafson's awe-inspiring image of a God who does not give priority to human interests, the model of decision-making being presented here encourages a thoroughly Catholic image of a God who is merciful, generous, and forgiving: a God who sent his Son into the world for our salvation, and who created humans to be blessed forever, as Luther's *Catechism* says.

While the Bible will be the major source of morality for Christians of all traditions, some will live their lives inspired not simply by the Bible's parables and metaphors, but by specific texts of Scripture—those that pertain to morality, for instance. For these Christians, the Bible will have unique authority as a source of "light." It is be a "*norma normans non normata.*" The lessons within Jesus' parable of the Good Samaritan, for example, and the explicit details in Matthew's Sermon on the Mount (chapters 5–7), will be shaping forces in the development of their moral self-consciousness, and in their understanding of discipleship and what it means to follow Christ in daily life. Christ, as both "*vorbild*" and "*lehrer*", will win their hearts and sway their minds, as the author of John's Gospel intends.

Other Christians, on the other hand, will read Scripture not in such a literal way, but in the light of their historically developed, twenty-first century faith-traditions. Such people will make moral decisions in the light of the "signs of the times," and the realization that while the Bible is God's revealed word, its books were written by men who lived in cultures that were economically, socially, politically, and religiously different from today's societies; that the Bible's moral norms were codified by authors who not only never faced the complex issues posed by modern warfare or contemporary medicine, but never foresaw today's issues.

Believing that the Church (as Newman taught), in spite of its faults and failings, is still the "pillar and ground of truth," these Christians will give greater weight in their decision-making to universally accepted developments in theology and changes in the Christian understanding of reality and life that the Church has sanctioned. They will be guided by papal, episcopal, and conciliar statements that have been written to throw light upon contemporary moral issues; they will be assisted in their decision-making by the Church's official stands on capital punishment, physician-assisted suicide, and birth control.[50]

Where there is disagreement within the Church, no definite direction—a clear sense, perhaps, that the Church's teaching is in transition because of the differing theological opinions (as there is at present about the morality of withdrawing nutrition and hydration from patients in persistent vegetative states, and the morality of capital punishment)—millions of Christians will be guided by respected commentators and charismatic leaders, aware (if they have completed college courses in ethics) that John Henry Newman, one of the great champions of respect for papal teaching, also saw specific instances (if few) in which Catholics might disobey papal directives in order to follow the dictates of their conscience.

Those educated by Jesuits will be made aware, no doubt, of Ignatius Loyola's rules for the discernment of "spirits"; they will know that it is lawful to follow the decision-making principles set down by "probabilists," while those who have the good fortune to be guided by pastors knowledgeable in the area of pastoral counseling will be assisted to make some personal moral decisions on the basis of *epikaia.*

In this age of the visual media (movies, TV), millions of educated Christians around the world will not inherit their central moral principles from listening to homilies or singing hymns, as many of their Irish, Italian, or German ancestors did. Rather, just as early Celtic Christians were taught their ethics from monks who carved the high Crosses that still dot Ireland's landscape, and came to know right and wrong, virtue and vice, from the carved Bible figures that told the story of God's creation, Adam's fall, Jesus' death and resurrection, likewise today's Christians will develop their ethics, and gain glimpses of God, the Father, Jesus, and the Holy Spirit when they prepare for First Communion and Confirmation.

Just as the Irish admired beauty, generosity, and bravery, they will come to understand the meaning of mercy, forgiveness, generosity, simplicity, and solidarity—the distinctive Christian virtues. As they grow from childhood, with its penchant for rigid obedience to strict rules, and become curious teenagers and maturing adults, today's Christians will (one hopes) advance in their ability to set aside the allure of dressing and talking like "pop" icons—seeing themselves living in the style of Hollywood's rich and famous. While it is natural for adolescents to model themselves after sports, movie, and music heroes (just as teenagers in past generations aspired to run like Jesse Owens or to have Elizabeth Taylor's looks), in time, many will outgrow such images. Britney Spears will give way to the Maori chieftain's teenage daughter in the recent box office hit from New Zealand *Whale Riders*. With the arrival of children (one of the great change events in self-consciousness and value development), most adults will come to see their lives in personally and socially responsible ways.

As young or older adults facing the responsibilities of work and marriage, many of today's Christians will come to appreciate the characters of the people they meet in local political and social communities—the moral strengths they find in friends and colleagues, in national business, political, religious, and sporting leaders. Some will grow to learn from the women and men who people the pages of Graham Green's *The Power and The Glory*, Henry Miller's *The Crucible*, James Baldwin's *Go Tell It on The Mountain*, Dostoevsky's *Crime and Punishment*, Conrad's *The Heart of Darkness*, or Toni Morrison's *Beloved*.

Contacts with contemporaries and these literary works (as well as Gerard Manley Hopkins's poetry that continues to move adults of all ages, religions, and cultures) will touch emotions and challenge reasoning powers; such face-to-face encounters and experiences with success and failure will provide the future's adults with their self-shaping and conscience-forming images and metaphors, words and stories, heroes and heroines—the grist that develops self-understanding, values, and character, as Herbert McCabe, Michael Polanyi, and Paul Ricoeur have reminded us.

At the same time, while some Christians (those in convents or monasteries who easily see that "the world is charged with the grandeur of God") will be motivated by Jesus' life and resurrection, or by some other conspicuously "religious" motive (God's glory, aspiration to heaven), the great majority of contemporary and future

Christians will live moral lives for imperfect and mixed motives. For some, it will be in order to be safe from legal or divine punishments; others because they possess the desire simply to do what is right and to show respect to others—or they have come to feel that acting and living ethically is its own mysterious reward.

And what will be the focus of moral decision-making? Will it be a search for the highest forms of pleasure, as J. S. Mill argued? Will it be a reasoned reflection on basic human goods, as John Finnis has proposed? Neither. In this model, moral "talk" (as argued already) is conversation about *responsibilities,* not principally about goods or values; it is discussion about *prima facie* duties, not consequences (benefits or burdens, potential for human relationships). It is "conversation" (with ourselves, others) about our *"responsibilities"* to ourselves, neighbors, state, church—because of who we are and the roles that we have chosen or been given.

Moral decisions come into existence because of the fact that life brings us face to face with specific options about what we ought to do here and now because of our own or other's past actions, as well as the fact that we are soldiers in combats, ICU physicians called to attend to a patient who might have AIDS, or exhausted teenage mothers on welfare who have to take two children to day care before being at work by 7:30 A.M.[51] Since moral decision-making involves "persons", it includes individual differences (we do not enter life or live life on the same playing field), personal histories—and unique vocations.

Prayerfully, and after careful data gathering and the thoughtful assessment of options, mature, sensitive moral decision-makers will be those who use their informed and Spirit-filled consciences to determine their *weightiest responsibilities* as they face choices about paying bills or keeping promises—as well as the more far-reaching decisions about entering or leaving religious life, or recommending passive or aggressive medical treatments in the case of terminally ill or comatose spouses. These decisions will be experiences in which one's emotions, tutored by one's cognitions (as Callahan says), are particularly important, just as they are in the less complex and day-to-day decisions throughout the Christian moral life, because significant decision-making events like the experience of conversion (as described in Paul's letters and Gerard Manley Hopkins's sonnets) involve options and choices about *human responsibilities*: i.e., what we owe to ourselves and others, and what others owe to themselves and to us as partners, parents, citizens, neighbors, and professionals.

These responsibilities are sometimes obvious, sometimes extremely difficult decisions involving the totality of our *rational* and *emotional* (affective) skills, training, education, and experience.

As people such as Chicago's Archbishop Bernardin and New York's Dorothy Day found, the awareness of another's or one's own approaching death, the drowning of a child due to one's carelessness, the sense that life is passing one by at a great pace, and, consequently, that one should put one's affairs in order—being "moments of grace"—such events leave impacts upon a person's self-image and self-consciousness that make them *"chairoi"* (lasting moments) that can (if properly used and rightly disposed) change one's *thinking and feeling* forever. They can take one's moral growth to new heights; they can change one's moral perceptions and ethical sensitivities forever. Like the judge-penitent in Camus' *The Fall*, persons can use such events to see themselves as they really are—and to take the first steps along the hard road that leads toward redemption.

Conclusion: Bravely Scaling the Silent Heights

A cautionary word. The Victorian statesman Lord Melbourne once said, "I wish I could be as certain about anything as Lord Macaulay is about everything." The opinions of Ross, Lonergan, Maguire, Gilligan, and Callahan about the role of the emotions and the central-ity of intuitions in morality, together with Ricoeur's, McCabe's and Sharon Welch's stands on the importance of language, communica-tion, and multiple communities in the process of moral growth and decision-making, are central to the positions taken throughout this essay, because of their inherent qualities. But, just like the theory that has embraced them, one knows they are fragmentary, fallible, and imperfect, because they are the fruits of "frail thinking reeds." Nevertheless, the positions lead to some significant—and closing— remarks about the growth of morality within individual and, particu-larly, Christian, consciousness:

- As stated already, there is ample evidence that whether they take place through time or across time, multi-disciplinary and cross-cultural decisions, inner dialogues, and public conversations about physician-assisted suicide, cloning, or capital punishment come about through processes similar to those involved in reading and discussing texts: e.g., Augustine's *Confessions, The Song of Roland,* Joyce's *Ulysses,* or Toni Morrison's *Beloved.*

- Such processes embody complex patterns of sensible, emotional, and rational insights, hopes, and dreams, as well as felt responses to hostile or friendly persons, to appealing or disturbing behavior.

- These exchanges with one's self or others, like studies in the arts, assist us to gain understandings and appreciations of complex issues; they allow us to grasp and relate things about knowledge inherited from others; they increase our self-knowledge; they fashion the "self" as well as a community of "selves." Such experiences provide humans with the meanings that are vital for personal growth.

- Individuals bring to these activities their own strengths and weaknesses, their insights and limitations. Just as they are frequently unable to articulate their artistic preferences or to communicate exactly why they consider a painting, a song, or a novel to be enjoyable or "excellent" literature, there are circumstances in which adults will not be able to "justify" their moral decisions, and this inability will sometimes limit or undermine the validity of their judgments, as Callahan notes. However, one must (as Callahan says) sometimes honor these decisions, since emotions and moral sentiments arise partly from nonverbally encoded interpersonal experiences, and persons should not be denied rights simply because they lack the communication skills or confidence of "self" to justify what they know to be right—what they know should be done.

- In spite of these and other inherent difficulties, just as the majority of humans possess a moral sense, they are usually able to communicate with others through the medium of terms and images: formulae and symbols whose meanings, while singular, are also capable of being generalized. If, as Herbert McCabe argues, "Ethics is just the study of human behavior in so far as it is a piece of communication, in so far as it says something or fails to say something," it requires some knowledge of moral terminology and some acquaintance with the language structures of ethics to communicate well. However, the great majority of humans knows what is right and wrong, and develops the ability to communicate this knowledge, as Ross has argued and Lawrence Kohlberg's more recent cross-cultural and multicultural research into the moral judgments of children has shown.

- Given the importance of "community" in personal moral growth, educators and pastors should take heed again of Newman's words that can apply to parishes and church-sponsored schools: "A university is … an Alma Mater, knowing her children one by one, not a factory, or a mint, or a treadmill." Wise counsel and forgiving guidance, inspired leadership and genuine spirituality—not that associated with Aristotle's "philosopher king," but with Jesus' "compassionate servant"—must be the distinctive marks of all those who aspire to teaching or pastoral positions within Christian communities.

- While, one the one hand, James Gustafson situates his theocentric ethic within God's cosmic ordering of the universe and encourages decision-makers to examine the divine and created patterns and potentialities within Nature; and, on the other hand, the American novelist Edward Whittemore, author of the four-part epic *Sinai Tapestry* (1977) rejects the notion that underlying history's apparent randomness there is some sort of direction, and that "somebody" conspires to make things happen—the ethic being proposed in this book recommends a humbler and more realistic stance than that implied by either Gustafson and Whittemore. It asks that Christians use all the resources of history, as well as their own hearts and heads, religions and sciences, in order to make decisions about their personal responsibilities in view of their own or others' (friends, neighbors) past or present actions, and what they owe to themselves and to others because of their past generosity or selfishness and their ties of blood, loyalty, or citizenship.

- With Gerard Manley Hopkins, this ethic believes in God's providence, but sees it to be as "mysterious" as the mercy shown to those who witnessed "The Wreck of the Deutschland." This ethical theory sees insights into moral order in Hobbes's remarks about human motivation, and (to a lesser degree, perhaps) in the results of the human desire for justice and peace, as well as in the protective social, legal, and cultural structures created from humankind's knowledge of gross immorality and its awareness of obvious goodness—results embodied in such documents as the U.S. Constitution, the UN Declaration of Human Rights, and in less formalized ways within civilization's lasting plays and novels in which one comes face to face with humanity's dreams and hopes, its joys and sorrows—"the things we come to know in time

... the endless farewells of life," as the grandmother-to-be reminds us at the end of Edward Whittemore's *Jericho Mosaic.*

- The legend of *Antigone*, like Shakespeare's *Hamlet*, is one such story that embodies humanity's sense of morality and immorality, and has shaped Western culture in its countless readings and presentations. Coming from classical antiquity rather than from Elizabethan England, the mythic tale has been told and retold for over two thousand years, inspiring poets, philosophers, historians, and constitutional lawyers living in cultures and societies as different as Paul's, Augustine's, and our own. In spite of the myth's particularities, it speaks loudly to its audiences who are able to grasp the play's general meaning because:(1) reason, the imagination, and the human heart focus on limited horizons infused with the sun's colors; (2) "The world is charged with the grandeur of God/It will flame out, like shining from shook foil/ It gathers to a greatness, like the ooze of oil/ Crushed"; (3) these capacities are suffused by their agents' common desires for security, peace, and order in a constantly changing world that lacks (as Job saw) any easily seen stable or universal order, that knows Satan's machinations and human cruelty and frailty. In times and places in which darkness rules, the basis of piety and ethics is preserved in the hearts and minds of the *anawim* who still believe (as Job did) in God's inexplicable revelation, and are able not to "curse God and Die" but to rise to prayer and feel awe.[52]
- Patently and ironically, the Christian church's, indeed, humanity's ethical insights, even after Babel, remind us that language—for all of T.S. Eliot's words about its shortcomings—inherits the legacy of the passionate spirit's creative if always earth bound and life-in-death quest for unity and order in beauty, truth, and goodness.
- Finally, by construing moral decisions in terms of judgments about options and one's responsibilities (as Ross does), a person is better able to settle complex issues in ways that are more realistic than neo-Scholastic "natural law" philosophy—and the approach puts one squarely within the Aristotelian and Thomist traditions which, since the days of Ambrose's "*De Officiis Ministrorum*", have described morality in terms of "duties" to self, others, state, church, and God. In adopting this approach, a person will not be stifling their inherent creativity or limiting their God-given freedom, but accepting the implications of "reality"—which, as Iris

Murdoch rightly notes, means "truth." Their decisions will be filled with the same features that characterize those of Robert E. Lee when he made the decision to put his responsibilities to Virginia ahead of others. They will mirror the morality embodied in Joe Cruzan's decisions concerning his daughter Nancy; and they will reflect the "truth" within the decision made by Graham Snyder, the father of the young Canadian hockey ace, Dan Snyder, to embrace and forgive Danny Heatley, the driver of the sports car in which his son was killed on a narrow Atlanta road, early in the morning on September 29, 2003.

- We *are* partners and neighbors; we *are* God's daughters and sons. Correct moral decision-making in the case of Christians means successfully determining what is one's existentially *correct* responsibility—what one *really* should do—in the light of God's saving-work-in-Christ as understood and interpreted by one's Christian community. Right living means doing what one "believes"—after careful study, thought, and prayer—to be the right thing to do—because one sees and feels that this course of action embodies one's *responsibility*—God's will for oneself.

- Such a model of moral decision-making unites professional decisions and life choices; it combines all of one's personal powers and focuses them on the religious person's and community's central life-question, "how to attend in truth to God and to all else in relation to God?"[53]

- And at the center of the Christian's effort to answer this question must lie the words, "The ways of God are not our ways" (Isaiah 58). In God's plan, the least of history become the first. God's preference for the weak and oppressed runs throughout the Bible ... ." (Gustavo Gutierrez, *The God of Life*).

Notes:

[1] On this subject, Robin M. Hogarth, *Judgement & Choice: The Psychology of Decision,* 2nd Edition (New York: Yale University Press, 1987). Also, William D. Boyce and Larry Cyril Jensen, *Moral Reasoning: A Psychological-Philosophical Integration* (Lincoln: University of Nebraska Press, 1978).

[2] For a useful summary of past and present views about conscience, Walter J. Woods, "Conscience," in *New Dictionary of Catholic Social Thought,* Judith A. Dwyer, editor (Collegeville: Liturgical Press, 1994), 223–228.

[3] Fagothey's work (2nd edition, 1959) was republished by Tan Books, New York, in 2001.

[4] On this subject, Bernard Lonergan, "The Transition from a Classicist Worldview to Historical Mindedness," in *Law for Liberty*, edited by J. E. Biechler (Baltimore: Helicon Press, 1967), 126–133.

[5] Texts used in philosophy courses taught at Roman Catholic colleges and universities with a dedication to Thomism took the same stand, as seen, for instance, in the widely used Paul J. Gleeson, *An Introduction to Philosophy* (St. Louis: Herder Book Company, 10th Printing, 1955), 375. The same emphases—with their tensions—can be seen in Martin Harrison's chapter on conscience in his *Credo: A Practical Guide to the Catholic Faith* (Chicago: Henry Regnery, 1954), where the author defines conscience as "an act of judgment deciding the legality or otherwise of an action" (121)—while at the same time creating confusion by making such contradictory statements as (a) conscience is a "deciding faculty" with which each human being is endowed to guide him in discerning law and applying it to any specific act (121–122); and (b) conscience is "not a virtue, a habit, but a decision or judgment of the practical reason about a certain act as to whether it is or is not in accordance with the law of God. It has been called 'the voice of God' but is in fact an act of the practical reason ..." (121–122).

[6] On the changing meaning of 'conscience' in Western thought and the contradictions within Vatican II's statements on this subject, James Gaffney, "Conscience: The Evolution of Ambiguity," in his *Matters of Faith and Morals* (Kansas City: Sheed & Ward, 1987), 115–133. Also, "Conscience" in Timothy E. O'Connell, *Principles for a Catholic Morality* (San Francisco: HarperSanFrancisco, 1990), 103–118; Michael E. Allsopp, "Conscience, the Church and Moral Truth: John Henry Newman, Vatican II, Today," *Irish Theological Quarterly*, 58, 3 (1992), 192–208; George V. Lobo, "The Mature Christian Conscience," in *Guide to Christian Living* (Westminster: Christian Classics, Inc., 1985), 281–311; Walter J. Woods, "Conscience," in *New Dictionary of Catholic Social Thought*, edited by Judith A. Dwyer (Collegeville: Liturgical Press, 1994), 223–228; "Moral Conscience," in *Catechism of the Catholic Church,* op. cit., 1776–1802,1849,1453; Richard M. Gula, "Conscience" in *Christian Ethics: An Introduction*, edited by Bernard Hoose (London: Cassall, 1998), 110–122—and Michael E. Allsopp, "The Catechism's Teaching on Conscience: Reading It Right," in *Ethics and the Catechism of the Catholic Church,* edited by Michael E. Allsopp (Scranton: University of Scranton Press, 1999), 45–59.

[7] For a more up-to-date analysis of decision-making, but one still clearly within the neo-Scholastic Catholic tradition, James E. Royce, *Man and Meaning: A Successor to Man and His Nature* (New York: McGraw-Hill Book Company, 1969).

[8] On this subject, Mary Midgley, "The Flight from Blame," *Philosophy*, 62 (1987), 271–291, where the author construes solving moral problems to involve facts, feelings, and action, and states that pitting these factors against themselves rather than relating them has been a "real misfortune."

[9] Barnard Lonergan, *Insight: A Study of Human Understanding* (New York: Philosophical Library, 3rd edition, 1970).

[10] Daniel Maguire, *The Moral Choice* (Garden City: Doubleday, 1978).

[11] On the importance of these features for an adequate ethics, Rita C. Manning, *Speaking from the Heart: A Feminist Perspective on Ethics* (Lanham: Rowman & Littlefield, 1992), 28–30.

[12] Shanon Brownlee, "Inside the Teen Brain," *U.S. News & World Report* (August 8, 1999), 44–54.

[13] Mark Reardon, "The Brain," *Adult Learning*, Vol. 10, 2 (Winter 1998–1999), 10–17. Also Sarah Jane Fishback, "Learning and the Brain," ibid., 18–22—and Owen Flanagan's, *The Science of the Mind* (Cambridge: MIT Press, 2nd edition, 2001) that covers Western thought from Descartes to E. O. Wilson. Also, the useful historical and research data found in Steven Rose, *The Conscious Brain* (New York: Vintage Books, 1976); Colin Blakemore, *Mechanics of the Mind* (Cambridge: Cambridge University Press, 1977); Anthony Smith, *The Mind* (New York: Viking Press, 1984).

[14] Bateson has left a significant mark upon the social sciences as a result of his work on the biology of the intellect, and his analyses of the links between logic and function. On these subjects, I highly recommend Bateson's *Mind and Nature: A Necessary Unity* (New York: Bantam Books, 1980).

[15] Research shows that the work and relationship experiences of parents, siblings, aunts, and uncles play dominant roles in shaping career and professional decisions. Sadly, domestic violence and child abuse in one's childhood home seem to lead to patterns of similar behavior in one's own home as an adult.

[16] Stephen D. Brookfield, *Developing Critical Thinkers: Challenging Adults to Explore Alternative Ways of Thinking and Acting* (San Francisco: Jossey-Bass, 1987). Also, Richard Paul and Linda Elder, *Critical Thinking: Tools for Taking Charge of Your Learning and Your Life* (Upper Saddle River, NJ: Prentice Hall, 200; Michael Andolina, *Practical Guide to Critical Thinking* (Albany, NY: Thomson Learning, 2002).

[17] Jacques Barzun, *Begin Here: The Forgotten Conditions of Teaching and Learning* (Chicago: University of Chicago Press, 1991), 154–155.

[18] Sidney Callahan, "The Role of Emotions in Ethical Decision-making," *Hastings Center Report* (June-July 1988), 9–14; *In Good Conscience: Reason and Emotion in Moral Decision Making* (San Francisco: Harper Collins, 1991), and "Conscience," in *Riding Time Like A River: The Catholic Moral Tradition Since Vatican II*, edited by William J. O'Brien (Washington: Georgetown University Press, 1993), 99–112.

[19] All citations are taken from Callahan's essay as reprinted in *Life Choices: A Hastings Center Introduction to Bioethics*, 2nd edition, edited by Joseph H. Howell and William Frederick Sale (Washington: Georgetown University Press, 2000).

[20] While Callahan accepts that the emotions have a self-preserving role in keeping with the goals of evolution, she does not go quite as far as Robert Frank, Professor of Economics, Cornell University, in her arguments about the place of the emotions in the moral life. Frank, whose writing has been called "extremely important," contends that the Enlightenment position that humans are essentially rational, self-interested calculators is erroneous, and establishes a hazardous basis for students of economics, psychology, and other social sciences. Using contemporary evolutionary theory as his guide, Frank makes the case that human behavior exists for one purpose only—to promote the survival of the genes carried by the individuals that bear them—and that moral sentiments besides sympathy—the emotions in general—play strategic roles in the emergence of important social behaviors; they act as incentives, solve problems, strengthen self-control, and lie behind moral choices. For further on this, Robert H. Frank, *Passions within Reason: The Strategic Role of the Emotions* (New York: W.W. Norton & Company, 1988).

[21] On the theme of conscience as "God's voice" in the writings of Newman and Josef Fuchs, as well as a valuable discussion of the place of prayer and discernment in decision-making, John Mahoney, "Conscience, Discernment, and Prophecy in Moral Decision-Making," in *Riding Time Like a River: The Catholic Moral Tradition Since Vatican II*, edited by William J. O'Brien, op. cit., 81–97; James Keating, "The Conscience Imperative as Prayer," *Irish Theological Quarterly*, 63, 1 (1998), 65–89.

[22] On this subject, Sir W. David Ross, *Foundations of Ethics* (Oxford: The Clarendon Press, 1939), 196–201.

[23] Jonathan Bennett, "The Conscience of Huckleberry Finn," *Philosophy* 49 (1974), 123–134.

[24] On the place of communities in ethics, and the difference that taking this starting point means, Alasdair MacIntyre, *After Virtue* (Notre Dame: University of Notre Dame Press, 1981), 1–5, 64–67, 204–205.

[25] On the place of creativity, distinguished by "divergent thinking," in human life, Robert J. Sternberg, "The Development of Creativity as a Decision-making Process," and Jeanne Nakamura and Mihaly Csikszentmihalyi, "Creativity in Later Life," in *Creativity and Development* (Oxford: Oxford University Press, 2003), 91–138 and 186–216, resp.

[26] As the *Catechism of the Catholic Church* says, "According to Scripture it is the heart that prays ... The heart is our hidden center ... the place of decision ... the place of truth, the place of encounter" (#2562–2563). Nowhere, however, does the author of the *Catechism* reconcile this position about the importance of the heart with what the *Catechism* says elsewhere about conscience "as a judgment of reason" (#1796).

[27] In spite of Richard McCormick's major contributions to the renewal of Catholic moral theology, the definitive motif of his moral theory, namely, "reason informed by faith," exhibits a rather limited vision of moral decision-making, conscience, and the shaping role of religion within the moral subject.

[28] Ross, *Foundations*, ibid., 171.

[29] Sir David Ross, *The Right*, 30–31. While Ross does not develop the subject, his construing of the rational aspects of intuition are quite compatible with what Michael Polanyi has said about the intuitive and subjective aspects of "tacit knowledge" in his Terry Lectures at Yale University in 1962, and earlier at the University of Virginia. For these remarks, Michael Polanyi, *The Tacit Dimension* (New York: Doubleday, 1966).

[30] On these subjects, in particular the differences between Lawrence Kohlberg's analyses and Carol Gilligan's, Lawrence Kohlberg, "Stage and Sequence: The Cognitive-Development Approach to Socialization," in D.A. Goslin, editor, *Handbook of Socialization Theory and Research* (Chicago: Rand McNally, 1969); Lawrence Kohlberg, *The Philosophy of Moral Development* (San Francisco: Harper and Row, 1981); Carol Gilligan, *In a Different Voice: Psychological Theory and Women's Development* (Cambridge: Harvard University Press, 1982). Also, Robert Coles, *The Moral Life of Children* (Boston: Houghton Mifflin, 1986).

[31] Iris Murdoch, *The Sovereignty of Good* (London: Ark Paperbacks, 1985), 37.

[32] For firsthand reflections on this process, Carol Gilligan, *In a Different Voice*, op. cit., 151–174.

[33] On this subject, Richard M. Gula, "Conscience," in *Christian Ethics: An Introduction*, edited by Brian Hoose, op. cit., 110–122, at 118.

[34] This listing of primary emotions has been drawn from Callahan's essay on the role of emotion in ethical decision-making, p. 25.

[35] For further insights into these ideas, Paul Ricoeur, *The Rule of Metaphor* (London: Routledge & Kegan Paul, 1978); *The Symbolism of Evil* (Boston: Beacon Press, 1969); *Oneself as Another*, translated by Kathleen Blamey (Chicago: University of Chicago Press, 1992). Also, *The Philosophy of Paul Ricoeur: An Anthology of His Works*, edited by Charles E. Reagan and David Stewart (Boston: Beacon Press, 1978); David Wood, *On Paul Ricoeur: Narrative and Interpretation* (London: Routledge, 1991). For Wilson's emphasis on the importance of "consilience," and his grand conception of the unity between the sciences, humanities, and religions, Edward O. Wilson, *Consilience: The Unity of Knowledge* (New York: Alfred A. Knopf, 1998). Also Carol Gilligan, *In a Different Voice*, op. cit., 151–177. And, Carol Gilligan, "Women's Conceptions of Self and Morality," *Harvard Education Review* (1977), 492ff.

[36] Gabriel Marcel, *Philosophical Fragments 1909–1914* (Notre Dame: University of Notre Dame Press, 1965), 35–36.

[37] Marcel tells us in the book's epilogue that he became convinced about the truth of these youthful insights though the power of personal contacts (he speaks about the impact of meeting a Marcel Legaut, author of the *Christian Condition*, in 1940, a man who had left academia to spend his life in solitary union with God), and the moving power of Bach's cantatas and passions (ibid., 126–127).

[38] On this subject, Hunter Lewis, *A Question of Values: Six Ways We Make the Personal Choices That Shape Our Lives* (New York: HarperCollins Publishers, 1991).

[39] Herbert McCabe, *What Is Ethics All About: A Re-Evaluation of Law, Love, and Language* (Washington: Corpus Books, 1969), at 68.

[40] Carl Elliott, "Where Does Ethics Come From and What to Do About It?," *Hastings Center Report* (July 1992), 28–35.

[41] On this subject, Sharon D. Welch, *A Feminist Ethic of Risk* (Minneapolis: Fortress Press, 1990), 123–136, at 123–124.

[42] This last remark is adapted from Page Smith, *Killing the Spirit: Higher Education in America* (New York: Viking, 1990), 202—a volume that I warmly recommend to all involved or interested in this nation's past and future.

[43] Welch's observations explain why those who have lived and worked outside their own societies are able both to appreciate and to see the shortcomings within their native communities. Welch's words also explain why Catholics educated in economics, law, or health care find many of the Church's social statements unconvincing, and consequently why they do not accept them. Since today's Catholics possess worldviews and values drawn from multiple "worlds"—Church, society, university—with their different ways of thought and visions of reality—Catholics will either possess multiple visions and values (one for work, the other for church), or they will develop for themselves coherent visions and value systems that seem to make the most sense— i.e., ones that have the most support in terms of their education, reading, travel, social and professional associations. Given the Church's penchant for neo-Scholastic philosophy, its antipathy toward current linguistics, psychology, biology, and sociology— not to mention the official Church's general rejection of feminist hermeneutics—the majority of contemporary Catholics will not (I believe) be willing to accept as their own the Church's largely anti-natural values, its "medieval" worldview, and class-warfare economics and politics.

[44] On this point, the useful remarks by John Mahoney, in his "Conscience, Discernment, and Prophecy in Moral Decision-making," in *Riding Time Like A River: The Catholic Moral Tradition Since Vatican II*, op. cit., 81–97, at 86–92; Sidney Callahan, "Conscience," ibid., 99–112, at 110.

[45] Those familiar with the philosophy of the medieval Franciscan scholar Duns Scotus (1264–1308) will know that he held that the human will played a more important part in the process of human behavior than human reason, that the mind did have the ability to directly know singular objects (even if confusedly), and that humans did, therefore, possess direct knowledge of external objects. In this Scotus showed greater realism than Aquinas, and stands closer to Lonergan, Callahan, and Ross, of course. For an explanation of Scotus's positions, in particular, the priority of singulars as objects of knowledge, the priority of intuition in cognition, the primacy of the will, and the will's unconditional freedom, Donald Walhout, "Scotism in the Poetry of Hopkins," in *Saving Beauty: Further Studies in Hopkins*, edited by Michael E. Allsopp and David Anthony Downes (New York: Garland Publishing, 1994), 113–132.

[46] For Ross's understanding of the ground of morality, and his answer to "What Makes a Right Action Right?", his *Right,* ibid., 16–47, *Foundations,* ibid., 42–86.

[47] On this subject, Gilligan's "Visions of Maturity", in *In Her Own Voice,* op. cit., 151–174.

[48] One useful self-help book (because lighthearted in its seriousness), is Steve Allen, *Dumbth: And 81 Ways to Make Americans Smarter* (New York: Collins, 1989).

[49] For Christians, and those like myself who believe that an authentic Christian ethic must be God-focused, Christ-centered, and Spirit-filled—such activities (and conscience itself) are guided not simply by intellect and will, but also by God's Spirit.

[50] As stated above, while Richard McCormick's central image of decision-making ("reason informed by faith") is too narrow and limiting, McCormick's essays on religion and ethics do contain valuable insights into the role that doctrinal beliefs should play in coloring consciousness and shaping specific decisions. On this subject, Richard A. McCormick, "Moral Theology in the Year 2000," "How My Mind Has Changed," in *Corrective Vision: Explorations in Moral Theology* (Kansas City: Sheed & Ward, 1994), 23–39, 46–54. Also Richard A. McCormick, *Health and Medicine in the Catholic Tradition* (New York: Crossroad,1984), 30–43, 46–62. For another author who provides a consciously "theocentric" ethic that stands firmly in the Catholic tradition, Gustavo Gutierrez, *The God of Life* (New York: Orbis Books, 1991).

[51] The practice of developing concrete moral "responsibilities" from a person's natural or chosen "roles" is part of a tradition that predates Cicero's *De officiis.* It can be found in Greek and Indian philosophies, in Luther's understanding of vocation, and the writings of the Oxford philosopher F. H. Bradley, author of "My Station and Its Duties." Early Christian writers developed this approach when they expanded upon the image of society or church as an organic body in which people have their roles or places. The most influential example of such a work is St. Ambrose's *De officiis ministrorum*—that joins pre-Christian and Christian ethics in a structured analysis of the philosophical basis of morality—both ordinary (expected of everyone) and honorable (beyond the normal call of duty).

[52] George Steiner, one of the 20th century's most respected literary critics and prose writers, provides a masterful analysis of the Greek legend and its enduring power in the context of a study of poetry and the act of reading in his *Antigones* (New York:

Oxford University Press, 1984). What is Steiner's answer to the question, "Why the unbroken authority of Greek myths over the imagination of the West?" "Greek myths encode certain primary biological and social confrontations and self-perceptions in the history of man [*sic*], they endure as an animate legacy to collective remembrance and recognition. We come home to them as to our psychic roots .... The very foundations of our arts and civilization, we are assured, are mythical" (300–301). At the same time, as seen in the wide variety of readings of the climax of Walker Percy's *Lancelot*— cultural and religious influences will sometimes distort myths and lead to unintended interpretations.

[53] This is the all-encompassing question for Christian theology, according to David F. Ford in his *The Modern Theologians: An Introduction to Christian Theology in the Twentieth Century*, 2nd edition (Malden: Blackwell, 2001), 721–722.

Chapter XI

A Christian Ethic of Responsibilities: Cases, Illustrations

By its very nature Christian love counts men to be things of value, ends to be served in spite of everything.

Paul Ramsey
Basic Christian Ethics

Traditionally, the magisterium and Catholic tradition have not made Jesus Christ central to the moral life. Until recently human reason has discovered the moral intentions of God in human nature. Scripture confirmed the values and principles which have resided in human nature since the creation and which remain even after the fall from grace.

William C. Spohn
"The Use of Scripture in Veritatis Splendor"

If I could deny myself enough I would achieve some kind of innocence, despite those intermittent nightmare promptings of my true nature. I thought I could negate myself and wipe myself out.

Carol Gilligan
In a Different Voice

The ways of God are not our ways (see Isaiah 58). In God's plan, the least of history become the first. God's preference for the weak and oppressed runs throughout the Bible....

Gustavo Gutierrez
The God of Life

233

"I'm growing old. I'm falling apart. And it's very interesting," the novelist William Saroyan once said. Something similar might be said about every effort to construct an ethical theory. As the thought matures and takes its complex shape, it shows signs of imploding or falling apart due to its own weight or the lack of adequate strength at its foundations. This feeling increases as one attempts to illustrate not only how to use the ethical theory in daily life, but as one tries to demonstrate that the approach has enjoyed wide support within the lived-experience of the human family.

In spite of the problems involved, it will be helpful to readers, perhaps, to provide some examination now of a number of "cases" from the fields of medicine, military affairs, politics, and day-to-day life in which this ethic's existence is demonstrated or its application is illustrated. The following six existential examples have been chosen because they shine light upon the *authenticity* of the decision-making process outlined in this book; and because they highlight—by their presence or absence—*Christian* moral principles. These real-life cases drawn from life and literature should assist readers to better understand this theory's answer to the questions, "How should we live?" and "What makes a right action right?"

One cautionary point: given Freud's analyses of the human person and decision-making, we should not presume to say that we "know" exactly why any man divorces his wife of thirty years, or why a soldier throws himself on a land mine to save his buddies. Only those who have spent their lives reading superficial romance novels—and who have never attempted to climb the psychological mountains contained in *The Brothers Karamazov* or *The Heart of Darkness*—would ever dare to say, "I can read you like a book!"

Sometimes hospital ethics committees, juries, and family members cannot avoid the difficult task of assessing the innocence and guilt or the mental status of their peers. They have a duty to weigh facts, motives, pain, suffering, and other extenuating circumstances. Always, as Ross says (wisely), we should remember that such judgments are never more than "considered opinions." Obviously, where the facts or the law, public opinion or Christian ethics, are ambiguous or motives are ambivalent (are they ever otherwise?), there will be divisions and disagreements. As mentioned above, where community attitudes (about homosexual behavior, for instance) are conservative, individual Christians, as well as church communities, will look upon these actions as "immoral"—regardless of an individual's life-history, psychological condition, spirituality, integrity, maturity, or self-identity.

Among another community of Christians, however, this same behavior might be looked upon as "moral" given that community's knowledge of the individual's family-history, attitudes, community involvements, personality, and the specific circumstances.

In examining the following cases, therefore, we should keep the above in mind. Also, we should remember that "life is messy," and that—with very few exceptions—a person's vocational, political, or moral decisions, especially those made in past centuries, in difficult circumstances, or stressful conditions, are far from easy to understand or assess. Some of the Christians mentioned below possessed a vivid sense of God's presence in their lives: they were Bible-reading and actively committed to faith communities. Others were less educated, more indifferent toward organized religion, and less influenced by any sense of personal or general providence or eschatology. However, in every case, the decisions made by these individuals reflect the "objective" basis for the insights into morality incorporated in this theory—that there is a "common" morality (even if it is colored by culture, history, and politics); moral awareness is largely intuited and unexplained; a person's appreciation of the "good" is separate from his or her decisions about the "right"; that right actions are associated with one's sense of relationships, community bonds, and the circles that bind a person to others and groups.

Most of all, moral decisions—at their best—are personal, thoughtful, but always fallible judgments about one's responsibilities, about what one ought to do, because of one's perception (subjective, limited) about the "goods" involved assessed in the light of one's past, present, and future—one's family and friends, children and grandchildren, the safety and security of one's nation, the health and reputation of one's faith community—and most of all, perhaps, the peace and happiness of oneself.

Robert E. Lee's Decision to Support Virginia in 1861: Solidarity's Responsibilities

Every nation has its heroes. Some are famous for their successes in sport; others for their deeds on the battlefield. Abraham Lincoln and Martin Luther King, Jr. stand at the summit of the pantheon of America's moral heroes—but not too far below stands the figure of

Robert E. Lee, famed not only for his role as the South's heroic leader during the Civil War, but also because of his successes as a student at West Point, his father's exploits during the Revolutionary War, and his connections by marriage to George Washington.

When Confederate guns fired on Fort Sumter, Lee was an officer in the U.S. Army. In view of his commission and the oath he had taken to defend and protect the U.S. Constitution, one might have thought that Lee's religion (he was a deeply committed Christian), family history, and sense of duty would have drawn him to accept Lincoln's offer to take command of the Union Army. However, Lee, as all know, did not.

Why? Was it because Lee was motivated to make moral decisions in terms of "rational self-interest" (Ayn Rand)? Did Lee decline Lincoln's invitation because of his reading of the Bible? Or was it because Lee construed moral decisions in terms of Mill's "greatest happiness" principle or Jesus' "love" commandment? Were his judgments based upon "natural law" or a desire to liberate the oppressed?

From what we know, Lee's decisions were not grounded on any of these concerns. Rather, Lee's decisions—first, to decline Lincoln's tempting invitation, then, second, to give up his commission (Lee held the rank of lieutenant colonel and was in command of the Second Regiment of Cavalry stationed at Fort Mason, Texas, when he was summoned to Washington to meet with Lincoln), third, to support Virginia (his home state), and finally, to accept Governor Letcher's invitation to take command of Virginia's Provisional Army in April 1861—were all based upon a sense of responsibility, that ultimately became defined in terms of Lee's personal (existential, contextual) understanding of *his* duties toward *his* people, *his* state, and *his* home.

The Civil War novelist Jeff Shaara describes Lee's judgments in his award winning book *Gods and Generals*. First, Lee told General Winfield Scott when they met in March 1861, "If Virginia sides with the southern states ... General, I cannot fire upon my home."[1] Later, when Lincoln began to raise an army to strike against the South, and Lee was told he was Lincoln's pick to command the Union's forces, Lee asked Francis Blair to inform Lincoln, "I must decline your offer. ... I hope, with all prayers to God, that Virginia stays within the Union, but I fear that with this call for an army, this building of an invasion force ... I fear that the president will now unite his enemies. I have never taken my duties lightly, not to my country nor to my home. But I have no greater duty than to my home, to Virginia" (ibid., 103).

Lee was a Virginian. He was as proud of that fact as Sam Houston was proud to be a Texan. By birth and by marriage, Lee was closely tied to the oldest families in the state. He knew that when Lincoln's army moved to invade the Confederate states, Virginia would be one of the first to be invaded. Lee also knew war. He had served with distinction in Mexico. With Sherman, Lee realized as early as May 1861 that the conflict between North and South would not be a brief affair; with Jackson, Lee believed from the start that Federal forces under the command of his former colleagues, Winfield Scott Hancock, John Buford, George Custer, Dan Sickles, and John Reynolds, would fight well.[2]

However, neither this knowledge nor personal danger to himself, his wife and family—concerns about loss of property, damage to his military career or his reputation—would force Lee to decide in favor of putting his skills at the service of the Union or retiring from the army to lead a civilian's life.

Robert E. Lee prized solidarity. While he wore his best military uniform to Appomattox Court House when he met with U.S. Grant to discuss the surrender of the Army of Northern Virginia, Lee was a person of marked simplicity. And, although like "Stonewall" Jackson, Lee did not shrink from severely punishing soldiers who ran in the face of Union troops, he was a merciful and forgiving commander, admired by his fighting men.

Clearly, Lee's morality was grounded upon dedication to what he saw to be his duty. And history's estimate of Lee as an ethical hero rises (or falls) in terms of recognition of the two interrelated features at the center of his ethic and the theory proposed in this book: (a) the soundness of Lee's moral judgments; (b) his fidelity to what he saw to be his *weightiest* duties.

Joe Cruzan's Commitment to His Daughter: Let Nancy Die

> As the parents and legal guardians of Nancy Beth Cruzan, and after long and careful consideration, we have decided the time has come to request the cooperation of the Missouri Rehabilitation Center in discontinuing the life support system that provides nutrition and hydration to our daughter.

> We are aware that the consequence of this action will be her
> death. It is not a decision we have arrived at lightly.

This is how Joe Cruzan began the letter that he handed to Donald
Lamkins, director of the Missouri Rehabilitation Center on May 28,
1987.[3] From this letter, and conversations that led up to it, Joe
Cruzan's landmark decision was based upon his love for his daughter
and his respect for her wishes (expressed in statements Nancy made at
the time of their grandmother's death when she spoke about the sense-
lessness of prolonging life when there was no purpose left to that life).

There is nothing in this letter about ending Nancy's treatment
because it was "futile," or because she was no longer a "person." Joe
Cruzan's words say nothing either about Nancy's treatment involving
the use of "ordinary or extraordinary means" or his having weighed
the treatment she was receiving in terms of its "benefits or burdens."
At no point does Joe Cruzan mention anything about Nancy's
"potential for human relationships"—all of which are "principles" or
"standards" central to contemporary Roman Catholic or mainstream
Anglo-American biomedical ethics.[4]

From the time that Joe Cruzan's decision became public—actually
for months before—friends and neighbors in Carterville, Missouri, a
"blue-collar town of about 2,000 people," did not agree with him,
some because of their belief in the Bible's command (shared by
Donald Lamkins) "Thou shalt not kill" (ibid., 49); Others because they
did not want to feel "bad" in later years about how they had treated
their children, when, as one older couple who also had a
daughter in the rehabilitation center put it, "There'd be nothing they
could do to undo what they'd done."

Joe Cruzan respected these beliefs—and although religion did not
play a major role in his decision, he expected others in his community
to respect it.[5] Furthermore, after hours of conversation with Bill Colby,
the Kansas City attorney who took up his legal battle, Joe was
convinced that Nancy had a constitutionally protected right to privacy,
a right (in other words) that prevented any outside (community, state)
interference with her decision to determine her own death.

Making sure (as best he could) that Nancy's wishes were respected
and carried out became Joe's Cruzan's *weightiest duty* as her father and
court-appointed guardian. This is obvious to any reader of William
Colby's *Long Goodbye*, which provides not only a day-by-day history
of this American tragedy, but also a lasting portrait of Joe Cruzan, his

character, and motivation. The book's chapters are filled with extracts from letters and conversations that reveal the man's determination ("Mr. Cruzan is very insistent about what he wants and getting his way, and he tends to become somewhat intimidating," Dr. Anita Isaac testified in March 1988). The book illustrates Joe's relentless (shall we call it—obsessive?) efforts to learn about PVS (persistent vegetative state), and to know what was happening with the progress of his case ("Joe called Shook Hardy on our toll-free line often, sometimes twice a day .... He was desperate for any information. By the time Joe finished with the mail and phone calls, he'd often revved himself up so high that he could not fall asleep until late into the night." (ibid. 223).

As one reads and rereads all references to Joe Cruzan, the man's suffering is obvious—the pain he felt for his daughter (incontinent, drooling, unable to communicate) and the pain he suffered from unsolicited mail—"the mailbox was driving him nuts," daughter Christi told Bill Colby after the Missouri Supreme Court ruled against the family in November 1988 (ibid. 260). Given the years of agony and frustration, the roller-coaster ride that his emotions experienced for so long, it's not hard to understand Joe Cruzan's fatigue and bitterness—his depression—and his end.

The most significant insight into Joe Cruzan as a moral being can be found (I believe) in his court testimony on November 1, 1990, where he said, "I made a commitment to my daughter that I wouldn't let this go on, and I intend to fulfill that commitment" (ibid. 353). Clearly, these decisions embody what Joe Cruzan came to see as his *weightiest* duty—one for which he was prepared to give all his heart, all his mind, and all his strength.[6]

Joe Cruzan's decision to honor the promise he made to Nancy did not involve the mental gymnastics we find in some descriptions of moral decisions contained in the writings of John Finnis or Germain Grisez, for example. Joe Cruzan's decision did not involve making a judgment directly against a "basic human good" (Nancy's life), but rather making a decision in terms of his personally felt responsibilities toward his daughter. Further, his decision did not involve any use of the "principle of double effect" (as Finnis's analysis demands). Rather, using W. D. Ross as a guide, as proposed above, when Joe Cruzan made his decision, or a judge who sits on a death penalty case makes a decision that will lead to a criminal's execution, she or he makes this decision without necessarily having to resort to the "principle of double effect"—because (as Finnis sees it) each of these decisions involves the inevitability of making a decision directly against a basic human good.

Mrs. Bergmeier's "Loving" Decision: Duty Toward Husband and Family

Mrs. Bergmeier's act of "sacrificial adultery," as Joseph Fletcher describes it in his *Situation Ethics: The New Morality* (1966), arguably is the most written-about case in Christian ethics since WWII.[7] While Fletcher sees Mrs. Bergmeier's action in terms of "the loving thing" in her situation, another (and more coherent) analysis is possible: The German mother of three children (Ilse, twelve, Paul, ten, and Hans, fifteen) did what she did (asked a friendly Volga German camp guard to impregnate her), because, after "she turned things over in her mind," she felt that returning to Germany so that she could take care of her family was her *weightiest* duty.

In describing Mrs. Bergmeier's situation, Fletcher tells us that "She more than anything else was needed to reknit them as a family in that dire situation of hunger, chaos, and fear" (ibid., 165). Mrs. Bergmeier had been told "through a sympathetic commandant that her husband and family were trying to keep together and find her" (ibid., 165). It is impossible to know with certainty what guided Mrs. Bergmeier, I accept. She might have been motivated by "rational self-interest" (who would wish to remain in a Soviet prison camp in the Ukraine?). As some cynical college students sometimes say when discussing this case, she might have simply been lonely or wanted to have sex with the camp guard.

However, a sense of responsibility cannot be ruled out—and it is the most likely justification, in my humble (and always liable to error) opinion. Many of us will disagree with Mrs. Bergmeier's decision. We will not condone how she achieved her freedom, because the means she used are hard to reconcile with Christian principles. At the same time, many will appreciate the power of a mother's love, the force of a deeply felt sense of responsibility—and the power involved when a person of character sets out to achieve passionately held goals.

Sean O'Casey's *The Plough and the Stars:* The Conflicts of Jack and Nora Clitheroe

It is easy to understand why Sean O'Casey's play, *The Plough and the Stars,* caused riots when it was first performed. Opening night on

February 8, 1926, at Dublin's Abbey Theatre was just ten short years after the Easter Rebellion, when James Connolly and Patrick Pearse declared Ireland a republic and their volunteer forces attempted to take over Dublin and other major cities throughout Ireland.

Some in O'Casey's audience had been responsible for Sinn Fein's rise to power, and for the creation of Dial Eireann in January 1919. Others had fought in Ireland's war for independence and suffered at the hands of the Black and Tans. They had welcomed the signing of the Anglo-Irish Treaty in December 1921; they had mourned Michael Collins's assassination (the deaths too of Arthur Griffith and Erskine Childers) during the nasty civil war when the Sinn Fein's party split into two armed factions following the acceptance of the treaty.

The majority in the well-dressed audience that night had rejoiced openly when Britain's Union Jack was lowered for the last time, and the Irish Free State's orange, white, and green tricolor was seen flying—at last—over Dublin Castle.

O'Casey's two-act play is intended to shock. Its cast includes patriots and parasites, an unseen "The Voice" that presents the case for revolution with the words, "It is a glorious thing to see arms in the hands of Irishmen .... Bloodshed is a cleansing and sanctifying thing, and the nation that regards it as the final horror has lost its manhood."[8] There is a blue-collar Marxist (The Covey), and a working-class British soldier (Corporal Stoddart) who justifies himself with the words, "Oi'm a Sowcialist moiself, but Oi 'as to do moi dooty.'" There are Bessie Burgess, Rosie Redmond, and Mrs. Gogan ("a doleful look-ing little woman of forty, insinuating manner and sallow complexion. She is figety and nervous, terribly talkative .... Her heart is aflame with curiosity, and a fly could not come into nor go out of the house without her knowing").

The play's action focuses, however, on Jack and Nora Clitheroe—he, "a tall well-made fellow of twenty-five," and she "your own little red-lipped Nora". In Act I, Jack learns to his surprise and embarrass-ment that he has been appointed commandant of the Dublin Battalion of the Irish Citizen Army—something he should have known two weeks earlier, but for the fact that Nora had burnt the letter of appoint-ment, afraid that "General Connolly an' the citizen army" is going to be Jack's "only care." And she is right.

For Jack: "Ireland is greater than a wife." For a variety of reasons—and pressures—he is committed to "Death for th' independ-ence of Ireland!" However, for Nora: "... there's no woman gives a son or a husband to be killed—if they say it, they're lyin', lyin' against God, Nature, an' against themselves! I cursed them—cursed the rebel ruffians an' volunteers that had dhragged me ravin' mad into th' streets to seek me husband."

Jack is no Jason; Nora is no Medea. Jack's rough-and-ready determination, in spite of his fears and Nora's pleadings, is to be "true to me comrades." Nora's desperate desire is more specific and personal: "I want you to be true to me, Jack ... I'm your dearest comrade; I'm your truest comrade ... They only want th' comfort of havin' you in th' same danger as themselves ...."

When Jack happens to get back home to the two-room Dublin tenement toward the climax of the fighting in the streets and around Dublin's general post office, Nora begs him not to leave her and hysterically holds onto him in panic, crying, "No, no, no, I'll not let you go. Come on, come up to our home, Jack, my sweetheart, my lover, my husband."

Jack's reply. "What are you more than any other woman?" To which Nora responds, "No more, maybe; but you are more to me than any other man, Jack .... I didn't mean any harm, honestly, Jack .... I couldn't help it .... I shouldn't have told you .... My love for you made me mad with terror."

Jack Clitheroe's sense of duty, his mindless patriotism, and sense of mateship combine to blunt him to Nora's desires; they blind him toward her less than romantic realism. Jack's patriotism tears apart the thin fibers of Nora's dreams. Her desperate anxiety cripples her love (O'Casey make neither of his heroes wise—or strong).

Finally, late in Act II, Captain Brennan (now wearing a business suit to avoid capture) repeats Jack's last words to Bessie, "Tell Nora to be brave; that I'm ready to meet my God, an' that I'm proud to die for Ireland."

It is too late—Nora appears, clad only in her nightdress, her hair uncared for some days and "her eyes are glimmering with incipient insanity."

As Joe Cruzan's death by suicide also teaches, some enduring commitments—some *weightiest* duties—are death-dealing, sometimes destroying minds too sensitive to stand life's terrors, sometimes ruining lives like Jack Clitheroe's ("shot through th' arm, an' then through th' lung ...").

Christian assessments of the morality of such self-killing or -other-killing decisions will rest (I believe) upon carefully made and prayerful opinions (communal, individual) as Ross argues, about: (a) the "right" and the "good"—and (b) an individual's always-contextual and ever-personal living-out or abandoning of his or her decisions about the past, present, or future implications of such decisions. The Church will rarely condone such decisions—but guided by compassion, mercy, and forgiveness, the Church will understand. And like the father in Jesus' parable of the prodigal son, will welcome these children into its home.

Nano Nagle's Decision Not to Seek Vatican Approval for the Presentation Sisters

Nano Nagle (1718–1784) was one of the pioneers of Catholic education in Ireland. She was also the founder of the now worldwide religious congregation for women called the Sisters of the Presentation of the Blessed Virgin Mary. Toward the end of her life, Nano faced a major crisis of conscience—should she and her "sisters" (women who'd joined her work) continue to teach in the schools they had set up (between 1752–1772 they set up seven schools in Cork), and should they continue to work among Cork's poor who lived in squalor and sickness throughout the major port city? Or should she apply to the Vatican for the official approval of the congregation, an act that would mean she and her sisters would be forced to accept regulations along the lines of the Ursuline Sisters (whom Nano had brought to Cork), who were bound (as all congregations of religious women were at that time) by the "rule of enclosure"—a restriction that would severely limit the sisters' daily work throughout the city?

While this might seem just another example of scholastic hair-splitting, it was a major ethical dilemma for this dedicated Catholic woman, the daughter of an old Irish family, who had been educated in Paris, and who, as a young woman, had enjoyed an active social life among the Irish émigrés who supported the Stuart cause.

Nano knew that the application for Vatican approval would mean the end of the sisters' open and active apostolate that took them morning and night to where she believed they were most needed. She also knew that not applying for Vatican approval would mean the sisters had no official place within the Catholic Church.

After a lot of reflection, Nano chose **not** to seek the Vatican's approval. Clearly, as her letters indicate, she saw that her responsibility toward poor Catholic families in Cork—and elsewhere in Ireland—was greater than her responsibility to submit to the Church's canon law. And in spite of the ecclesiastical difficulties it brought (and it did), Nano stuck firm to her decision throughout the final years of her life. She died—without the Vatican's blessing on her work–on April 26, 1784— loved by Cork's poor as the "best of benefactors and patronesses."[9]

Conclusion: Holiness and Personal Fidelity to One's *Weightiest* Duties

"I wanted to hang out with my buddies, but I didn't want to make things hard on them, so I stayed to myself," recalled Reggie Jackson when talking about his time playing baseball in Alabama in 1967. The star athlete, who had served with distinction in the U.S. Army before being selected to play in the major league, knew his *weightiest* duty— as much as he might have wanted to spend time with teammates or have a steak after a game—he knew what he *ought* to do, for his own sake and his friends.[10]

John Stuart Mill might have been convinced that his ethic embodied Jesus' love commandment. However, Jesus' greatest act of love— his submission to God's will for him—assumes its moral stature not because it contains an extraordinary amount of "love," but because it is an act of heroic "fidelity." Further, Christ, as Pope John Paul II argues in his historic encyclical on the foundations of Christian morality *Veritatis Splendor,* is our great ethical "model"—because he is the great martyr—the "suffering servant," the "man for others"—the one who (as Gerard Manley Hopkins says) "gave glory to God by *sacrifice"*— sacrifice of himself, his hopes, dreams, and ambitions.

Acceptance of God's will in daily life—and faithfully fulfilling (as best we can) what we see to be our *weightiest* duties—this is Christian morality, righteousness, and the road to paradise. This is the true meaning of "goodness" and "holiness" in Christian thought. And it is what the "voice of conscience" responding to God's Spirit, as well as God's presence in "dappled things," dictates and encourages, warns and guides. Our sense of duty—and our commitment to fulfilling our weightiest duties—shapes us and destines us for Absolute Goodness.

Finally, a Christian's fidelity to his or her duties in keeping with Jesus' example of *kenosis* (self-giving for others) is central to the belief that "The Church is a Church of the small and poor, and hence of saints. It is not because the dome of St. Peter's is so vast that the Catholic Church is the Church of Christ, but because so many ordinary people have been declared blessed or saints under that dome. They are a sign of countless others who remain nameless."[11]

During these years—the time between the outpouring of Christ's Spirit at Pentecost and Christ's Second Coming—the personal effort to seek moral truth, and the faithful living out of the results of that search, are eternally significant. They are what makes the grain glorious, and the harvest ripe, abundant, and running over.

Notes:

[1] Jeff Shaara, *Gods and Generals* (New York: Ballantine Books, 1996), 100.

[2] In June 1962, Lee told his daughter, "It is plain we have not suffered enough, laboured enough, to deserve success. Our people have not been earnest enough, have thought too much of themselves ... and instead of turning out to be men, have been content to leave the protection of themselves and families to others." From *An Illustrated History of the Civil War: Images of an American Tragedy*, William J. Miller and Brian C. Pohanka, editors (Alexandria: Time-Life books, 2000), 161–162.

[3] For the full text of this letter, and a complete account of this story, William H. Colby, *Long Goodbye: The Death of Nancy Cruzan* (Carlsbad: Hay House, Inc., 2002).

[4] As early as January 1988, it is clear that Joe Cruzan had a thorough knowledge of the legal and ethical arguments pertaining to his daughter's case. On this subject, Colby, op. cit., 106–110. For useful ethical analyses of the ethical issues involved in this case, Richard A. McCormick, "The Cruzan Decision: Missouri's Contribution," "'Moral Consideration' Ill-Considered," and "The Case of Nancy Cruzan: A Reflection," in *Corrective Vision: Explorations in Moral Theology*, op. cit., 210–218, 219–224, 225–232; Eileen P. Flynn, "Artificially Provided Nutrition and Hydration," in *Issues in Health Care Ethics* (Upper Saddle River: Prentice Hall, 2000), 112–126; Tom L. Beauchamp and James F. Childress, *Principles of Biomedical Ethics*, 4th Edition (New York: Oxford University Press, 1994), 12, 170, 175, 216, 235, 251, 253, 257.

[5] During court testimony on Thursday, March 10, 1988, Joe Cruzan said that "religion played no role in the family decision" to let Nancy die. Colby, op. cit., 171.

[6] It is important to remember here Ross's remarks that judgments about one's weightiest duties are simply *opinions*—nothing more—and that they are therefore always open to dispute. One may be quite convinced on the basis of the evidence that Joe Cruzan's decisions were *subjectively* correct, while still certain that his opinions were *objectively* wrong—not in keeping with Biblical morality or Roman Catholic moral theology. Such aspects as being Nancy's father, a deep sense of compassion, solidarity, mercy—need to be factored into any assessment of Joe's decision about Nancy's wishes and her ongoing ordeal.

[7] For this case, Joseph Fletcher, *Situation Ethics: The New Morality* (Philadelphia: Westminster Press, 1966), 164–165. For comments on Fletcher's ethic, N. H. G. Robinson, *The Groundwork of Christian Ethics*, op. cit., 249–250; William Barclay, *Christian Ethics for Today* (San Francisco: Harper & Row, 1984), 80–83; J. Charles King, "The Inadequacy of Situation Ethics," *The Thomist*, 34 (1970), 423–437; Gerard J. Dalcourt, "The Pragmatist and Situationist Approach in Ethics," *Thought*, 51

(1976), 135–146; Michael E. Allsopp, "Joseph Fletcher's Situation Ethics: Twenty-Five Years after the Storm," *Irish Theological Quarterly,* 56, 3 (1990), 170–190.

[8] All quotations are taken from Sean O'Casey, *The Plough and the Stars* (London: Macmillan and Co., Ltd., 1926).

[9] During a visit she made to Sydney, Australia, during the 1970s, Dorothy Day was asked what she would do if the Archbishop of New York told her to close her soup kitchen in the city. She replied—without any hesitation—"I would close it." I do not know what Nano Nagle would do if she had been placed in such a position. Fortunately, she was not—as the Irish hierarchy allowed Nano and her companions (there were only three when she founded the congregation on Christmas Eve, 1775), to continue their work without applying for Vatican approval. Concerning Dorothy Day's idealism and pursuit of moral excellence, Robert Coles, *Dorothy Day: A Radical Devotion,* Radcliffe Biography Series, Merloyd Lawrence, General Editor (Reading, MA: Addison-Wesley Publishing, 1987).

[10] Concerning what happened on the one time when Jackson went to a restaurant, John Whitcomb and Claire Whitcomb, op. cit., 77–78.

[11] Bishops of the Netherlands, *A New Catechism: Catholic Faith for Adults* (New York: Herder and Herder, 1967), 351.

INDEX